T0390761

LEWIS CARROLL
AND THE VICTORIAN STAGE

To the memory of
George Rowell
and
John Russell Stephens

Lewis Carroll
and the Victorian Stage
Theatricals in a Quiet Life

RICHARD FOULKES
University of Leicester, UK

Routledge
Taylor & Francis Group
LONDON AND NEW YORK

First published 2005 by Ashgate Publishing

Published 2016 by Routledge
2 Park Square, Milton Park, Abingdon, Oxon OX14 4RN
711 Third Avenue, New York, NY 10017, USA

Routledge is an imprint of the Taylor & Francis Group, an informa business

Copyright © Richard Foulkes 2005

Richard Foulkes has asserted his moral right under the Copyright, Designs and Patents Act, 1988, to be identified as the author of this work.

All rights reserved. No part of this book may be reprinted or reproduced or utilised in any form or by any electronic, mechanical, or other means, now known or hereafter invented, including photocopying and recording, or in any information storage or retrieval system, without permission in writing from the publishers.

Notice:
Product or corporate names may be trademarks or registered trademarks, and are used only for identification and explanation without intent to infringe.

British Library Cataloguing in Publication Data
Foulkes, Richard
    Lewis Carroll and the Victorian stage : theatricals in a quiet life.—(The nineteenth century series)
    1.Carroll, Lewis, 1832-1898—Knowledge—Theater 2. Theater—England—History—19th century
    I.Title
    828.8'09

Library of Congress Cataloging-in-Publication Data
Foulkes, Richard.
  Lewis Carroll and the Victorian stage : theatricals in a quiet life / Richard Foulkes.
    p. cm.—(The nineteenth century series)
  Includes bibliographical references and index.
  ISBN 0-7546-0466-7 (alk. paper)
  1. Carroll, Lewis, 1832-1898—Knowledge—Performing arts. 2. Amateur theater—England—History—19th century. 3. Performing arts—England—History—19th century. 4. Theater—England—History—19th century. 5. Authors, English—19th century—Biography. I. Title. II.
Series: Nineteenth century (Aldershot, England)

PR4612.F68 2004
828'.809—dc22

2004020741

ISBN 13: 978-0-7546-0466-2 (hbk)

Lewis Carroll at the Play by Harry Furniss

Contents

General Editors' Preface	*viii*
List of Illustrations	*ix*
Acknowledgements	*x*

Introduction		1
1	Juvenile	5
2	Unwillingly to School	21
3	Oxford	34
4	*Alice*	51
5	Home Entertainments	69
6	The Terrys	88
7	Minors and Protégées	108
8	Photography	124
9	Carroll at the Theatre	138
In Conclusion		198

References	*204*
Index	*216*

The Nineteenth Century Series
General Editors' Preface

The aim of the series is to reflect, develop and extend the great burgeoning of interest in the nineteenth century that has been an inevitable feature of recent years, as that former epoch has come more sharply into focus as a locus for our understanding not only of the past but of the contours of our modernity. It centres primarily upon major authors and subjects within Romantic and Victorian literature. It also includes studies of other British writers and issues, where these are matters of current debate: for example, biography and autobiography, journalism, periodical literature, travel writing, book production, gender, non-canonical writing. We are dedicated principally to publishing original monographs and symposia; our policy is to embrace a broad scope in chronology, approach and range of concern, and both to recognize and cut innovatively across such parameters as those suggested by the designations 'Romantic' and 'Victorian'. We welcome new ideas and theories, while valuing traditional scholarship. It is hoped that the world which predates yet so forcibly predicts and engages our own will emerge in parts, in the wider sweep, and in the lively streams of disputation and change that are so manifest an aspect of its intellectual, artistic and social landscape.

Vincent Newey
Joanne Shattock
University of Leicester

List of Illustrations

Frontispiece Lewis Carroll at the Play by Harry Furniss
(By courtesy of the Alfred C. Berol Collection, Fales Library,
New York University)

1	Marionette Theatre	10
	(*Queen* 18 November 1931)	
2	The Westminster Play 1847	30
	(*Illustrated London News* 1 January 1848.	
	By courtesy of Westminster School)	
3	*The Merchant of Venice*, Oxford 1883	43
	(Alan Mackinnon, *The Oxford Amateurs*)	
4	Surrey Theatre *Harlequin King Chess*	57
	(*Illustrated London News* 30 December 1865)	
5	Phoebe Carlo as Alice with the Dormouse	63
	(*Theatre* 1 April 1887)	
6	Isa Bowman as Alice	66
	(Isa Bowman, *The Story of Lewis Carroll*)	
7	Una and the Lion	74
	(*Illustrated London News* 23 December 1872)	
8	Ellen Terry as Marguerite [Margaret] in *Faust*	101
	(Lyceum Theatre programme in author's collection)	
9	Engaging children for the Drury Lane pantomime	111
	(*Illustrated London News* 7 December 1867)	
10	Charles Kean as Leontes and Ellen Terry as Mamillius	
	in *The Winter's Tale* at the Princess's Theatre. Photograph	
	by Laroche in the Theatre Museum, London.	128
	(By courtesy of the Board of Trustees of the Victoria and	
	Albert Museum)	
11	Queen Katherine's Dream in *Henry VIII* at the Princess's Theatre	144
	(*Illustrated London News* 2 June 1855)	
12	Frederick Robson as Daddy Hardacre at the Olympic Theatre	152
	(*Illustrated London News* 25 April 1857)	
13	Miss Florence St. John and Miss Emily Duncan in *Olivette* at	
	the Strand Theatre	183
	(*Dramatic Notes 1879-82*)	
14	Richard Corney Grain	194
	(David Williamson, *The German Reeds and Corney Grain*)	

Acknowledgements

I am grateful to the British Academy for awarding me a Small Research Grant for travel expenses relating to research for this book and to the University of Leicester for a semester's study leave in which to write it.

I acknowledge the permission of A. P. Watt Ltd on behalf of the Trustees of the C. L. Dodgson Estate and Morton N. Cohen to quote from Lewis Carroll's letters and diaries.

I am indebted to the staff of the following libraries: Christ Church, Oxford University; the British Library; Darlington Library (Centre for Local Studies); Eastbourne Reference Library; the Folger Shakespeare Library; the Garrick Club; Guildford Museum; the H. A. Jones Theatre Collection at the University of Leicester Centre in Northampton; Harvard University (the Theatre Collection and Houghton Library); Hatfield House; New York University (the Berol Collection in the Fales Library); the Pierpoint Morgan Library; in Richmond, North Yorkshire: The Georgian Theatre Royal and Richmond School; the Ripon Local Studies Research Centre; the Royal Archives at Windsor Castle; Rugby School; the Surrey History Centre; the Theatre Museum; Westminster Public Library; Westminster School and of course the University of Leicester Main Library and School of Education Library.

Anyone embarking on research into Lewis Carroll has the inestimable advantage of the Lewis Carroll Society with its journal (*The Carrollian*) and other publications including the diaries under Edward Wakeling's editorship, its meetings in London and expeditions to places associated with Carroll. Mark Richards, the society's chairman, has responded unfailingly to a series of queries over several years. Morton N. Cohen, the doyen of Carroll scholars, has placed his unrivalled knowledge of Carroll at the disposal of a relative novice. Hugues Lebailly has most generously made his doctoral thesis ('Charles Lutwidge Dodgson et la Vie Artistique Victorienne', Université des Sciences Humaines de Strasbourg, 1997) available to me. Edward Wakeling, as editor of the aforementioned edition of the diaries and co-author of *Lewis Carroll Photographer*, has helped to clarify a number of points.

The following individuals have provided valuable assistance and encouragement: Professor J. S. Bratton, Bobby Brown, Hugo Brunner, Don Chapman, Professor Carol J. Carlisle, Dr Katharine Cockin, Dr Julie Coleman, Allan and Suzanne Cook, Dr Victoria Cooper, Miss Margaret

Acknowledgements xi

Cottier, John Cunningham, the late Charles Edwards, Dr Richard Gardner, Jane Hatcher, Dr Martin Halliwell, John H. B. Irving, Trevor Mantle, Peter Selley (Sotheby's), George Speaight and Dr Georgianna Ziegler.

I am grateful to Professor Vincent Newey and Professor Joanne Shattock as editors of the Nineteenth Century series for their support for this volume and to Erica Gaffney and Ann Donahue at Ashgate for their attention to it. For the preparation of the camera-ready copy I owe incalculable thanks to Angie Kendall who has carried out the task with her customary efficiency and care. The Photographic Unit at the University of Leicester has prepared the illustrations.

This book is dedicated to two outstanding scholars of the Victorian theatre, George Rowell and John Russell Stephens, who died within days of one another in late 2001. George Rowell laid the foundations for the study of the Victorian theatre with his early pioneering work and continued to add to his own achievements and set an example to others for over forty years. In a life cut cruelly short John Russell Stephens established his reputation with two important monographs and numerous articles and other contributions. As Ashgate's reader for this volume he offered much valuable advice and information from which I have benefited. For me, as for many fellow theatre historians, their loss is personal as well as professional.

Finally I must thank my family for their interest and encouragement especially my wife Christine who, as with previous labours of this kind, has lovingly sustained me through the processes involved in bringing *Lewis Carroll and the Victorian Stage Theatricals in a Quiet Life* to completion.

Introduction

My interest in Lewis Carroll can be dated to 1998, the centenary of his death, when I attended a conference entitled the Lewis Carroll Phenomenon at Cardiff University. The distinction of the speakers, the number of different countries represented and the range of the papers given all testified to the importance of Lewis Carroll and his continuing attraction to scholars in several disciplines (literature, mathematics, physics, photography) as well as his appeal to ordinary readers and enthusiasts, such as members of the Lewis Carroll Society.

I have to say that I approached the conference and its subject with the suspicion of an outsider. I had worked on the Victorian theatre for over thirty years and Carroll had featured moderately in a book (*Church and Stage in Victorian England*) that I had just completed. It was because of this that I had offered a paper on 'Lewis Carroll and the Victorian Theatre', which in due course I was called upon to deliver at an inconveniently timed slot which, I hoped, accounted for the rather sparse attendance. I remember that at the end of my delivery someone remarked that: 'You don't like him [Carroll] much, do you?' That was a fair response to what I had said and my answer could only have been: 'No, I don't.'

Looking back now at the notes for that talk I see that I covered much that I have returned to in this book: the marionette theatre at Croft Rectory, Carroll's first visit to a play, his father's editorship of Tertullian, the issue of whether the theatre was inherently evil or (only) capable of being put to ill effect, child performers, his failure to take priest's orders, the Terry family, Liddon and the trip to Russia, pantomimes, soliciting gifts for his young companions, the snobbish tone of his attempts to find work for his cousin Minna Quin, his increasing prudery, his disinclination to support OUDS and his rejection of the Church and Stage Guild. In fact so much did I squeeze into that slot that I wonder that it has taken me another five years to complete this expanded study. However it was not just what I covered in that talk, but the impression that I had formed of Carroll and had evidently relayed to my auditors.

Though the enthusiasm of his early theatregoing was undeniable, his comment on Queen Katherine's vision in *Henry VIII*: 'so could I fancy (if the thought be not profane) would real angels seem to our mortal vision' struck me as rather sanctimonious. His delight in children of five

2 *Lewis Carroll and the Victorian Stage*

appearing on stage at 11pm was not clouded by any concern for their wellbeing. His own continuing absorption in his marionette theatre well into his twenties was surely highly inappropriate, as was his fascination with charades and other childish pastimes. His letter (12 May 1892) to A. R. H. Wright justifying his attendance at 'good plays' smacked of casuistry, as did his letter to Ellen Terry about 'the selfish man' (13 November 1890). His behaviour in relaying his young companion's (alleged) remark 'Where is it going to stop?' about Ellen Terry 'undressing' as Margaret in *Faust* was not only deeply ungrateful and tactless, but bordered on the salacious. His attitude towards the new playwrights (Pinero, Wilde and Jones, as well as Ibsen and Shaw) was completely hidebound and he became increasingly intolerant of even middle-of-the-road plays. His lobbying for his cousin Minna Quin to the actor-manager Wilson Barrett – 'I think real *ladies*, even of less dramatic ability than those who come from the lower rank, deserve consideration'– was just appallingly snobbish. And then there was still the whole question of Carroll's fascination with little girls, which, though it features in most aspects of his life and work, is particularly prominent in the theatre.

This is the point at which the reader might wonder not only why I went further, but also whether he or she should do so. My reason for exploring the subject of Carroll and the theatre further was twofold. By any yardstick Carroll was a remarkable individual and he attended the theatre over 400 times during forty-two years, recording his impressions in his diaries and letters. During that period (1855 to 1897) the British theatre underwent an unprecedented process of expansion, rejuvenation and diversification. Though theatre historians and specialists in other kindred disciplines have increasingly recognised the importance of what happened, hardly any of them have summoned Carroll as a witness for his account of Kean at the Princess's Theatre, Robson at the Olympic, the Terrys, in particular Ellen but also Kate and Marion, and Gilbert and Sullivan, or for his record on child performers and the changing social composition of the theatrical profession. This then is one objective: to alert theatre historians and others to Carroll as a rich resource of information, a resource that is not limited to the professional theatre as it also covers the ambit of Victorian domestic pastimes and takes us into the world of charades, marionette theatres and home theatricals.

My other objective is to see whether by focusing specifically on Carroll's lifelong interest in – or rather enthusiasm for – the theatre in so many forms and manifestations we can gain new insights into his personality. I essay this task under various headings covering his childhood and youth, Oxford, photography and so on. Although there is a forward moving chronology within each chapter and from chapter to

Introduction 3

chapter the main focus is on themes, but having said that it is as well to point out that certain subjects do come up in more than one place. A key strategy has been to place Carroll's particular tastes and preferences in the context of his time. To ask, for instance, how odd it actually was to be interested in a marionette theatre at the age of twenty-three in the 1850s or to attend pantomimes performed entirely by children in the 1870s or to prefer J. M. Barrie to Shaw in the 1890s.

It would be premature to anticipate my conclusion here, but, if for no other reason than to counter the discouragement which I may have caused readers earlier, I should say that at the end of this book I am generally much more favourably disposed towards Carroll than I was at the conclusion of the short paper in Cardiff in 1998.

As far as possible I have sought to give information about sources and references in the text rather than in unwieldy footnotes. The two major sources for Carroll's own views on the theatre are his diaries and letters. The diaries were first edited in a condensed form by Roger Lancelyn Green in two volumes published in 1954 by Oxford University Press and reprinted in 1971 by the Greenwood Press. Lancelyn Green undertook this task with the co-operation of the Dodgson family and by the standards of the day his editing (omissions) was unexceptionable. However expectations change and the Lewis Carroll Society is in the process of publishing 'the first complete version of the nine surviving' volumes of Carroll's diaries edited by Edward Wakeling. Volume 1 appeared in 1993 and volume 7 (up to June 1883) in 2003. Thus when writing this book Lancelyn Green has been my only published source for July 1883 onwards, though I have supplemented this by consulting Carroll's own manuscript (in the British Library) or rather a microfilm of it. In view of this somewhat complicated and *changing* situation I have (with very few exceptions usually pertaining to notes) given the date of the diary entry that I am quoting without citing a particular edition so that the reader can follow that up in whichever edition may (now and in the future) be available.

I have adopted the same policy with letters. Morton N. Cohen produced his two-volume edition *The Letters of Lewis Carroll*, 'with the assistance of Roger Lancelyn Green', in 1979 (published by Macmillan). However this is not easily obtained now, though some readers may share my good fortune in acquiring volume I in one place (Stratford-upon-Avon) and volume II in another (Saffron Walden). Cohen's single volume *The Selected Letters of Lewis Carroll* first published in 1982 has been reprinted and may be easier to track down. With the date of each letter available to them readers can look for it in whichever edition they have access to.

4   *Lewis Carroll and the Victorian Stage*

There remains – at this stage – the fraught issue of nomenclature which confronts all writers on Lewis Carroll born Charles Dodgson. I have resolved to call him Lewis Carroll throughout. Of course Charles Dodgson did not become Lewis Carroll until he was over thirty years old, but my case rests on two points: one that the use of Carroll from his birth avoids confusion with his father whose namesake he was and second that it is really only because he was also Lewis Carroll that we are interested in Dodgson. Even in the early diaries and letters Dodgson was Lewis Carroll in the making and after he assumed that (additional) identity his life could never be the same again.

1 Juvenile

'...his childhood was sharply severed. It lodged in him whole and entire.'
Virginia Woolf, *The Moment and other essays*

In a letter of condolence to Henry Sinclair dated 22 March 1879 Lewis
Carroll described the death 'of my own dear father', which had occurred
over a decade earlier in June 1868, as 'the deepest sorrow *I* have known in
life'. Despite this affirmation of his close feelings for his father, Carroll's
biographers have painted an altogether more complex picture. Karoline
Leach likened the son's mind to mercury, his father's to granite (1999, p.
101) and characterised his effect on the rest of his children as 'hyper-
passivity' (p. 97). Mercury and hyper-passivity are not natural bedfellows,
but nevertheless Leach detects that in later life Carroll 'even began to
adopt certain aspects of his dead father's persons, echoes of the man's
pomposity, a humourless sententiousness that had previously been alien to
him' (p. 222). Morton N. Cohen also addresses the father-son relationship
and identifies 'two forces in Charles's life that were working at cross-
purposes: filial devotion and filial rebellion' (1995, p. 329) and poses the
question: 'What did the father think of his eldest son?' (p. 340).

The facts of Charles Dodgson's life are succinctly summarised by Ivor
Ll. Davies in his *Jabberwocky* (1976) article 'Archdeacon Dodgson':

Charles Dodgson was born in 1800 at Hamilton in Lanarkshire. He was
educated at Westminster School and Christ Church, Oxford, where he took a
double first in classics and mathematics and obtained a studentship. In 1827
he married his cousin, Frances Jane Lutwidge, by whom he had eleven
children, Lewis Carroll being the third. He became Perpetual Curate of
Daresbury in Cheshire (1827), Rector of Croft in Yorkshire (1843), Canon of
Ripon (1852) and Archdeacon of Richmond (1854). He died in 1868. (p. 46)

Born on 27 January 1832 Lewis Carroll, or Charles Lutwidge
Dodgson as he was christened, therefore spent the first eleven years at
Daresbury, where, according to his nephew and first biographer Stuart
Dodgson Collingwood: 'Mr Dodgson from the first used to take an active
part in his son's education' (1898, p. 22). Mrs Dodgson was also involved,
as her son's small notebook chronicling his reading with his mother
reveals.[1] According to this he read Bunyan's *The Pilgrim's Progress* in
February and March 1839 and went on to *The Cheapside Apprentice*, in

6 *Lewis Carroll and the Victorian Stage*

which Anne Clark notes the extreme disrepute of the theatre (1979, p. 16). Whilst his young son was engaged in this purposeful reading, Dodgson senior was immersed in what was to be the most monumental undertaking of his entire life.

Dodgson was an exact contemporary of Edward Bouverie Pusey (1800-1882) with whom he had been at Christ Church. Pusey became Regius Professor of Hebrew at Oxford when he was only twenty-eight and thereafter took a prominent part in the Oxford movement, contributing to *Tracts for the Times* and aligning himself with Newman's controversial *Tract XC* (1841) (Donaldson, 1902, p. 149) after which he (Pusey) assumed the leadership of the movement. Dodgson was what was widely known as a 'Puseyite'; that, together with his undisputed ability as a classical scholar, led to him contributing to Pusey's ambitious series 'The Library of the Masters' which he had devised with Newman. Pusey himself edited the first volume *St Augustine's Confessions*, which appeared in 1838 with a further forty-seven volumes to follow, the last in 1885, three years after his death. As Pusey's biographer, Maria Trench, observed: 'The task of finding translators, editing, and writing prefaces to translations, was no light one', though it was no doubt ameliorated by the 'increasing sales', rising from 800 at the outset to 3700 in 1853 (1900, p. 105). How much say Dodgson had in the allocation of the volume with which Pusey entrusted him is not at all clear, though as Morton N. Cohen remarks he 'could not have undertaken so massive a labor...had he felt no sympathy for Tertullian' (1995, p. 324), for his lot was Tertullian (c150-230), whom Cohen describes as 'a second-century pagan who converted to Christianity, lived an exceedingly ascetic life, and preached strict personal discipline and restraint in all things'. It was to this stern father of the Latin Church that Dodgson devoted much of his time, surrounded though he was by his ever-increasing young family.

Of all the activities in which Tertullian counselled personal discipline and restraint none loomed larger than the theatre, launching as he does (in *De Spectaculis*) what Jonas Barish calls a 'systematic onslaught...against the frequenting of the shows by Christians' (1981, p. 44). Tertullian knew whereof he spoke since he had regularly attended such spectacles in his youth. Tertullian did not confine his objections to the undeniable degeneracy of many such performances, but went further and asserted the innate evil of all such activities. As for acting it involved 'an escalating sequence of falsehoods. First the actor falsifies his identity, and so commits a deadly sin. If he impersonates someone vicious, he compounds it...' and so on (p. 46).

Sadly for any aspirations Dodgson might have had for the lasting value of his translation Barish does not use it, though to do so can of

Juvenile

course be revealing about the translator, who inevitably makes his own presence felt through his choice of words and overall tone. In his preface Pusey refers to the 'exceeding difficulty' of the translator's task in view of 'the condensed style of Tertullian', which in places had necessitated the sacrifice of 'his own ideas of English style'. But Dodgson had remained his own man: 'The Translator has purposefully abstained from the use of any previous translation, in order to give his own view of the meaning unbiased.' (Dodgson, 1842, pp. xvii-iii) The footnotes are of course Dodgson unalloyed, such as the following example which occurs early in the (for us crucial) section 'OF PUBLIC SHOWS': 'in like way in Greek, "the phrenzied pleasures...of the theatre"' (p. 188) as well as the circus and such like. In the passage about scriptural justification for condemning plays Tertullian had cited Psalm 1 verse i, which Dodgson renders: 'Blessed is the man, saith he, who hath not gone into the council of the ungodly, and hath not stood in the way of sinners, nor sat in the seat of pestilences' (p. 191). Dodgson deftly observes 'yet Divine Scripture hath always a wide bearing...so that even this passage is not foreign from the purpose of forbidding the public shows' (p. 192), a recurrent and unacceptable feature of which was 'immodesty' (p. 207): 'Thou hast therefore, in the prohibition of immodesty, the prohibition of the theatre also...tragedies and comedies are originators of crimes and lusts, bloody and lascivious, impious and extravagant' (p. 208). Dodgson certainly seems to be entering into the spirit of the original here as he does in another key passage: 'we fall from God...when we touch aught of the sinful things of the world. Wherefore, if I enter the Capitol, or the temple of Serapis, as a sacrificer or a worshipper, I shall fall from God, as also if I enter the Circus or the theatre as a spectator.' (p. 198) The ban, it is important to note, is total. There is no discretion, no distinction between good and bad, moral and immoral plays:

> The Heathens, with whom there is no perfection of truth, because God is not their teacher and truth, define good and evil according to their own will and pleasure, making in one case good, which in another is bad, and that in one case bad, which in another is good. (p. 210)

These were to be abiding concerns for Lewis Carroll who, despite spending his early years under the same roof as his father who was translating one of the most virulent anti-theatrical texts ever written, became an inveterate theatregoer. Fifty years after the publication of Dodgson's translation of Tertullian, Lewis Carroll wrote to A. R. H. Wright on 12 May 1892 that 'we ought to abstain from...all things that are essentially evil', from which he excluded the theatre: 'I take them [his young friends] to good theatres, and good plays; and I carefully avoid the bad ones'. And on the subject of pleasure he wrote to Ellen Terry on 13 November 1890 clearly with the theatre in mind:

> The 'selfish man' is he who would still do the thing, even if it harmed others, so long as it gave *him* pleasure: the 'unselfish man' is he who would still do the thing, even if it gave him no pleasure, so long as it pleased *others*. But, when both motives pull together, the 'unselfish man' is *still* the unselfish man, even though his own pleasure is one of the motives! I am very sure that God takes *pleasure* in seeing his children happy.

Sure though the adult Lewis Carroll was that 'God takes *pleasure* in seeing his children happy', it is uncertain how much as a child he was on the receiving end of such an attitude from his own father. Indeed Carroll's dedication to giving such pleasure to children and – belatedly – to himself might very likely have been in compensation for what he had experienced – or rather *not* experienced – in his own childhood.

Through Dodgson's translation of Tertullian and his son's letters the two engage in a virtual debate about the theatre across the decades. Whether they engaged in such a debate face to face, and if so when, can only be speculation. Violet Dodgson, the fifth daughter of Wilfred Longley Dodgson and therefore Carroll's niece, recalled her grandfather as 'a dignified but genial man' whose presence at dinner ensured 'an amusing and exhilarating evening': 'He had a great fondness for a good argument and plunged, good-humouredly but eagerly, into controversy. So did his sons after him and Charles not least.'[2] Of his position in an argument about the theatre Violet Dodgson was in no doubt: 'the Archdeacon, though allowing private theatricals and charades, set his face against theatre-going and none of his 7 daughters ever went inside a real theatre'. Such an attitude was by no means unusual. The Revd Stewart Headlam, from whose advocacy of the music hall – as well as the theatre – Carroll dissented, grew up in an evangelical family at Wavertree, near Liverpool with his father Thomas, 'a great hand at charades', who completely proscribed attendance at theatres (Bettany, 1926, p. 6).

Another dispensation from the Revd Charles Dodgson was also very typical of such families at the time: a toy theatre, made, according to family tradition as vouched for by Collingwood (1898, p. 28) and Violet Dodgson, by Lewis Carroll 'with help from the village [Croft] carpenter'. As George Speaight has shown, Juvenile Drama in the form of printed sheets depicting the theatre, characters and scenes (as published by Robert Dighton, Hodgson and Co. and Skelt) to be cut out and assembled 'was in its origins and in its heyday entirely pre-Victorian and mainly Regency in

Juvenile 9

character' (1946, p. 60). Lewis Carroll's theatre at Croft obviously belonged to a later generation, in George Speaight's opinion it 'must be one of the very earliest German stages to have reached England' (p. 157), though as he acknowledged it would have been considerably earlier than any other known example. If anything the uncertainty was increased by the evidence provided in 1928 by Mrs Marion Parrington, described as a distant cousin, who wrote to Louisa Dodgson, the last surviving sibling of Lewis Carroll, about a toy theatre which had been passed on to her twenty-seven years earlier and was 'a quaint shabby old thing these days...[it] must be 70 years old, the funny figures with long wires, in their old fashioned clothes are so amusing they all have their names on the back'.[3] What Mrs Parrington was trying to do was to obtain family approval for her intention to sell the theatre, which she proceeded to do at Sotheby's on 14 November 1928 when it was bought by one John Cresswell Brigham for £10. He displayed it in his private museum in Darlington. According to Florence Becker Lennon it was shown at a centenary exhibition in London in 1932 (1947, p. 321). Thereafter any trace of the theatre disappears, but interest was aroused by a short report in *The Times* (10 October 1972) which included a tiny reproduction of a photograph, which had originally appeared in the *Queen* magazine (18 November 1931) on the basis of which Mrs Dodie Masterman 'identified the theatre as made up from engraved sheets published by Adolf Engel...in about 1880!' (Crutch, 1973, p. 3). Clearly this now apparently lost theatre could not have been that used by the young Carroll.

The idea of Carroll constructing his own theatre with the village carpenter is in any case rather more appealing, but the important thing is that he indulged in this pastime when it was hugely popular, not only as a hobby, but also professionally. George Speaight has researched the Royal Marionette Theatre, located off the Lowther Arcade in the Strand, where in 1852 Signor Brigaldi directed puppets 'from the theatres at Naples, Milan, Genoa etc.' accompanied by 'their own orchestra' (1955, p. 240). In total Brigaldi had about 150 marionettes, each between two and three feet high made of wood, cork and *papier maché*. They were manipulated from a high bridge. The pieces in which they performed were burlesques or parodies, which satirical though they often were evaded censorship because they were performed by puppets. The marionettes were very much the vogue. Their season ran for six months until July 1852 after which they toured the provinces spending three months in Manchester and two in Liverpool. They returned to London and 'were eventually established at Cremorne Gardens in 1857 in a magnificent Marionette Theatre, with an imposing Italianite façade, capable of seating a thousand people which had been specially built for them' (p. 242). Cremorne

Gardens had previously hosted a rather more modest marionette installation in 1852 when they were 'great favourites of the public and of the proprietor, who liked "the little beggars who never came to the treasury on Saturday"' (Wroth, 1907, pp. 7-8). As Henry Morley observed: 'Puppets have at various times, therefore, and in various countries, had a larger following than one might have thought fairly due to the merits of wooden actors in the abstract. Wooden actors in the concrete (flesh and blood) have been so much worse.' (1891, pp. 28-9)

1.   Marionette Theatre

Juvenile

Marionette theatres clearly appealed strongly to large numbers of adults principally as spectators, but whereas there is no evidence of Carroll attending such performances, though he must have been aware of them, there is evidence of him still working with his own theatre in the summer of 1855, when he was twenty-three. George Speaight has written: 'The early Toy Theatre was, in fact, never intended for children, in the sense that paper toys were. It was quite obviously intended for the enthusiasts of the theatre, who were mainly young men and boys; and it was the boys who insisted upon making the thing work, and compelled its evolution from souvenir sheets of characters to complete plays.' (1946, p. 119) Speaight is of course referring to early nineteenth-century toy theatres for which, as we have seen, he adopted the term 'Juvenile Drama', but the point about the appeal being to 'enthusiasts of the theatre...mainly young men and boys' may have had equal – or greater – application to the more complicated mid nineteenth-century toy theatres. That Lewis Carroll's continuing fascination with his marionette theatre was not all that unusual is evident from the fact that it was shared by his cousin, Charles Robert Fletcher Lutwidge, who, being three years his junior, was twenty in 1855. On 9 July Carroll wrote in his diary of his activities helping at the new National School at Croft, adding 'Fletcher has been here since Friday'. He refers to Fletcher again on 13 July: 'Fletcher still here. During his stay he painted one scene, a palace interior, for the Marionette theatre. I am convinced now that calico is the best material for painting on.' For Fletcher this was valuable experience for his contribution to ADC productions at Cambridge as F. C. Burnand recorded:

Mr. Gage was the local paid artistic talent, but in the year 1857 Charles Lutwidge, of Trin Coll., painted a proscenium for us, representing the figures of Tragedy and Comedy standing in niches under the busts of Shakespeare and Molière. A scroll ran along the width of the proscenium with the motto 'All the world's a stage', and the club initials, 'A.D.C.', in the centre. The same amateur artist also painted for us 'the conservatory flat' in *Still Waters* – a very effective set-piece – and some other set-pieces for the burlesque of *Turkish Waters* and *Lord Lovel*. He had also commenced a design for an act-drop...

As we came to depend more on our members for everything, stage carpentry, stage mechanism, painting, etc., so we dispensed with all extraneous help, and Lutwidge and Merthyr Guest – a worthy successor of our first manager Polwhele – might be seen, in paper caps and aprons, hard at real work on the stage, thus saving the Club great expense, while adding to the interest of the performance. (1880, p. 169)

12   *Lewis Carroll and the Victorian Stage*

Whilst his cousin concentrated on the scenery, Lewis Carroll was more interested in the plays to be performed. Earlier that year he had staged a performance with the sons of his father's curate Mr Webster: 'Ap: 11. As our own family are all at home now, and likewise the Webster boys, we got up an entertainment for the assembled party with the Marionette Theatre. I chose the Tragedy of King John, which went off very successfully.' Carroll's choice of *King John* reflects his awareness of the contemporary stage. It had been revived by Charles Kean on 9 February 1852 at the Princess's Theatre. Such was his interest in the production that he copied out *The Times* review (Clark, 1979, p. 146). Like all Kean's productions *King John* was elaborately staged with painstaking attention to historical accuracy (see Shattuck ed., 1962), which Carroll no doubt sought to emulate. By April 1855 *King John* was no longer in Kean's repertoire, but on 16 May another pageant of English history *King Henry VIII* began its lengthy run at the Princess's where on 22 June, 'after much searching of heart and consultation with Dr Liddon, [he] decided his conscience was his own' and 'went to see his first play'.[4] As for so many of Carroll's contemporaries, the permitted indulgence in toy theatres led to the overthrow of parental proscription against attending the professional theatre. Thus toy theatres might be said to have assisted in the formation of a new generation of middle-class theatregoers.

Carroll calculated that for *King John* 'we have managed to get up the whole thing with about 20 figures, for a very few shillings' and turned his mind to producing:

> Ap: 11. (W)…A Christmas book for children that would sell well. Practical hints for constructing Marionettes and a theatre… – this might be followed by several plays for representation by Marionettes or by children. All existing plays for such objects seem to me to have two faults – either (1) they are meant for the real theatre, and are therefore not fitted for children, or (2) they are overpoweringly dull – no idea of fun in them.

It is worth noting here that at the age of twenty-three, Carroll, who in later life was to take a succession of children to the theatre, was already considering their special needs, pre-eminent amongst which was 'fun'.

On 10 July 1855 Carroll wrote of his 'idea for a new Drama for the Marionette theatre, *Alfred the Great*, but have not yet begun to write it. His adventures in disguise in the neatherd's hut, and in the Danish Camp, will furnish two very effective scenes.' If he ever wrote such a play Carroll's would not have been the first on the subject, Nelson Lee having completed *Harlequin Alfred the Great* in 1850 (Booth ed., 1976, p. 47), as Carroll might possibly have known. One marionette theatre play which

Juvenile   13

Carroll did get around to writing has happily survived, his sister Louise in November 1928 having 'chanced on the MS of a play Uncle Charles wrote for the theatre, written out in his own hand'.[5] Soon after the discovery the family sold the manuscript at Sotheby's on 14 February 1929 when it fetched £570. It was subsequently published in the *Queen* (18 November 1931) together with a photograph of the marionette theatre on which it had allegedly been performed, but which, as we have seen, has since been dated 1880. Described as 'A Hitherto Unpublished Ballad Opera', *La Guida di Bragia* was 'the Opera' which Carroll performed on 31 July 1855 'for the benefit of Menella Wilcox', a cousin whose own daughter Menella (Minna) Quin was to embark on a stage career with Carroll's help. The title of the opera refers to *Bradshaw's Railway Guide*, but the use of Italian not only imbues the subject with absurd grandeur, but also reflects the contemporary enthusiasm for Italian marionette theatres. Carroll had already given expression to his interest in railways by constructing a model in the garden at Croft, which was of course near to Darlington, the birthplace of such important developments in this revolutionary form of transport. The connection between the railways and the theatre was not unique. E. L. Blanchard, many of whose pantomimes Carroll later attended, entitled one *The Birth of the Steam Train, or Harlequin Locomotive* in 1846, the year after the anonymous *Harlequin and the Steam King*. There was even a skit published in *Punch* (24 May 1856) which Roger Lancelyn Green acknowledged had 'similarities' with *La Guida di Bragia*, but he did not 'imagine LC had anything to do with it'.[6] This is probably true. The *Punch* playlet, entitled *Bradshaw A Mystery*, is far less ambitious and sophisticated than *La Guida di Bragia*, with which it has one character name in common: Orlando, who in both plays is rather better endowed socially than he is intellectually. Percy Fitzgerald provides a further connection between the theatre and railway guides since as well as writing *Principles of Comedy and Dramatic Effect*, about which Carroll sent him a complimentary letter of 18 October 1872, he was also the author of *The Story of Bradshaw's Guide*, which provides the context for Carroll's play: the introduction in 1847 of the 'Continental Guide' and the price (half-a-franc) of the Italian guide the 'Orario Civelli' (1890, p. 57 and p. 66).

As with Italian marionette theatre, which was currently so popular, Carroll's play began with a prologue, but one which was entirely concerned with the British theatre. It was spoken by 'Mr. B. Webster' (see Webster, 1969), actor, manager and dramatist who had run the Olympic and Haymarket theatres and was particularly renowned for his performance as Triplet in *Masks and Faces* (by Charles Reade and Tom Taylor), later revivals of which Carroll attended.

14 *Lewis Carroll and the Victorian Stage*

PROLOGUE
By Mr. B. Webster
Scene: Green curtain at back – green floor – green paper sides.
Draw up P. curtain
Shall soldiers tread the murderous path of war,
Without a notion what they do it for?
Shall pallid mercers drive a roaring trade,
And sell the stuffs their hands have never made?
And shall not we, in this our mimic scene,
Be all that better actors e'er have been?
Awake again a Kemble's tragic tone,
And make a Liston's humour all our own?
Or vie with Mrs Siddons in the art
To rouse the feelings and to charm the heart?
While Shakespeare's self, with all his ancient fires,
Lights up the forms that tremble on our wires?
Why can't we have, in theatres ideal,
The good, without the evil, of the real?
Why may not Marionettes be just as good
As larger actors made of flesh and blood?
Presumptuous thought! To you and your applause
In humbler confidence we trust our cause. (*Queen* 18 November 1931)

If Charles Dodgson attended the performance he would surely have noted not only his son's knowledge of the theatre (Kemble, Liston, Siddons), but also the lines 'Why can't we have, in theatres ideal, / The good, without the evil, of the real?' which amounted to a claim that the theatre could be 'good' and was not (*pace* Tertullian) inherently 'evil'.

The play proper combines two plots: the first two comic characters Mooney and Spooney who on securing jobs at a railway station change their names to Moggs and Spicer; the second an aristocratic couple Sophonisba and Orlando, who undertake a journey to Birmingham. There are also a Mrs Muddle, a Kaffir and at the end Bradshaw himself who reveals that he 'altered all the train-times in my book / And made the world go wrong' as a result. The play includes a fair amount of reported speech, necessitating Mooney and Spooney to assume other voices, numerous 'Airs' including 'Should all my luggage be forgot, / And never come to hand' to '*Auld Lang Syne*' and extensive Shakespearian parody such as 'Tunes, music, thorough-bass, lend me your ear.' It concludes (as did the Italian marionette plays) with an epilogue, spoken by Richard Flexmore, the renowned clown, judged by Clement Scott as 'one of the best clowns and dancing masters since the days of Grimaldi' (1899, vol. I,

Juvenile

15

p. 263), another indication of Carroll's theatrical knowledge and taste. In the best theatrical tradition Flexmore appealed to the audience:

Both strangers and relations, we thank you, one and all,
We asked you for your plaudits and you answered to our call,
Pit, gallery (if such there be) and stalls, and private boxes,
Spectators all of many names, especially Wilcoxes!

There can be little doubt that Lewis Carroll's efforts were a triumphant success with his audience, but what of his father? How did that stern *pater familias* regard his twenty-three-year-old son who was devoting so much time to a toy theatre and other equally light-hearted activities?

Some of these had taken place at an age at which they would generally have been considered appropriate. Collingwood dates the earliest magazine *Useful and Instructive Poetry* to 'somewhere about the year 1845' and refers to 'a host of equally short-lived ventures' concluding about 1850 with *The Rectory Umbrella* (1898, p. 38). As Jean Gattegno points out 'his parody of *Henry IV*, Part II, [in *Useful and Instructive Poetry*] merits special attention for the way in which it combines a sense of parody with an early taste for logic.' (1977, p. 115). The serial story 'The Walking Stick', which runs through *The Rectory Umbrella*, includes elements of popular entertainment, notably a magician (Collingwood, 1898a, p. 618). Carroll's lifelong fascination (see Fisher, 1973) with magic began early and his delight is apparent in a lengthy letter of 9 November 1853 to his sister Mary describing 'a conjuring performance in Oxford last night'. Then there are the charades for which on 25 August 1855 he proposes 'a plan...suited to inferior actors', though he later (4 September) reports that: 'Freddy acted far better than I expected' (in *Box and Cox* which followed the charade 'Den-mark') and he accorded the event his highest mark of approbation, a white stone.

On occasion Carroll dispensed with other performers altogether. On his first ever theatre visit on 22 June 1855 *Henry VIII* had been preceded by 'a capital farce, *Away with Melancholy*' by John Maddison Morton, the author of the aforementioned *Box and Cox*. Carroll evidently lost no time in acquiring a copy and on 3 September he read it aloud, 'a decidedly more successful performance than *Henry VIII* the other evening was'. He repeated his performance on 18 September and gave reprises on 24 March 1856, 29 September 1856, 6 April 1857, 4 August 1857 when he referred to it with ample justification as 'my often repeated performance, *Away with Melancholy*'. That was not all, he also introduced the voice of his favourite character Mr Trimmer into other entertainments such as that on 31 December 1856 when he 'employed seven different voices'. Running

16   *Lewis Carroll and the Victorian Stage*

to twenty printed pages with a cast of six (three male: Windsor Brown, Mr Trimmer and the servant David; three female: Mrs Maynard, Miss Kitty Cobb and Dainty) and numerous songs including the title 'Away with melancholy', this fairly typical 'boarding-house' (the same type of setting as *Box and Cox*) play would have placed very considerable demands on a solo-performer (see Maddison Morton, 1850).

Though *Away with Melancholy* was Carroll's favoured piece, he also performed Henry Thornton Craven's *Done Brown*, which he had seen at the Lyceum Theatre, Sunderland on 21 September 1855 as the afterpiece to *Henry IV*. On 11 July 1857 his performance was part of a packed day which included photography and charades and on 5 August 1857 it was on the day following *Away with Melancholy*. Similar in length to *Away with Melancholy*, *Done Brown*'s six characters are if anything rather more fantastic: 'Fitzlang, Inheritor from Nature of most available Property – impudence; Monsieur Octave Alfred Leclef, a Gallic Apollo, dwelling adjacent to the heavens – a garret; Murphy O'Filliloo, a Bricklayer – a (H)odd Fellow and a very Free Mason; Mr Boosey, a retired Spirit Dealer, with two weaknesses – irascibility & strong grog; Alfred Bingham, the young Lover – well dressed and amiable, of course; Mrs Winks, a Lodging House Keeper – a Widow eligible' (Craven, nd). As the characters' names suggest, the piece gave Carroll abundant scope to employ a range of voices and accents. As their names also imply, several characters have a penchant for drink, under the influence of which they burst into song punctuated by repeated requests for 'more brandy', though *Done Brown* is 'A Vaudeville' free from the moralising of temperance melodrama. The frontispiece depicts the following exchange:

> *FITZLANG* – Here – you arm yourself with the coffee pot, and I'll arm myself with the poker.
> *LECLEF*   Be dam! – dat is not fair!

Carroll was not merely performing a play, he was depicting the vice of drunkenness and uttering a word ('dam') to the use of which on the stage he took great exception in later life. What emerges most strongly from Carroll's public play readings is his sense of fun and comic flair. Of his first effort *Henry VIII*, on 28 August 1855, he wrote of 'feeling angry with myself for the miserable way in which I fell short of even my own concept of that glorious play'. As well as this feeling of his own inadequacy Carroll must have been aware of how little scope this play ('the whole reading took about an hour') offered for him to engage with his audience in terms of the response which he almost certainly most craved: their laughter. In contrast lighter fare such as *Away with Melancholy* and *Done*

Brown released him as a performer and drew frequent and no doubt encouraging reactions from his audiences.

Carroll's evident interest – and skill – in projecting different voices may have attracted him to Henry Cockton's novel *The Life and Adventures of Valentine Vox The Ventriloquist*, first published in 1840, to which he refers on 16 January 1855: 'Read *Valentine Vox* in the morning instead of working'. As Donald Thomas (1996, p. 126) points out, lunacy is one of the novel's themes, but to assume that, because of his uncle Skeffington Lutwidge's post as a Commissioner in Lunacy, this constituted Lewis Carroll's main interest in it is to endow it with a seriousness which Carroll's own diary entry scarcely justifies. In fact much of Valentine's life and many of his adventures are to do with various forms of entertainment. He exercises his voice; appears on the stage of the Italian Opera; attends a masquerade at Vauxhall Gardens with regard to which the following observation is made: 'When men say, that vice invariably attends them [masquerades], they say but that which is applicable to all entertainments; but if they be properly conducted, a more delightful kind of amusement can scarcely be conceived.' (p. 181)

Further locations include a civic pageant, the Zoological Gardens with 'talking animals' (thanks to Valentine's skill!), Greenwich Fair, the Royal Academy and Ascot Races. The episodes set in a lunatic asylum notwithstanding, *Valentine Vox* virtually constitutes a gazetteer of leisure and recreation in early Victorian England. Carroll's own tally was far from meagre as his list of 'Events' and 'Theatricals' at the end of his 1857 diary indicates, including as it does a magic lantern in addition to other home amusements and a burgeoning list of theatres visited.

Although it was a rapidly expanding town (largely because of the railways), nearby Darlington does not feature in Carroll's list. As Chris Lloyd has chronicled, the Quakers who dominated the town were categorically opposed to the theatre. He quotes a notice issued to their employees by the mill-owners Henry Pease and Co in 1859 in response to a licence being granted for a theatre: 'We ask you then – as you value the confidence of your employers, your health, your character, your claim to the title of Christians – never to go within the doors of a Theatre' (1991, p. 15). A firsthand account of the fears and frustrations of a youthful theatregoer in Darlington at the time when the like-minded Lewis Carroll was at Croft Rectory a few miles away is given by J. M. Dent, the eminent publisher. He describes how to the Quakers 'the theatre was taboo...looked upon...as the very gate of hell' (in Dent, Hugh R, 1938, p. 5). As with Carroll, Dent's first visit to the theatre was unforgettable:

> I have dreamed about that first night quite lately. Having once tasted blood the theatre became the one desire of my boyish life, and I would perpetrate any meanness, deceive the homefolk by any kind of prevarication, get money how and where I could – it was only threepence a night – that I might be thrilled with excitement in melodrama and romance and farawayness in Shakespearean comedy and tragedy. (p. 17)

He admitted to having 'a conscience loaded with guilt', but felt that 'even from the crudest melodrama, I was being taught a code of morals' as he became 'so rabid a theatre haunter' (p. 18).

Close by in Croft Rectory Lewis Carroll had by 1855 set his course as a rabid theatregoer. Though in his father's eyes this must have been his son's worst calumny it was at least conducted at a distance whereas during each vacation from Oxford the Revd Charles Dodgson was confronted by an apparently unrelenting sequence of home entertainments, which though they were not in themselves reprehensible, probably seemed increasingly inappropriate for a student (fellow) in mathematics at Christ Church, who was fully expected to follow his father into the holy orders in the Church of England. There his duties would include conducting services and delivering sermons which he would experience great difficulty in doing because of a stammer, a stammer which in no way affected his performances in marionette plays, charades and other entertainments including the solo public reading of six-character plays. As he revealed in a letter of 2 February 1874 to H. F. Rivers, Carroll had seven sisters who stammered in varying degrees, but for his father the plight of his eldest son for whom he had such high expectations must have been profoundly disturbing. It was not until 1859 that Carroll consulted Dr James Hunt, described by Cohen as the 'foremost speech correctionist' of the day (1995, p. 76). Hunt provided some insights into contemporary attitudes in his books beginning with *Stammering and Stuttering Their Nature and Treatment* in 1854. Naturally he defined the two maladies: stammering 'difficulty of properly enunciating some or many of the elementary speech-sounds' and stuttering 'a vicious utterance, manifested by *frequent repetitions*' (pp. 12-13). On the question of causes and treatment Hunt wrote of the problem in detecting 'the difference between real and pretended stammering, and many children really afflicted have been treated with great injustice on that account. A susceptible, timid child, constantly in awe of an ignorant parent, or a brutal master, may be made to stutter by cruel treatment.' (p. 147) In 1859, the year in which Carroll consulted him, Hunt delved further into the causes of speech disabilities in his *A Manual of the Philosophy of Voice and Speech Especially in relation to the English Language and Art of Public Speaking*, which he dedicated

Juvenile 19

to Charles Kingsley. With George MacDonald also a client (Carroll met him for the first time at Hunt's), Hunt might be said to have cornered the market in leading authors for children. With chapters on 'Ventriloquism and Speaking Machines' (Chapter 9) and 'The Cultivation of the Voice' (Chapter 20), which included references to actors from Betterton to Charles Mathews, Carroll must have felt that he was in the hands of a kindred spirit, though the contents of 'Disorders of the Voice' (Chapter 16) might well have disconcerted him. In it Hunt dealt with the possible causes of psellism (the generic term for all speech disorders) identifying three types: organic, dynamic and psychical. Organic was straightforward: a cleft palate for instance, but under dynamic Hunt listed nervous debility, solitary vices, spermatorrho/ea and under psychical depressing emotions, want of energy, self control etc. (1859, p. 312).

A timid child in awe of an overbearing parent, a practitioner of solitary vices or a depressive lacking in self control. Which, if any of these causes, applied to Lewis Carroll? There is no evidence that he was depressive nor that he practiced solitary vices, though even if he did it would probably not exist. The case for the Revd Charles Dodgson as an overbearing parent has of course already been given considerable weight by several of his son's biographers. The fact that his seven daughters all suffered from speech defects and what Karoline Leach called 'hyper-passivity' is certainly consistent with this interpretation, as is his attitude to his sons Skeffington and Wilfred when they were staying in Keswick in the spring of 1856. Dodgson had 'arranged with Mr Webster that you shall continue as his Pupils until the end of the year'. He then seeks to reassure them that 'in making arrangements for you I have always endeavoured to fix upon that plan which I thought would make you both the most happy', though he does not appear to have consulted them and it must be doubtful that he would have deferred to their preferences if he had. Dodgson then proceeds to impose a strong sense of obligation on his sons: 'You must receive it also as a mark of confidence which I have in you both that you will not let the attractions of the Lakes & Hills prevent your attending to the *chief* purpose for which you are placed under a Private Tutor – This extra stay at Keswick will cost me an additional 200 Guineas' (Amor ed., 1990, p. 13). In an earlier letter dated 6 February 1856 Dodgson's concern was not the attractions of 'the Lakes & Hills', but 'the <u>young ladies</u>, into whose company you are introduced' (p. 12). Given the Revd Charles Dodgson's prohibition on 'Lakes & Hills' and '<u>young ladies</u>' for his younger sons, what was his likely attitude towards his eldest, most talented son, then in his mid-twenties, spending much of his time on a marionette theatre, charades and other home entertainments as well as

20 *Lewis Carroll and the Victorian Stage*

disregarding the absolute injunction against attending a professional theatre?

The Revd Charles Dodgson's relationship with his eldest son remains elusive: a disapproving and long-suffering onlooker or a benign and indulgent presence? My own view tends to the former, but I acknowledge that a case could be made for the latter. His son's character though emerges much more clearly. He found applying himself to serious, professional tasks quite difficult and was easily and willingly distracted. He must have been a natural performer, someone who delighted in an audience – especially their laughter – and attention, not only for himself but also for the pleasure (fun) he found that he could give other people, particularly children. He may well have had to withstand a certain amount of disapprobation, but if so it was clearly worth it in order to shed his shyness and stammer and to express what he considered to be his true self. As Virginia Woolf put it: 'For some reason, we know not what, his childhood was sharply severed. It lodged in him whole and entire.' (1947, p. 70)

Notes

1   DFC (Dodgson Family Collection) A/1/1, The Surrey History Centre, Woking.
2   Typescript of talk given to the Leamington Literary Society by Miss Violet Dodgson on 17 October 1949. DFC/C/1/1-15.
3   DFC/F/64/1/1-2.
4   DFC/C/1/1-15.
5   Letter dated 8 November 1928 from Frances Menella Dodgson to her brother Wilfred about their aunt's discovery of the manuscript DFC/F/60/2. The DFC also contains further letters on this subject and an exchange between Menella Dodgson and John Cresswell Brigham on the marionette theatre which he offers to sell to her for £50. Further contemporary correspondence about the theatre and the play are to be found in the Berol Collection at the Fales Library, New York University, where the manuscript of *La Guida di Bragia* is now located. The Lewis Carroll Scrapbook recently acquired by the Library of Congress includes *Bradshaw A Mystery*. See *The Gazette* 20 August 2004 and http://international.loc.gov/intldl/carroll.html.
6   Letter dated 23 March 1961 from Roger Lancelyn Green to Violet Dodgson DFC/F/64/11/1-3.

2 Unwillingly to School

'What were you sent to Rugby for?'
Thomas Hughes, *Tom Brown's Schooldays*

The performance of plays has a longstanding place in the school curriculum. Tudor education provides many examples: St Paul's, Winchester, Eton, Shrewsbury, and Westminster, whose headmaster Nicholas Udall, previously head of Eton, was the author of *Ralph Roister Doister* (see Lobb, 1955). Whether *Ralph Roister Doister* was first performed at Eton or Westminster, it was at the latter establishment during the headship (1543–55) of Dr Alexander Nowell that the annual performance of a Latin play was instituted, being included as a clause in the statutes when the school was re-founded in 1560. With the notable exception of Dr Richard Valpy at Reading School, dramatic activity in schools declined in the eighteenth century, but by the beginning of the nineteenth a revival was underway. William Charles Macready, 'the Eminent Tragedian', did not greatly enjoy his time at Rugby, where he was bullied, but highlights included a performance of M. G. Lewis's *The Castle Spectre* on 15 October 1807, supported by his own father who provided costumes and scenery, and the headmaster Dr Wooll. A couple of decades later William Gladstone recorded details of a performance of a play at Eton (see Foulkes, 1997, pp. 36–8).

The first school attended by Lewis Carroll was Richmond School, which he entered on 1 August 1844 at the age of twelve. Factors influencing the Revd Charles Dodgson's choice of this school included its proximity (ten miles) to Croft and its 'excellent reputation as an educational establishment' with 'the fees...over one hundred guineas a year, comparable with that of the foremost public schools of the day' (Amor, 1995, p. 31). Carroll boarded (at additional cost) in Swale House, which was presided over by the school's headmaster James Tate II, whose father had preceded him in the post. James Tate I was born in Richmond on 11 June 1771, the son of a working maltster, and became a pupil at the school from whence he proceeded to Sidney Sussex College, Cambridge. Tate was appointed head of Richmond School on 27 September 1796 and: 'On 29th September, 1796, two days after his appointment as Master of the School – Tate married in London at Kensington Parish Church, Margaret

Wallis, second daughter of Fielding Wallis, actor, and Jane (née Miller) his wife.' (Wenham, 1958, p. 67) Margaret Wallis's elder sister Tryphosa Jane had a successful stage career encompassing Bath and Covent Garden.

Sybil Rosenfeld has unravelled the complex web of professional and family relationships which, she states, 'must begin ...with the birth at Barnard Castle in 1727, of Tryphosa Brockell, daughter of the Rev. Christopher Brockell, granddaughter of the Rev. John Brockell, and great-granddaughter of the Rev. John Brockell' (1984, p. 2). Tryphosa herself was the grandmother of Margaret and Tryphosa Wallis. As Sybil Rosenfeld observes, because of this background their '[theatrical] company always had a strong reputation for respectability and this must have been enhanced by the family's connections with the church' (p. 2). When the seventeen-year-old James Tate attended the opening of the Richmond Theatre on 2 September 1788 the stage was occupied by many members of the family into which he was to marry. In his diary he wrote: 'The New Theatre opened. A Prologue by Stanfield spoken by Butler. Inkle and Jarico [comic opera by George Colman the Younger] and the midnight hour [Mrs Inchbald's comedy *The Midnight Hour*]...The Theatre very elegant'. (p. 13) Tate continued to patronise the theatre and with his marriage to Margaret Wallis and his appointment to the headship of Richmond School: '[he] encouraged his pupils to take an interest in the Theatre Royal, Richmond, most unusual for a schoolmaster in those days. Theatre bills are still in existence advertising performances "by command of the Gentlemen of Richmond School"' (Wenham, 1958, p. 67) In November 1799 'the Gentlemen of Richmond School' went further as Tate wrote to Mrs Ottley:

> And now to tell you of a very good thing done by our boys this week. Mrs Darley the wife of Mr. Darley, one of Mr. Butler's company, was confined the very morning on which the company left for Whitby. Here she was left with two children besides...Well amongst our boys my own scholars that board in the house particularly, Mrs Darley's success was mentioned when a thought struck one of them, which was heartily embraced by the rest, that they would act a play in the school for her benefit, of course my consent was soon obtained & my hearty concurrence too. (in Rosenfeld, 1984, p. 27)

As it was for similar requests such as that craving permission by 'your humble petition to perform *Cato* for the good of the poor' and a play entitled *The Earl of Warwick* for which they only awaited 'the sanction of your leave to begin', pointing out that 'it will be a very good exercise in oratory' (in Wenham, 1958, p. 67). Tate I served thirty-six years as

Unwillingly to School 23

headmaster of Richmond School during which time he produced eleven children, one of whom succeeded him as head: James Tate II.

By 1830 the fortunes of the Richmond Theatre had declined and it 'was from time to time taken for a season by various managers' (Rosenfeld, 1984, p. 92), which meant that the family connection with Richmond School lapsed. Donald Thomas has speculated that: 'It may have been here [Richmond] that Charles Dodgson saw his first theatre. Richmond's Theatre Royal, built in 1788, was plain but elegant with its boxes on their Tuscan pillars and its graceful proscenium arch.' (1996, p. 48) Although he certainly did not attend a performance at the Richmond Theatre, Carroll may have glimpsed its interior and must have known its exterior and been aware of such visiting luminaries as Charles and Ellen Kean whom Lord Russell recalled appearing there (Rosenfeld, 1984, p. 99).

The theatre was closed by the time Carroll was attending Richmond School and there are no records of dramatic activity at the school then, but there seems to be no reason to suppose that Tate II was unsympathetic to such activities. What he undoubtedly supplied for the twelve-year-old son of the Revd Charles Dodgson was a family environment, which must have greatly eased his removal from Croft. In a letter to his sisters Frances and Elizabeth and his brother Skeffington on 5 August 1844, Carroll describes 'two tricks' played on him by boys during their games and identified 'as the boys I think that I like best' as 'all the Tates of which there are 7 besides a little girl who came to dinner the first day, but not since'. With most of the Tate children his junior in years, Carroll would have had the opportunity to form the sort of relationship which he was to replicate throughout his life. That he formed a bond with the family is evident from his references to them in his diaries. On 4 August 1855 he records that:

> Walked over to Richmond, and called on the Tates; Charles, Thomas, and John, are away from home: Lucy Tate has grown from a romping girl into the most staid of young ladies, so much change can 2 years produce. I dined and had tea there. And, missing the last evening train, walked home again, the last mile or so being a most painful performance.

Perhaps this was the first of what was to become a recurrent experience for Carroll: 'a romping girl' transformed 'into the most staid of young ladies'. The following year Lucy Tate 'came over to be photographed' at Croft after which 'I read aloud *Done Brown*, which was followed by a story-charade, in which Lucy Tate, William, Katie, Georgie, Lucy [all the rest were Wilcox cousins] and I appeared, "Win-dough"'. Lucy was then thirteen. Although he does mention other members of the Tate family

24   *Lewis Carroll and the Victorian Stage*

(James on 18 September 1855; Charles on 20 March 1856), significantly it is Lucy whom Carroll photographs, entertains with his performance of *Done Brown* and involves in charades.

Entering Rugby School, nigh 200 miles from home, in the midst of winter (January 1846) must have been a bleak experience. Why the Revd Charles Dodgson chose Rugby at all, let alone that particular time of year, is somewhat puzzling. He himself had attended Westminster School as a King's Scholar, but Westminster was in a slough whereas Rugby still basked in the glow of the recently deceased (in 1842) Dr Arnold's achievements. The Revd Charles Dodgson can hardly have been drawn to Rugby by Arnold's replacement, the future Archbishop of Canterbury Archibald Campbell Tait, who whilst a Balliol don had been prominent in the opposition to Newman's *Tract XC*, a leading supporter of which was Edward Bouverie Pusey, Dodgson's contemporary and patron. As a member of School House Carroll was under Tait's direct superintendence; his surviving letters home are to his sister Elizabeth, through whom he channels communications to his father such as the request on 9 October 1848 for a copy of 'Liddell and Scott's Larger *Greek-English Lexicon*'. Although according to H. C. Bradley many of the school's more 'barbarous customs' had been abolished by Dr Wooll (1900, p. 49), amongst those which had survived was a rite of passage observed on the last Saturday night of the half when:

> it was an established rule that every new boy should be obliged to sing, or in case of his refusal, be pumped upon. By such as were of a shy disposition their turn would be looked forward to with much the same feelings as those which occupied the mind of a young sailor on approaching 'The Line', when Neptune's visit and particular style of shaving were in vogue. The extreme severity of this regulation was seldom inflicted, even in case of an absolute refusal to sing. (Newark, 1848, p. 122)

It is natural to speculate on how Carroll would have dealt with that situation. Shy he undoubtedly was, but he was also a natural entertainer. Which side of him would have come to the fore? Was he as intimidated as the unfortunate Arthur in *Tom Brown's School Days*:

> 'Can you sing?'
> The poor boy was trembling and hesitating. Tom struck in – 'You be hanged, Tadpole. He'll have to sing, whether he can or not, Saturday twelve weeks, and that's long enough off yet.' (Hughes, 1966, p. 131)

Hughes's novel, first published in 1857, is of course set in the Arnold era and ends with his death, but in some respects Carroll might be seen as a

Unwillingly to School

prototype for Arthur, or rather vice versa, with his clergyman father 'full of faith, hope, and love', who 'as he [Arthur] reached his thirteenth year...after much debating with himself had resolved to send him there [Rugby]' where 'the timid weak boy, had points in him from which the bravest and strongest recoiled' (p. 142). Thus Claudia Nelson is right when she says that

> Hughes's novel contrasts the various possibilities for male character, weighting the boyish Tom Brown and Scud East against the bully Flashman, the eccentric Martin and the frail George Arthur...In fact Hughes seems to have intended his tale as 'an exposition of Arnold's method' of inculcating moral responsibility. Viewing matters in this light, we must conclude that of all the boys at Rugby it is Arthur who is the most adult and the most genuinely manly. (1991, pp. 40–41)

Nelson goes on to underline the affirmation of feminine power: 'Manliness involves motherliness...the boy (Tom) has become a real man, gentle, pious, humble, obedient, disciplined, and ready to cry on affecting occasions' (p. 44). Undeniably these are qualities which Carroll displayed. Be this as it may, the reality was that Carroll was unhappy at Rugby. Although he wrote home on 9 October 1848 asking: 'Is W.L. and L.F.'s *Useful and Instructive Poetry* finished binding yet?' there is no evidence that he involved himself in what J. B. Hope Simpson described as 'plenty to do indoors' at Rugby:

> For the intellectual there was the Debating Society, stated in 1845, or the excitement of producing one of the many ephemeral School or House magazines, such as the *Rugby Miscellany* of 1845, which produced ten numbers; or the *Rugbaean*, which was started by T. W. Jex-Blake in 1850 and ran through twenty numbers before its death in 1850. (1967, p. 34)

The first issue of the *Rugby Miscellany*[1] in March 1845 carried a lengthy report of an event which tantalisingly took place before Carroll's admission to the school, but is nonetheless a useful indicator of the attitude of Tait[2] and his staff towards drama: a performance of *As You Like It* by the boys. The author, Y.L., pays tribute to 'the ruling powers' not only for disregarding the 'many objections...raised to the theatrical performances, by parents of boys, at the school; on the ground, chiefly, I suppose, of its withdrawing the attention too much from the work of the school', but also insisting on 'Shakspeare, or nothing'. In the event the production was prepared in ten days at little expense and the cast acquitted themselves very creditably. To have Rosalind performed by a boy was of course to return to Elizabethan practice and 'though there was some

26 *Lewis Carroll and the Victorian Stage*

difficulty in the part being performed by a male, yet the transformation was complete, and the acting very spirited and lively, a very great point in character'. Orlando was considered to display 'a certain Byronic style', Jaques –'Macready's own character'– 'seemed to feel and understand his author thoroughly…his intonation was rather unnatural, both in the speech of the seven ages and the last scene', Duke Frederick 'was in no possible way suited for his part', the Banished Duke needed 'a little more animation', Audrey 'took with the audience, but was too gross, though very amusing', Adam 'by the same hand, was very well done', and 'Celia was a very pretty figure, and acted very neatly'. Y.L. concluded:

> Let us hope, then, that this practice will not be suffered immediately to die; but let us look for a time not far distant, when again, under propitious auspices, we may see at Rugby the curtain rise on some other of Shakspeare's plays. Vivant Regina et princeps.

Unfortunately succeeding volumes of the *Rugby Miscellany* contain no reference to further productions, leading to the conclusion that none took place during Carroll's time at the school. However, the allusion to Jaques as 'Macready's character' shows that the actor was known and honoured at his *alma mater*, something that with his strong interest in theatre history Carroll would have fully endorsed. Frustratingly for him, Carroll, who had left Rugby earlier that year, narrowly missed the great tragedian's visit to his old school on 14 November 1850. The occasion was a reading of *Hamlet* in aid of the fund to purchase Shakespeare's house in nearby Stratford-upon-Avon. As Macready was at pains to point out to the thronged schoolroom, he was doing this at 'the suggestion of their own praepostors' (Pollock ed., 1876, p. 643). Self-critical as ever, Macready judged that 'I think I succeeded in keeping alive the interest of the audience', a view endorsed in the first issue of *The Rugbaean*, which recorded that during his performance 'he received that most gratifying of all applause, silence and attention, but at the end the approbation was loud and long'. Edward Dodgson, unlike Skeffington and Wilfred, did follow his eldest brother to Rugby, but not in time to attend this theatrical treat and give a full account to his stage-struck sibling. Macready returned to London with £50 for the fund, marvelling that thanks to the railway his entire expedition had been completed in about twelve hours.

After a protracted series of 'farewell' performances, Macready retired from the stage on 26 February 1851 and on 1 March was guest of honour at a magnificent farewell banquet attended by leading politicians, authors, artists and fellow-actors…upwards of six hundred in all with speeches by Bulwer Lytton, Charles Dickens, Sir Charles Eastlake, John Foster, the

Unwillingly to School　　　　　　27

Prussian Minister (Chevalier Bunsen) and W. J. Fox MP. The banquet celebrated not only Macready's distinction as an actor and manager, but also his huge contribution to making the theatre respectable, in which enterprise he had of course been assisted by many of those present. Someone who was not present, but undoubtedly counted himself in that number, was the future Dean of Christ Church Dr Liddell, then headmaster of Westminster School, who wrote to Macready on 3 March 1851:

> I should very much have liked to have been one of the clergy who attended on Saturday to express by their presence their thanks to one who had done so much for elevating the drama to its own high and noble office. But all efforts to get tickets were, for me at least, in vain. (Pollock ed., 1876, p. 675)

Liddell's presence would indeed have been appropriate since through his commitment to the Latin play at Westminster he had made his own not inconsiderable contribution to 'elevating the drama'. Macready had made common cause with Liddell by attending a performance on 20 December 1847: 'Went to the Westminster Play, "The Adelphi." Mr Liddell welcomed me very kindly.' (p. 593)

The particular significance of the 1847 Latin play was that in the previous year there had been no performance. This was not, as had been the case some years (1817 and 1818 for instance, Sargeaunt, 1898, pp. 270–72), because of factors beyond the school's control such as court mourning or illness, but because of a conscious decision by someone in authority: Samuel Wilberforce. Wilberforce's tenure of the Westminster deanery was brief indeed. He was not installed there until May 1845 and by that autumn he had accepted the bishopric of Oxford (Meacham, 1970, p. 46). He is now best remembered for his ill-judged contribution to the evolution debate at the meeting of the British Association for the Advancement of Science at Oxford in June 1860. During his short incumbency of the Westminster deanery Wilberforce exhibited more zeal than tact, especially with regard to the Latin play. Dropping the Latin play in 1846 was 'attributed to new staff though the real reason was probably the hostility of the late Dean, Dr Wilberforce' (Carleton, 1965, p. 57). The use of 'probably' here was undoubtedly redundant. The longstanding tradition of the Latin play meant that over the centuries many old boys traced their interest in the theatre to their involvement in it and some went on to professional careers: Thomas Sheridan, Thomas King and George Colman (p. 155). The strength of feeling towards the Latin play amongst Old Westminsters surfaced in July 1847 when a petition with over six hundred names on it was presented 'To the Very Reverend the Dean of

28   *Lewis Carroll and the Victorian Stage*

Westminster', who by then was Wilberforce's successor William Buckland, whose 'appointment to the deanery preceded by a few months Williamson's resignation of the headmastership' and the appointment of Liddell (Sargeaunt, 1898, p. 241).

The names on the list make impressive reading, being headed by the Archbishop of York (Edward Vernon Harcourt) and three dukes (Beaufort, Richmond and Bedford). The large number of clergymen on the list of course reflected the preferred career options of the day, but it also indicated that if there was any anti-theatrical prejudice in those quarters it did not extend to the Latin play about which the petition expressed itself in no uncertain terms: 'we seek...to record our firm and deliberate belief, founded on experience and reflection, that the abolition of the Westminster Play cannot fail to prove prejudicial to the interests and prosperity of the School'.

However, the names absent from a petition such as this one can be as telling as those on it. In this respect the Dodgsons represented a divided house. 'Hassard Hume Dodgson, Esq., Temple' did sign, but his brother Charles did not.[3] Charles Dodgson had been admitted to Westminster on 14 January 1811, rising to Captain of School and Captain of King's Scholars in 1817 (Barker and Stenning eds, 1928, vol. I, p. 273). In the latter capacity, since it was the scholars – known originally as 'the children of the grammar school'– who performed the Latin play, it would have been his duty to speak the prologue, a fate from which he was spared by the cancellation of the play because of the death in childbirth of Princess Charlotte (the only child of the Prince Regent – later George IV – and Caroline of Brunswick) on 19 November. Charles Dodgson did not appear in the Latin play in previous years when his involvement would have been voluntary. In contrast Charles's younger brother Hassard Hume Dodgson, who was admitted on 15 June 1813, appeared twice: in 1820 as Geta in *Phormio* and in 1821 as Simo in *Andria*. Furthermore Hassard Hume Dodgson sent his sons Francis Hume and Percy to Westminster, the former appearing as Thais in *Eunuchus* in 1851. Lewis Carroll was no doubt aware of his cousin's performance, his Christ Church friend Vere Bayne having pasted newspaper coverage in a scrapbook,[4] but he evidently did not attend a performance of the Latin play until he saw the *Adelphi* in 1853, as he recalled when he saw it again on 21 December 1857. The Latin play at Westminster therefore affords insights into the Dodgson family. Hassard Hume Dodgson took part in two productions, signed the petition for the reinstatement of the play, and sent his two sons to Westminster, where one appeared in the play. Charles Dodgson did not take part in any production of the Latin play and was saved from having to deliver the prologue in 1817 by court mourning, he did not sign the

Unwillingly to School

petition and sent none of his sons to Westminster. The height which clerical opposition to the play could reach is indicated by Samuel Wilberforce's intention to suppress it, which Charles Dodgson did not oppose. It seems plausible that the tradition of the Latin play may have been a factor in the Reverend Dodgson's decision not to send any of his sons to Westminster.

The Westminster play also provides insights into the future Dean of Christ Church, H. G. Liddell's character, in particular his attitude towards the theatre. His own schooldays were spent at Charterhouse where he recalled:

> It was my lot to sit next W. Makepeace Thackeray. *He* never attempted to learn the lesson, never exerted himself to grapple with Horace. We spent our time mostly in drawing, with such skill as we could command. His handiwork was very superior to mine, and his taste for comic scenes at that time exhibited itself in burlesque representations of incidents in Shakespeare. I remember one – Macbeth as a butcher brandishing two blood-reeking knives, and Lady Macbeth as the butcher's wife clapping him on the shoulder. (Thompson, 1899, p. 8)

Thackeray went to Cambridge and Liddell lost touch with him 'till I went to Westminster as Headmaster in 1846'. Whether or not Thackeray, whose *Vanity Fair* was being issued in monthly parts at the time, was amongst Liddell's distinguished guests at the Latin play in 1847, it is clear from Macready's diary entry that it was a gathering of notables including the Dean of St Paul's (Henry Hart Milman, whose *Fazio* was his most successful play), Dean Buckland, Lords Lansdowne and Morpeth (later the seventh earl of Carlisle, an accomplished poet who presided over the Shakespeare tercentenary – 1864 – celebrations in Stratford-upon-Avon) and the dramatist Thomas Noon Talfourd. Macready also saw his son Willie, for whose education he had chosen Westminster, rather than Rugby – the direct opposite of Charles Dodgson's decision.

However, the most important visitor to the Latin play that year 'could not come to Town before Christmas Day' and so 'the Adelphi was acted a fourth time on Thursday 30 December' for Prince Albert who 'came attended only by the Marquis of Abercorn and Colonel Phipps. He expressed great satisfaction at the Play and Epilogue'.[5] Liddell had become Prince Albert's domestic chaplain in 1846, giving his first sermon before the court at Windsor in April. Liddell was not an outstanding preacher, but Prince Albert clearly rated his other abilities highly to the extent of 'placing the Prince of Wales under his charge at Oxford in 1859'

2. The Westminster Play 1847

Unwillingly to School   31

(Thompson, 1899, p. 54). Amongst the many worthy causes to which the prince applied himself was the elevation of the theatre both as a profession and a form of entertainment. On 28 December 1848 Queen Victoria, herself an enthusiastic – if rather less serious-minded than her husband – theatregoer, instituted the Windsor Theatricals under the direction of Charles Kean with a performance of *The Merchant of Venice* (Rowell, 1978, p. 48). By securing Prince Albert's presence at the reinstated Latin play, Liddell had shrewdly capitalised on one of the prince's known enthusiasms, outmanoeuvring its opponents in the process and linking the school's revival to one of its most ancient traditions. As Lawrence Tanner put it:

> By 1848 the numbers had risen to 124. Old Westminsters had been reassured by the revival of the Play in 1847 in the presence of Prince Albert, after it had been dropped in the previous year (before Liddell's appointment) in response to a determined attempt of Dean Wilberforce to abolish it altogether. (1951, p. 64)

Liddell's involvement with the Latin play was by no means restricted to an edict that it should take place. In *The Westminster Play, Its Actors and Its Visitors*, Germain Lavie, who was admitted to Westminster in 1849 and appeared in the 1852 play, wrote of 'the beauty of the dresses, which thanks to Mrs Headmaster, improve in grace and elegance year by year' (1855, p. 16) and the reception accorded to her on her entrance:

> Old Westminsters stand, and everybody in the house imitates their example to welcome Mrs Headmaster, who appears on the arm of the Captain, who for this minute or two looks as happy as any one in knee breeches and buckles can be expected to look. (p. 12)

Thus encouraged by the headmaster's wife, the Captain proceeded to deliver the prologue, which from 1847 to 1854 (except 1853 when 'the Queen's Scholars, sympathising with their master, visited by a severe domestic affliction, declined to act the play') was written by Liddell (see *Lusus Alteri Westmonasterienses*, 1867).

Indeed in 1847 Liddell wrote two prologues, one for the 'customary nights... December 13, 16, 20' and a 'Prologus Alter' for Prince Albert's visit on 30 December. It fell to Hervey Vaughan Williams, as Captain of the Queen's Scholars, to deliver both of these. The opening lines of the first prologue:

> GAUDERE multos, qui nunc audiunt, puto,
> Quod prodit in scenam iterum nostra fabula:

Gaudemus et nos: anno namque proximo
Omissa multos terruit, haud injuria. (p. 96)

were greeted by 'a burst of applause: the pleasurable excitement or rather enthusiasm shown by so many refined and intelligent faces' (Thompson, 1899, p. 96). This quatrain has been translated as follows: 'I think that many people who hear me now will rejoice that our play is appearing once again on stage. We too rejoice, its omission last year put many people off, not without cause.'[6] Liddell goes on to refer to the opponents of the play: 'They want these Terence plays to be done away with once and for all', by which he meant – as all present realised – Samuel Wilberforce. In contrast, Liddell commends the 'almost six hundred men...Dukes, Counts, Clergy and Laiety, [who] all zealously deny that charge', 'our Archbishop [Vernon Harcourt] who recently died' and 'our Dean [William Buckland], whom it is fitting we hold in highest honour'. He pointedly rejects the charge of the immorality of the stage: 'We hope, I say, that we ourselves may be able to express Athenian wit with elegance in the Latin language, nor does it follow that we shall fall into a wanton way of life.' There is no mention of these issues in the Prologus Alter for the performance attended by Prince Albert in which Liddell invokes Queen Elizabeth, who re-founded the school, plays with the meanings of word 'hospes' as 'guest' and 'foreigner' both of which Prince Albert was, and draws attention to the common Saxon heritage of his home and adopted countries.

Liddell and Wilberforce never engaged directly in the dispute over the Latin play at Westminster School, but their relative positions are clear enough. Such was Wilberforce's hostility to the theatre that he used his position as Dean of Westminster to suppress it even in what was obviously its most privileged form: a classical play in Latin authorised by Queen Elizabeth herself. His attitude to ordinary, commercial theatres in London and elsewhere can readily be surmised. Liddell on the other hand clearly lost no time in reinstating the Latin play to which he welcomed Prince Albert as an honoured guest. Furthermore, Liddell wrote the prologue for the play each year (two in 1847) and his wife lent enthusiastic support, particularly with the costumes. Christ Church, of which Liddell became dean in 1855, was the cathedral church of the Oxford diocese of which Samuel Wilberforce was bishop. The two men were inevitably involved with one another in their professional lives, not least the ordination of fellows (or 'Students' as they were called at Christ Church), one of whom was a certain Lewis Carroll.

Notes

1 I am grateful to Mr Rory MacLean, librarian and archivist at Rugby School, for his help, including access to copies of *Rugby Miscellany* and *The Rugbaean*.

2 Tait's biographers suggest that Tait was fairly indulgent towards pupils' taste in entertainment: 'Even when a boy, whom he had locked up for the afternoon, broke out, and was found riding on one of Wombwell's elephants, all he did was to rebuke him sternly, ending with the usual twinkle, and "Remember I won't be disobeyed, even for an elephant".' (Randall Thomas Davidson and William Benham, *The Life of Archibald Tait*, London, 1991, vol. I. pp. 140–1)

3 Copy of the petition in the Westminster School archives. I am grateful to Mr E. A. Smith for his assistance with this and related material.

4 Vere Bayne (1829-1908) was, as Edward Wakeling writes, a 'close friend from his [Carroll's] childhood days' who also became 'a fellow graduate and don at Christ Church' where: 'For a time he was Archivist, and many ephemeral works by Dodgson survive in his carefully kept scrapbooks.' (Wakeling ed., vol. 1, p. 61, n. 35).

5 'Westminster Play Ledger' in Westminster School archives.

6 I am indebted to Mr A. Trevor Mantle for translating Liddell's prologues. Mr Mantle described Liddell's Latin as 'quite challenging to translate', a little verbose for such a succinct language and prone to the use of 'somewhat obscure words, particularly in old spellings (poene for paene etc.) or rare forms (possiet for potest, etc.)'.

3 Oxford

'Few of Oxford's famous men have been so inconspicuous in her midst'
J.B., *Academy*

Five years before his appointment as Dean of Christ Church, Liddell had served on the first Oxford University Commission, the membership of which included Archibald Tait, then Dean of Carlisle. The secretary was Arthur Stanley, biographer of Thomas Arnold and later long-serving (1864-81) Dean of Westminster, with whom Liddell formed a close friendship that 'ripened into that close and affectionate intimacy which closed only with Stanley's death' (Thompson, 1899, p. 125). Thus well before he took up his post at Christ Church Liddell was unquestionably identified as a reformer, which may have accounted for Lewis Carroll's diary entry for 7 July 1855: '*The Times* announces that Liddell of Westminster is to be the new Dean: the selection does not seem to have given much satisfaction in the college.' Pusey, who in December 1852 had nominated Carroll for his studentship (fellowship), was even less enthusiastic: 'Now nothing but what is evil is threatened as his [the deceased dean Thomas Gaisford] successor' (in Bill and Mason, 1970, p. 38).

As Bill and Mason demonstrate, as with Westminster School, Liddell was taking on an institution in decline. Indeed, so close was the traditional relationship between the school and the college that the decline of the former had affected the latter. Its roll was low: 'The college at this time numbered about 180 undergraduates. The educational staff consisted of seven persons, six classical tutors and one mathematical lecturer...Mr Dodgson' (Thompson, 1900, p. 214). Nevertheless 'The House' (abbreviated from 'The House of God'), as Christ Church was known, maintained its sense of superiority within the university on the grounds that it was the Oxford diocese cathedral, not a mere college. Nevertheless many of the issues, such as reforming the syllabus, with which Liddell grappled concerned the whole university, but of particular concern to Carroll was the security of his studentship, which traditionally was held for life subject to certain conditions. The intricacies of the situation are explained by Bill and Mason:

Whether a Student entered the Church or a lay profession he was compelled to take Orders on entering the ranks of the Theologi or to surrender his

Oxford

35

Studentship. If he entered the Church he would normally take Orders on reaching the canonical age, but it was possible for him as for the Student destined for the law or for medicine to hold his studentship for six or seven years without taking Orders. (p. 18)

For Carroll this was a time-bomb ticking away, but in the short term he observed the Liddells and made his own assessment of the new dean, his wife, their son and three daughters Lorina Charlotte, Alice Pleasance and Edith Mary. The Liddells took some time to move in as their residence required extensive renovation, but as it neared completion they prepared 'to throw open our doors for an evening musical party next week' (Thompson, 1899, p. 148). Rumours about the nature of this entertainment were evidently rife as Liddell observed: 'This is a strange place for rumours. It has been reported that Mrs Liddell is getting up private theatricals, and that Dr. C- permits his daughter to personate one of the witches, while the Dean is expected to play Macbeth!' (p. 149) What the Liddells planned was

to get up the 'Macbeth' music, with choruses, some glees, and other music, by the help of some of the young men and some ladies, if they are not too prudish to join. The gallery will be a good place for sound, forty-four feet long, opening by a wide archway upon the stairs, so that a great number may be present – not to mention the drawing room. (p. 148)

As at Westminster School the Liddells intended to entertain in both senses of the word.

Carroll recorded receiving his invitation on 1 March 1856 'to the second' of two musical evenings (Bakewell, 1997, p. 70): 'Received an invitation to a musical party in the Deanery next Saturday [8 March].' Not that he had to wait a full week for entertainment, since that very evening he 'went to one of Mitford's Harmonic parties, and heard some fair ordinary songs, and capital comic singing and acting by Twiss, *Macbeth*, *The Country Fair*, and *Richard III*'. Just three years younger than Carroll, Twiss, who had attended Westminster School, became one of his first photographic models (as Dickens's Artful Dodger) and a talented amateur actor (*Alumni Oxiensis 1715-1886*, vol. iv, p. 1453). Carroll provided a typically succinct, but detailed diary account of the Liddell's party:

Mar: 8 (Sat) Went to the Deanery in the evening to a musical party: about half the college were there. The songs in *Macbeth* were the chief performance: a son of the Chevalier Bunsen sung some things magnificently: among others, *Blücher's War Song*. The choruses were taken by Pember and his brother, Mitford, Twiss etc. The party broke up about half past eleven. I

36   *Lewis Carroll and the Victorian Stage*

took the opportunity of making friends with little Lorina Liddell, the second of the family.

Born in 1849 Lorina, aged six at the time, was evidently allowed to stay up for at least part of the entertainment, an indulgence probably not extended to her younger sisters Alice (b. 1852) and Edith (b. 1854). As Carroll was aware from a visit to the Princess's Theatre on 16 January, there were other young children spending late hours entertaining rather than being entertained. Allowing their six-year-old daughter to stay up for their musical entertainment seems to reflect the Liddells' practice as parents. There was the occasion of Ruskin's visit, described in *Praeterita*, which had been planned for an evening when

the Dean and Mrs Liddell dined at Blenheim...Alice said that she thought, perhaps, if I would come round after papa and mama were safe off to Blenheim, Edith and she might give me a cup of tea and a little singing.

Encountering snow 'a fathom deep in the Woodstock Road', the Liddells returned early, but protested that '"we'll be good and quiet, and keep out of your way. Go back to your tea, and we'll have our dinner downstairs"', but 'after they had done dinner' their children 'couldn't keep papa and mama out of the drawing-room' (Ruskin, ed. Clark, 1949, pp. 470–1).

What song might Ruskin and the Liddell girls have sung together? The young Liddells' fondness for and knowledge of popular songs was recalled in later life by Alice ('On our way back we generally sang songs popular at the time', Hargreaves, 1932, p. 7) and is of course reflected in both *Alice's Adventures in Wonderland* and *Through the Looking-Glass and What Alice Found There*. A particular favourite was 'Villikins and his Dinah', after which they named 'two tiny kittens'; Dinah became a strong (and threatening) offstage presence in *Alice in Wonderland*. 'Villikins and his Dinah' was popularised by Sam Cowell, one of the earliest music-hall stars who performed it at the Grecian in 1851 and subsequently at the Canterbury and in America. The original song, which was dramatised by both F. C. Burnand (1856) and J. Stirling Coyne (1850) and became the centrepiece of Frederick Robson's performance in *The Wandering Minstrel* (see Sands, 1979, Appendix 3, pp. 143-5), consists of six verses of four lines each telling the story of the resolute Dinah, her wealthy father and her lover Villikins:

Tis of a rich merchant who in London did dwell
He had but one daughter, an unkimmon nice girl;
Her name was Dinah, scarce sixteen years old,
With a very large fortune in silver and gold.

Oxford 37

Her father informs Dinah that he has selected for her 'a husiband both gallant and gay' and when she rejects his plan her father threatens to give his 'large fortune to the nearest of kin, / And you won't reap the benefit of one single pin'. The headstrong Dinah consumes 'a cup of cold pison' and on the discovery of her corpse Villikins:

> Then swallowed up the pison like a lover so brave,
> And Villikins and his Dinah now lie buried in one grave.
>
> Now all you young maidens take warning by her.
> Never not by no means disobey your guv'ner,
> And all you gentlemen mind who you clap eyes on,
> Think of Villikins and his Dinah and the cup of cold pison.
> (in Disher, 1955, p. 130)

'Villikins and his Dinah' was still topical when *Alice in Wonderland* was published in 1865 and the following year when Ruskin featured it in 'Lecture VII. Home Virtues. *By the fireside in the Drawing-room. Evening.*':

> Dora. Now, the curtains, are drawn, and the fire's bright, and here's your arm-chair – and you're to tell us all about what you promised.
> L. All about what?
> Dora. All about virtue.
> Kathleen. Yes, and about the words that begin with V.
> L. I heard you singing about a word that begins with V, in the playground, this morning, Miss Katie.
> Kathleen. Me singing?
> May. Oh tell us – tell us.
> L. 'Vilikens and his –' (Ruskin, 1885, p. 82)

Carroll, Ruskin and Dean Liddell would all have regarded music halls as beyond the pale for themselves, let alone well brought up young ladies, but such being the power of popular culture 'Villikins and his Dinah' evidently enjoyed huge and prolonged popularity in such households and the delighted and exuberant rendition of its Cockney idiom 'unkimmon', 'pison' and ungrammatical multiple negatives –'Never not by no means'– might well have been heard ascending from the party returning along the river from Nuneham or even in the deanery drawing-room.

In 'Alice's Recollections of Carrollian Days' (Hargreaves, 1932, p. 4), in addition to singing popular songs Mrs Hargreaves recalls many forms

38   *Lewis Carroll and the Victorian Stage*

of amusement: learning to dance the quadrille, games from chess to croquet, riding, walking dogs, bathing kittens and being photographed. Another amusement that she might have mentioned was *tableaux vivants*, for it was one of these that the Liddells mounted to entertain Queen Victoria, Prince Albert and two of their children when they visited Christ Church whilst the Prince of Wales was studying at Oxford. In choosing *tableaux vivants*, Liddell was showing the same acuity that had brought Prince Albert to the Latin play at Westminster, since, as George Rowell has shown, the royal family were enthusiastic participants in, for example, 'a programme with a strongly Scott (and Scots) flavour' in February 1856 and 'for the younger children...The Princes in the Tower' in February 1860 (1978, p. 85). Belle Moses conjures up the scene at Christ Church later that year on 12 December: 'There was a brilliant reception that evening at Dean Liddell's and *tableaux vivants*, to which we may be sure our modest Lewis Carroll gave much assistance' (1910, p. 74). Whether or (more probably) not Carroll gave assistance he was certainly interested in *tableaux vivants*, since he used the same technique as a photographer and he proudly reported to his family his conversation with the Prince of Wales on the subject of photography. In the same letter (18 December 1860) he dealt – relatively briefly – with the *tableaux vivants*:

> The *tableaux vivants* were *very* successful, but I must leave the description of them for viva voce. Lady Williamson was there, and supplied the costumes, and herself appeared in one scene. One of the prettiest was Tennyson's *The Sleeping Princess*, acted entirely by the children. The grouping was capital, I believe by Lady W. I was sure it could not be Mrs. Liddell, of whose taste in that line I have already had melancholy experience in my photographs. I shall try to get them to go through it by daylight in the summer. It would make a beautiful photograph.

The Liddells' expansive entertaining attracted some adverse comment actually in dramatic form. 'The Masque of Balliol' contained the couplet:

> 'I am the Dean and this is Mrs Liddell,
> She plays the first and I the second fiddle.'

As Michael Bakewell observed 'Mrs Liddell was popularly supposed to be the dominant partner in the marriage' (1997, p. 70). The Liddells and Carroll were the targets of the more aggressive satirical masque *Cakeless* by John Howe Jenkins, a Christ Church undergraduate, in 1874. Apollo and Diana have three daughters (Ecilia, Rosa and Psyche) for whom they

Oxford 39

have ambitious matrimonial plans, which do not include Kraftsohn whose identification as Carroll becomes clear in his opening lines:

> KRAFTSOHN (*interrupting*) I do protest against this match, so let me speak.
> APOLLO (*irate*) Strip, strip him, scouts! This is the knave we seek.
> KRAFT By circles, segments, and by radii,
> Than yield to these I'd liefer die.' (in Anne Clark, 1981, Appendix II, pp. 256-62)

The fact that these exchanges took place in dramatic form reflects the upsurge in interest in theatricals at Oxford at the time, with Christ Church very much in the lead. Humphrey Carpenter detects the stirrings of dramatic activity at Brasenose, 'a college then notable in its high spirits' in 1847 (1985, p. 11) with the performance at the Henley Regatta of a burlesque of *Macbeth* by Frank Talfourd, himself at Christ Church, son of dramatist (and judge) Sir Thomas Noon Talfourd, whom Macready had seen at the Westminster Latin play in 1847. Other colleges followed suit. Carroll's close friend Vere Bayne's scrapbook contains programmes for Christ Church Theatricals on 4 and 5 December 1863.[1] The two men were present on Saturday 5th as Carroll records in his diary for that day:

> Dec. 5. (Sat) Ch. Ch. Theatricals, given in Berner's rooms. The pieces were *Number 1, Round the Corner* [by William Brough], *Alfred the Great* [by Robert Brough], and *Betsey Baker* [by John Maddison Morton]. Reid came out well in comedy in the first and Kenyon in the second and third being best as 'Guthrun'. Smith Barry made a beautiful 'Ina', and Baring also looked very well as a lady. The acting was nearly all fair, and the singing very nice. Mrs. Liddell and the children were there, but I held aloof from them, as I have done all this term.

The reason for Carroll's estrangement from the Liddells at this time is inevitably the subject of speculation. The fact that Mrs Liddell brought her still young family to the performance is a further manifestation of her enthusiasm for the theatre and that at least she and Carroll shared. Though he commented on the acting and the audience, Carroll did not refer to the scenery or (except by implication) the costumes, but the programme notes: 'Alfred the Great...Programme of Scenery and Incidents' and 'The Theatre and Costumes by Messrs L. and H. Nathan, 24 Tichborne Street, Regent Street' suggests a high standard.

Vere Bayne kept his programme for the Christ Church Theatricals, billing themselves as 'Her Majesty's Servants', in 1864 when they presented another triple bill (*My Dress Boots* 'the New Farce' by T. J. Williams, Esq.; *The Maid and the Magpie* the celebrated burlesque by

40 *Lewis Carroll and the Victorian Stage*

H. J. Byron Esq.; and *A Thumping Legacy* by J. M. Morton) on 6, 7, 8 December 1864. Carroll however made no mention of his attendance in his diary. The 'Programme of Scenery and incidents' for the Byron play comprised six different locations before reaching its 'HAPPY CLIMAX'. A further programme was performed on 19 and 20 June 1865, consisting of J. M. Morton's *A Most Unwarrantable Intrusion*, H. J. Byron's *La! Sonnambula* and J. M. Morton's 'screaming farce' *Ticklish Times*, confirming J. M. Morton as the Christ Church Theatricals' favoured author. It was Morton's *Away with Melancholy* that Carroll had performed as a one man show in the 1850s, which suggests that his tastes were fairly representative of the younger university generation at the time.

It was a time when, in Alan Mackinnon's words, Oxford went 'acting mad' with 'separate dramatic societies at Pembroke, at Christ Church, and perhaps half-a-dozen others' (1910, p. 39), one of which was St John's where on Sunday 21 June 1868 Carroll watched 'the burlesque, *Romeo and Juliet*' which he considered 'very good'. He followed this by attending dramatic readings by Mrs Scott-Siddons whom he tried unsuccessfully to persuade to sit for a photograph. There is then a break in the diary until 2 August when Carroll writes: 'On the evening of June 21, the day on which the above entry was made, it pleased God to take to himself my dear Father.' That Carroll should have been occupied attending two dramatic performances on the very day, and that a Sunday, on which his anti-theatrical father died was a coincidence upon which he must have pondered. It seems to lie beneath Carroll's injunction in the preface to *Sylvie and Bruno*:

> Let me pause for a moment to say that I believe this thought, of the possibility of death if calmly realised, and steadily faced – would be one of the best possible tests as to our going to any scene of amusement being right or wrong. If the thought of sudden death acquires, for *you*, a special horror when imagined as happening in a *theatre*, then be very sure the theatre is harmful for *you*, however harmless it may be for others; and that *you are* incurring a deadly peril in going. Be sure the safest rule is that we should not dare to *live* in any scene in which we dare not *die*. (Woollcott ed., 1997, p. 262)

Such was the enthusiasm for college dramatics that 'the fateful fiat went forth in 1869 in the shape of a Vice-Chancellor's decree. There were to be no more theatricals, amateur or otherwise, within the jurisdiction of the University.' (Mackinnon, 1910, p. 39) Enthusiasts were not so easily deterred, notably the Hon. J. G. Adderley who entered Christ Church in 1879: 'The son of Lord Norton, he belonged to a family celebrated at its

Oxford 41

Warwickshire home for the excellence of its annual amateur theatrical week' (Carpenter, 1985, p. 18). Adderley gave his own account of his experiences in an address to the Church and Stage Guild, which was published as *The Fight for Drama at Oxford*. He recalled an incident in December 1879 when 'the greatest consternation prevailed among the authorities at the sight of scenery and footlights being publicly carried through the College gates' for 'a performance in my rooms in Peckwater' (1888, p. 14). The Censors' tactic was to starve the performers whose programme 'consisted of "Area Belle," imitations of popular actors, and the inevitable "Box and Cox"'. In Adderley's version:

> A few days after this performance we were invited to the Deanery to give an entertainment to the late Duke of Albany; our scenery was carried in triumph to the Deanery; the Vice-Chancellor, was among the audience. A full account appeared in the local papers, and we awoke to find ourselves famous. (p. 15)

Humphrey Carpenter has established that the performance actually took place 'on the evening of 4 March 1880' (1985, p. 19) and was widely reported, but he could find no corroboration for the rest of Adderley's narrative.

The Philothespians as they called themselves mounted their next performance on 31 May 1880, evading the official ban by performing at J. W. Gilbert Smith's rooms in Cornmarket. The bill was lengthy and varied: a prologue spoken by Smith, *Içi on Parle Français* by T. J. Williams, the screen scene from Sheridan's *The School for Scandal*, and F. C. Burnand's burlesque of *Villikins and his Dinah*, which the Cambridge ADC had performed back in November 1855 (Burnand, 1880, pp. 60–1). 'Villikins and his Dinah' was not exactly resistant to treatment as 'A tragico-comico burlesque' and Burnand exploited such characteristics as the aberrant 'i' in 'Parient' and 'galliant' (1856). In the twenty-five years since he wrote his burlesque Burnand had established himself on *Punch*, of which he became editor in 1880, remaining in post until 1906. One family for whom the attraction of 'Villikins and his Dinah' was unabated in 1880 was the Liddells. Mackinnon, who played Mrs Spriggins (replete with 'corkscrewy curls') in *Içi on Parle Français* and Charles Surface in *The School for Scandal*, recalled the significance of Mrs Liddell's patronage:

> the pursuer [the proctor] was at our very door, but here we were saved by the first tender of help, outside the society itself, in the kindness of Mrs Liddell, who was bold enough to bring a party of ladies from the Deanery, and left her carriage at the door. (Mackinnon, 1910, p. 48)

42 *Lewis Carroll and the Victorian Stage*

Carroll made no reference to the occasion. On 31 May 1880 he met his former Rugby headmaster Archibald Tait, since 1869 Archbishop of Canterbury, and his two daughters, all of whom he photographed. It may be that he had outgrown undergraduate taste in drama and that his by then extensive experience of professional theatre in London made him more aware of the limitations of such fare in the university.

The year 1880 can be seen as a turning point for drama at Oxford. Benjamin Jowett, Professor of Greek and Master of Balliol, gave his consent to a performance of Aeschylus's *Agamemnon* in the college's great hall on 3 June 1880 with the future actor-manager Frank Benson as Clytemnestra. Like Liddell, Jowett was sympathetic to the cause of drama: 'Performance of Shakespeare or of Greek plays in the Theatre at Oxford' had been number fifteen (out of seventeen) on his 'Agenda, 1881-1886, during my Vice-Chancellorship' (Faber, 1957, p. 390). The success of this innovation, which Henry Irving and Ellen Terry attended, encouraged further activity with the Philothespians performing *The Merchant of Venice* in 1883 and the inauguration of the Oxford University Dramatic Society in 1884 and its first production Shakespeare's *I Henry IV* on 9 May 1885. Jowett's sympathetic attitude to drama was crucial, but the commitment of enthusiastic undergraduates and dons was also essential. W. L. Courtney of New College and Henry Scott Holland of Christ Church led for the dons as Etonian Arthur Bourchier, also of Christ Church, did for the undergraduates. Carroll, whose enthusiasm for the theatre and contacts amongst leading professional actors must have been unrivalled in the university, appears to have played no part in these developments, though they largely emanated from his college. The fact that he had resigned from his mathematical lectureship in 1881 is hardly a plausible explanation since in all other respects his position remained the same and he presumably had more time to devote to his preferred interests. The article 'The living embodiment of the old Oxford' (originally published in *Academy* 22 January 1898) by the unidentified author 'J. B.' seems to identify the nature of Carroll's later presence in the university:

> Few of Oxford's famous men have been so inconspicuous in her midst...In a sense he was the most old-world of all the elements in the place...his mind, alike in its piety, its ingenuities and its humours, belonged to an earlier and quieter world. His Oxford was sleepy and early Victorian, a haunt of people who played croquet and little girls with short frocks and smoothly brushed hair and quaint formal politeness. (in Cohen ed., 1989, pp. 68-9)

3. *The Merchant of Venice*, Oxford, 1883

It is true that Carroll attended two performances of the Philothespians in *The Merchant of Venice*. On 7 December 1883 he took his friend, the dramatist Augustus Dubourg,

> my object being to see Ethel Arnold as 'Portia'. She was a great deal better than I had expected. Shylock was well played by Bourchier of Christ Church, and Launcelot Gobbo in quite first rate style by W. Bromley Davenport. Julia Arnold made a fairly good Nerissa and Mrs Woods (Daisy Bradley that was) a pretty Jessica.

He returned the next night

> to see Ethel as Nerissa: but there was next to nothing to see. I had not realised what a trifling part it is: she did it nicely, but wants ease, in both parts. Mrs Courtney was a most artificial Portia.

Mrs Courtney, wife of don W. L. Courtney, was unwilling to play Portia for all performances so Ethel Arnold alternated with her. She and her sister Julia were grandchildren of Thomas and nieces of Matthew. Carroll

44 *Lewis Carroll and the Victorian Stage*

had known them since their childhood when they performed 'The Mad Tea-Party' at their home in Oxford on 7 December 1874. Bourchier was to marry another of his protégées, Violet Vanbrugh. Although Carroll's main reason for attending the performance was to see his young friends on stage, he applied objective standards to theirs and other performances. Other dons (Jowett and Liddell) were reported to have attended and the *Theatre* described 'a brilliant assemblage' at the Town Hall:

> This will be the beginning of a new era in university amusements. All credit is due to Mr. Bourchier, the President of the Club, to Mr. Scott Holland, a popular 'Don' at Christ Church, to Mr. Courtney of New, and other tutors for their liberal advocacy of a legitimate form of harmless amusement. (1 January 1884)

It was indeed 'the beginning of a new era', but during the remaining fourteen years of his life Carroll does not appear to have attended any OUDS productions. Nigel Playfair records consulting him about performing his own version of the two 'Alice' books in Worcester College Gardens in 1894, when he found him

> a queer and in some ways rather a pathetic figure. He kept up to the end his reputation as the friend and mentor of little girls, but he was faithful in his friendships and did not set about making new ones. Consequently many of his 'little girl friends' were plain and, at least so it appeared to me, rather middle aged females. (1930, p. 89)

Playfair underestimates Carroll's capacity for making new 'little girl friends', but his point about Carroll's loyalty and the greater maturity of some friends is well made.

The most glittering and prestigious event in the university's rehabilitation of drama was the address given by Henry Irving at Jowett's invitation as part of the Commemoration ceremony in the Examination Schools on 26 June 1886. His subject, 'Four Great Actors' (Richard Burbage, Thomas Betterton, David Garrick and Edmund Kean) (Richards ed., 1994, pp. 50-69), would certainly have appealed to Carroll, whose own interest in great actors of the past had been manifest in his prologue to *La Guida di Bragia*, but with over 4000 applications for the 1500 places he might not have secured a ticket even if he had tried. Amongst those who did were the Liddells: 'The Dean of Christ Church and Mrs Liddell condescended to come.' (Fitzgerald, 1893, p. 214) Fitzgerald may underestimate the Liddells' enthusiasm for the occasion and their determination to avoid a repetition of the disappointment at missing

Oxford 45

Macready's farewell banquet. Carroll's only recorded encounter with Jowett on the subject of the theatre took place on Thursday 1 March 1883 when he recorded: 'Called on the Vice-Chancellor (Jowett), at his request, to speak about the backs I wish to give to the seats in the gallery at St. Mary's. I also talked about "Vance", whom I want him to forbid in Oxford.' 'Vance the Great', as he was known, though his real name was Alfred Peck, was celebrated for his cockney songs (in the style of Sam Cowell of 'Villikins and his Dinah' fame), his celebration of Cliquot champagne and his so-called moral motto songs such as 'Act on the Square, Boys'. His regular visits to Oxford were an affront to W. L. Courtney, who complained:

> But of all the opposition to the theatre, the most unreasonable is that of those senior members of the University who, without any compunction of conscience, quietly permitted the vulgarities and indecencies of the Victoria Theatre. Every term the 'Vic' used to be the chosen home of Vance, Jolly Nash [John Nash], *et hoc genus omne*; nothing more refining than a music-hall was ever allowed to be exhibited on boards which would presumably have been defiled by a stage play. Only during the vacation, when the University veto was removed, was the Victoria Theatre ever respectable.' (in Adderley, 1888, 'Avant-Propos' by WLC)

The Victoria Theatre was never respectable enough for Carroll, who in nearly half a century resident in Oxford attended only fourteen public performances (excluding various entertainments in colleges). On 19 February 1855 he went to the Town Hall for Fanny Kemble's solo reading of *Henry V*. As he wrote he had 'never heard anything of the kind before, nor any Shakespeare on the stage', but he noted that the 'long speeches and soliloquies sunk at times into recitation' and how difficult it was 'labouring under such disadvantages as the want of dresses and scenery'. He was to echo these sentiments when he attempted to give a reading of *Henry VIII* at Croft on 28 August, though by then he had seen Charles Kean's production of that play. On 29 and 30 October 1856 Carroll attended the German Reeds' entertainment at the Star and was particularly impressed by Miss Priscilla Horton (Mrs German Reed), whose 'acting was wonderful, and not the least charm in her performance was her exquisite singing'. Fanny Kemble's readings and the German Reeds' entertainments attracted audiences who would not have dared attend full-scale theatrical productions, but once he had done so Carroll clearly preferred them, though not in Oxford.

He did not venture inside the New Theatre, the 1886 replacement of the 1868 building (Earl and Sell eds, 2000, p. 175), until 27 January 1894,

46 *Lewis Carroll and the Victorian Stage*

when he took Enid Stevens to a matinee of A. W. Pinero's *Sweet Lavender*, starring Edward Terry, to celebrate his own birthday. The explanation was partly the university restrictions and, in the early years, the widespread opprobrium attached to the stage, but in view of his extensive theatregoing in London the traits of a 'Bunburyist' do seem to be detectable in Carroll's behaviour: the sombre don in Oxford, the man about town in the capital.

There is an irony here. The resolution of the situation regarding Carroll's Studentship, with which this chapter opened, was crucial to Carroll remaining in Oxford, as he evidently very much wanted to do and in fact succeeded in doing. On 5 August 1861 Carroll wrote from Croft to the Diocesan Registrar, Oxford: 'I am intending to offer myself at the Bishop of Oxford's examination in September, to be ordained Deacon. I gave his Lordship notice of this about 4 months ago.' Having been appointed to his Studentship in 1852 Carroll had already considerably exceeded the customary six or seven years before either taking orders or relinquishing the Studentship. Even in 1861 Carroll seems to have needed reassurance from his friend Henry Parry Liddon, a Puseyite with a high reputation as a preacher, whom Bishop Wilberforce had appointed as the first Vice-President of Cuddesdon, the theological college that he had established close to his own palace (a safe six miles outside Oxford) in 1854. On 22 December 1861 Carroll was ordained deacon. Compared with his agonies over this decision, the next step of taking priest's orders caused even more. A 'Cuddesdon ordination' contrasted pointedly with 'the laxity of the past' (Wilberforce, 1905, p. 63). On 21 October 1862 he nerved himself to consult Liddell:

> Oct: 21 (Tu). Called on the Dean to ask him if I was in any way obliged to take Priest's Orders. (I consider mine as a Lay Studentship). His opinion was that by being ordained Deacon I became a Clerical Student, and so subject to the same conditions as if I had taken a Clerical Studentship, viz. that I must take Priests' Orders within four year from my time for being M.A. and that as this was clearly impossible in my case, I have probably already lost the Studentship, and am at least bound to take Priests' Orders as soon as possible. I differed from this view, and he talked of laying the matter before the electors.

Carroll returned the next day: 'The Dean has decided on not consulting the electors, and says he shall do nothing more about it, so that I consider myself free as to being ordained Priest.'

It had been a strange reversal of roles with the traditionalist, conservative Carroll pleading a special case in a procedure which the

Oxford

reforming dean probably regarded as obsolete anyway. Carroll remained cagey about his reasons for not taking priest's orders. In a letter (c. mid-1882) to an unidentified recipient he wrote: 'I am a member of the English Church, and have taken Deacon's Orders, but did not think fit (for reasons I need not go into) to take Priest's Orders.' (Cohen ed., 1979, vol. I, p. 463) Explanations have ranged over Carroll's sense of his own unworthiness, his stammer and Bishop Wilberforce's expressed opinion that the 'resolution to attend theatres or operas was an absolute disqualification for Holy Orders' (Foulkes, 1997, p. 132). As for Liddell, he has been described as relenting, sidling out and doing a complete reversal. In *In the Shadow of The Dreamchild A New Understanding of Lewis Carroll*, in which she argues that Carroll and Mrs Liddell were lovers, Karoline Leach takes the view that overnight Liddell had 'radically altered' his mind and taken the 'quite illegal, decision to let the matter drop', the alternative being to eject him:

> If, for example, as seems so possible from so much evidence, Dodgson had been or still was his wife's lover, and Liddell knew or suspected as much, then he would realise that Dodgson was potentially too dangerous to be handled without due care, and from this vantage point his actions do make some sense. A Dodgson who had been dismissed from the House...would seem to Liddell an infinitely more dangerous article than a Dodgson still dependent on Christ Church. (1999, p. 199)

Even if one were to accept Leach's (ingenious if implausible) hypothesis, the cuckolded Dean would surely have seized the opportunity to get rid of Carroll, who hardly seems likely to have been 'dangerous' either within or outside The House. If Carroll and Mrs Liddell did not love each other, they did both love the theatre, as did the Dean himself. The Dean had already experienced the aftermath of Bishop Wilberforce's hatred of the theatre and had resolutely and effectively reversed the situation that he had inherited with regard to the Latin play at Westminster School. If indeed Carroll's love of the theatre was the central issue, it seems highly likely that firstly Liddell would have been sympathetic towards Carroll and that secondly he would have been loath to cede victory to Wilberforce on that matter especially.

So it was that, thanks to Liddell, to whom and about whom he expressed little appreciation, Carroll remained securely at Oxford for the rest of his life. A key figure from his early days there was Henry Parry Liddon, whose name occurs frequently in the diaries and with whom he discussed his decision to attend the theatre for the first time and whether he should take deacon's and later priest's orders. In a letter on the subject

48   *Lewis Carroll and the Victorian Stage*

of the Church and Stage Guild to the Revd J. Oakley on 15 May 1879 Liddon stated:

> Speaking for myself, there is no form of entertainment which I should so entirely enjoy, as good acting. But I have never been inside a theatre since I took Orders in 1852, and I do not mean to go into one, please God, while I live.' (Johnston, 1904, p. 282)

In another letter of 8 June 1881 Liddon said that he had 'learnt it [his feeling against theatre] from Dr. Pusey, from Mr. Keble, from others' before going on to invoke Tertullian (p. 285). Liddon's self-denying ordinance against enjoying 'good acting' is given added weight by his experience at school in Lyme where 'he wrote several plays' including one about Napoleon, as whom he gave a very successful performance (p. 4). As Morton N. Cohen has spotted, the Revd Liddon did in fact go to a theatre with Carroll on 22 January 1858 when after dinner at the London Rooms they went to the Olympic Theatre where: 'We saw *The Tragedy Queen* [John Oxenford] (decidedly poor), *The Doge of Duralto* [Robert Brough] which only Robson made good, and *Boots at the Swan* [Charles Selby], best of the three.'

No such lapse occurred in the summer of 1867 when Liddon and Dodgson travelled to Russia together. Both men kept journals, a recurrent theme in which is Carroll's theatregoing, as for instance 25 July in Konigsberg: 'Dodgson went to the Theatre.' (Cohen ed., 1979 a, p. 10) Liddon, who was on a serious mission to meet members of the Russian Orthodox Church, refrained from being judgemental about his companion's indulgence. Carroll recorded his impressions, those on 25 July being 'fairly good in every way, and very good in the singing and some of the acting' which, since he could 'catch only a few words here and there' in the play *Anno 66*, was no mean achievement. The Nijni Theatre in Moscow was 'the plainest I ever saw – the only decoration inside being white wash', the very large theatre was only a tenth full, but though 'the performance, being entirely in Russian, was a little beyond us...by working away diligently at the playbill, with a pocket-dictionary, at all intervals, we got a tolerable idea of what it was all about'. The 'best piece' was '*Aladdin and the Wonderful Lamp*, a burlesque that contained some really first-rate acting...I have never seen actors who attended more thoroughly to the drama and the other actors and looked less at the audience'. As Edward Wakeling has noted (Wakeling ed., vol. 5, p. 311, n. 481) the Nijni 'had recently been burnt down' and Carroll was attending a temporary replacement.

Oxford 49

Three days later on 28 July the 'Little Theatre' in contrast was 'really a large handsome building. There was a good audience, and the pieces *The Burgomaster's Wedding* and *A Woman's Secret*, won great applause, but neither pleased me so much as *Aladdin*. It was all in Russian.' On 2 September in Dresden, Carroll 'went to the theatre in the "Royal Garden"...The performance (with the exception of the acting, which was commonplace) was a remarkable one', notably a 'Wonder-Fountain' with jets of water and coloured lights. On 9 September in Paris Carroll visited the Théâtre Vaudeville to see Victorien Sardou's comedy *La Famille Benoiton*

> a capitally-acted play – every part without exception being well and carefully played. 'Fanfan' was played by one of the cleverest children I ever saw (Mdlle. Camille as the bills called her) who could not have been more than 6 years old.

There remained the Opéra Comique on 12 September for '*Mignon* – a very pretty spectacle, with charming music and singing'. French imports were a feature of the London stage and some of them were far too racy for Carroll's taste, but in Paris as at home he chose carefully. Plays in French were a particular specialism of the St James's Theatre and over the years many foreign actors (Salvini, Rossi, Ristori, Bernhardt) graced the London stage, but Carroll was rarely tempted to see them. What he experienced during his Russian trip was, as Anita Gandolfo suggests, a sense of release, 'a creative responsiveness' combined with 'the level-headed reasonableness characteristic of the narrator of *Alice*' (1983, p. 93). It is surprising therefore that Carroll never ventured abroad again.

Liddon, like many other English clerics (Foulkes, 1997, Chapter 7), went to the Passion Play at Oberammergau in 1870: 'The Play quite exceeded my expectations; there was nothing throughout the whole that was not edifying, and the dramatic power, reverence, absence of self-consciousness – in fact, downright reality of the whole thing – were quite wonderful.' (Johnston, 1904, p. 138) Carroll in contrast would not see it, as he explained in a letter (12 April 1881) to Helen Feilden:

> And first, many thanks for your history of the 'Ober-Ammergau Passion-Play.' I am very much interested in reading accounts of that play: and I thoroughly believe in the deep religious feeling with which the actors go through it: but would not like to see it myself. I should fear that for the rest of one's life the Gospel History and the accessories of the theatre would be associated in the most uncomfortable way. I am very fond of the theatre, but I had rather keep my ideas and recollections of it *quite* distinct from those about the Gospels.

50 *Lewis Carroll and the Victorian Stage*

Carroll's separation of religion and the theatre is entirely consistent with his view that the latter should be entertaining. It should not of course offend morality and religion, but neither should it usurp their place.

Though they parted company about Oberammergau, Liddon and Carroll were united in their opposition to the Church and Stage Guild, Liddon's response to which has already been quoted. The Revd Stewart Headlam offended many in the church and on the stage by including the music hall in his attempt to 'break down prejudice against theatres...promote social and religious sympathy between Church and Stage' (Bettany, 1926, p. 101). J. R. Orens has observed that, compared with Headlam, Carroll's 'attitude towards the stage was much closer to Liddon's' (1978, p. 34), but what really emerges is that Carroll's attitude towards the theatre was made up of several different attitudes. He abhorred the music hall and declined to attend the Passion Play. Though exhibiting his youthful enthusiasm for the theatre to his family and friends he took little interest in later generations of undergraduate thespians. In Oxford he rarely attended the theatre, enforcing a distinction between his life as a don and his enthusiasm for the stage. And yet his very ability to do this was dependent on the resolution of his dilemma of taking priest's orders in a way that enabled him to remain a don and continue to attend plays.

4 *Alice*

> '...and what is the use of a book,' thought Alice, 'without pictures or
> conversation?'
> Lewis Carroll, *Alice's Adventures in Wonderland*

Alice's criticism of her sister's book at the beginning of *Alice's Adventures in Wonderland* can certainly not be levelled at Lewis Carroll's tale. It is interlaced with dialogue between the characters and furthermore Alice frequently talks to herself. As for the pictures, Carroll initially produced his own illustrations, but the first and still most celebrated published illustrator was of course John Tenniel (Cohen and Wakeling eds., 2003). Dialogue, scenery and costume are vital elements in theatrical performance, as Carroll was fully aware from staging plays on his marionette theatre. In the interim between those youthful activities and writing *Alice's Adventures in Wonderland*, he had become a regular theatregoer during a period when elaborate scenery, lavish costumes and considerable technical virtuosity were evident on the nation's stages.

As several critics have commented, Carroll's use of dramatic elements is by no means confined to the 'Alice' books. Early examples include *The Rectory Umbrella*. 'The walking Stick of Destiny', which Stuart Collingwood describes as 'a serial story of the most thrilling interest' (1898, p. 38), is conceived in emphatically theatrical terms with its dramatic setting, props, gestures ('Door thrown open'), dialogue, devices (swopped goblets), climax and curtain. 'The Vernon Gallery' shows a strong visual sense, which in 'The Scanty Meal', with the 'balloons' of dialogue coming out of the mouths of the family of six seated around the dining table and their servant, could be a scene from a play.

Of Canto I, 'The Trystyng', the first poem in the *Phantasmagoria* volume (1869)

> One wintry night, a half-past nine,
> Cold, tired, and cross, and muddy,
> I had come home, too late to dine,
> And supper, with cigars and wine,
> Was waiting in the study.

J. S. Bratton has written: 'The cosiness of this picture is later qualified by incidental revelations that the domestic situation described is actually less

52   *Lewis Carroll and the Victorian Stage*

than perfect' (1975, p. 237). In other words, it is an adroit piece of dramatic exposition. Bratton notes Carroll's adeptness in parodying Tennyson and Longfellow, though Carroll disclaimed any special skill in 'Hiawatha's Photographing' (1857): 'Any fairly practised writer, with the slightest ear for rhythm, could compose, for hours together, in the easy running metre of "The Song of Hiawatha"'. But Carroll had more than 'the slightest ear for rhythm', as he demonstrated in this poem and elsewhere. Of 'Hiawatha's Photographing' E. L. S. wrote:

> This can be most effectively rendered as a stage piece. Someone as 'chorus' recites the poem, while others come on, in different characters, 'the governor, the father' and so on, and carry out the verses in dumb show. We did it, one Christmas in my very young days, and L. C. was much taken with the idea, when, years after, I met him and told him of it. (*Cornhill Magazine* November 1932)

'Melancholetta' is almost like a short play telling of a brother's attempt to enlist 'three young dogs from town' to cheer up his 'dismal sister', first at a meal and then at Sadler's Wells Theatre, but all to no avail: 'The night's performance was "King John". / "It's dull", she wept, and "so-so."' (Woollcott ed., 1997, pp. 772-5). The very title of 'The Three Voices' proclaims the importance of the spoken word and the use of italics demonstrates Carroll's keen attention to rhythm and emphasis as in the First Voice's: 'The man that smokes – that reads *The Times* – / That goes to Christmas Pantomimes – / Is capable of *any* crimes!' (p. 778)

Carroll used the dramatic form for several of his Christ Church pamphlets. For instance in 1872 on the controversy concerning the new belfry for the college bell, known as Tom: 'The New Belfry of Christ Church, Oxford, A Monograph by D.C.L.' which is made up of twelve scenes of which the eleventh opens thus:

> XI. On the Dramatic Treatment of The New Belfry, Ch. Ch.
> Curtain rises, discovering the Dean, Canons, and Students, seated round a table, on which the mad Architect, fantastically dressed, and wearing a Fool's cap and bells, is placing a square block of deal.
> DEAN (*as Hamlet*). Methinks I see a Bell-tower!
> CANONS (*looking wildly in all directions*). Where, my good sir?
> DEAN. In my mind's eye. (*Knocking heard*) Who's there?
> FOOL. A spirit, a spirit; he says his name's poor Tom.
> *Enter* THE GREAT BELL, *disguised as a mushroom.*
> GREAT BELL. Who gives anything to poor Tom?...Do poor Tom some charity, Tom's a-cold...

Alice 53

DEAN (*as King Lear*). The little dons and all, Tutor, Reader, Lecturer – see, they all bark at me! (Woollcott ed., 1997, pp. 1032-3)

Whether, in view of their shared interest in the stage, Carroll's target Dean Liddell relished the dramatic treatment, this 'Monograph by D. C. L.' became 'the hottest item in Oxford' and at six pence a copy ran into five issues (Cohen, 1995, p. 386). 'The Vision of the Three T's A Threnody' followed in a similar vein, but with Isaac Walton's *The Compleat Angler* as the basis of the parody.

Carroll also used dramatic structure for his mathematical work:

Sep: 23. (Sun) [1877] The idea suddenly occurred to me of throwing my pamphlet on *Euclid and His Modern Rivals* into an entirely different form, *viz.* a series of dialogues between 'Geometer' on the one hand, and Euclid, Wilson, etc. on the other. The dramatic form will make any 'chaff' much less out of place than in a regular treatise.

The use of dramatic elements and/or dramatic form was therefore a feature of several of Carroll's works, ranging in time from juvenilia to his maturity and in subject matter from photography to mathematics. Carroll offers his greatest insight into the *writing* of the 'Alice' books in his article '"Alice" on the Stage', published in the *Theatre*, 1 April 1887:

In writing it out, I added many fresh ideas, which seemed to grow of themselves upon the original stock; every such idea, and nearly every word of the dialogue, *came of itself*. Sometimes an idea comes at night, when I have to get up and strike a light to note it down – sometimes when out on a lonely winter walk... – but, whenever or however it comes, *it comes of itself*. I cannot set invention going like a clock, by any voluntary winding-up: nor do I believe that any *original* writing (and what other writing is worth preserving?) was ever so produced?...Alice and the Looking-Glass are made up almost wholly of bits and scraps, single ideas which came of themselves.

Carroll's description of his method of writing may account for the schools of criticism which interpret the 'Alice' books either in terms of his own personality or by identifying every character and locality with people and places which he knew (Jones and Gladstone, 1995). On the face of it this method of creating a book does not seem very likely to result in a dramatic structure, and even Charles C. Lovett concludes his detailed account of early dramatisations of the 'Alice' books, especially that by Henry Savile Clarke, as follows:

54 *Lewis Carroll and the Victorian Stage*

The episodic nature of the book works quite well on the page, but drama requires a firm plot structure to hold it together. The audience must be curious as to what will happen next and what the consequences of the current action will be. In *Alice*, however, we have a series of loosely related episodes, each charming, which demonstrates no real dramatic coherency. (1990, p. 105)

Whilst acknowledging Lovett's point about the lack of 'dramatic coherency' in the 'Alice' books, it is still possible – and indeed necessary – to highlight the *theatrical* nature of many of those episodes. Jean Gattegno makes the interesting observation that Carroll 'seems to have gone to the theatre oftenest during the years 1864-5, when *Alice's Adventures in Wonderland* was being written, and 1888-92, when he was working on *Sylvie and Bruno*' (1977, p. 266). Thanks to Hugues Lebailly's[1] magisterial analysis of Carroll's visits to exhibitions and theatres, the required data is available. Since Carroll's diaries are the main source of information there is a gap because of the lost diaries spanning 1858-62. Lebailly lists 12 theatre visits in 1863, 21 in 1864, 20 in 1865 and 12 in 1866. The fact that 1867 is also quite high (14) is partly accounted for by the Russian trip, but thereafter Carroll's attendance declines noticeably until 1873, a factor in which might have been his sense of guilt following his father's death on a day (21 June 1868) when he [Carroll] was present at two performances. The writing and publication (1871) of *Through the Looking-Glass* cannot therefore be fitted into this argument and though 1892 is high with 25 visits, the rest of Gattegno's '*Sylvie and Bruno* period' is variable.

Even though the evidence is not quite as clear-cut as Gattegno implies, the connection between the theatre and the 'Alice' books is undeniable. Frankie Morris has rightly identified the pantomime as being highly influential. Except for short versions as part of a larger bill, Carroll did not attend a full-scale pantomime until he saw *Little King Pippin* with Percy Roselle at Drury Lane on 17 January 1866, but his familiarity with the form's essentials can be safely assumed. Alice's descent into the rabbit hole can of course be linked to similar devices in fiction, such as George MacDonald's *Phantastes A Faerie Romance for Men and Women* (1858), in Chapter XVII of which the narration runs:

I gazed into a chasm…At last I saw it was almost a perpendicular opening, like a roughly excavated well, only very large…I discovered a sort of natural staircase…descending spirally into its abyss…I commenced my tortuous descent. (1905, p. 208)

However, in comparison, Carroll's treatment of Alice's experiences is lighter and faster and her changes in size, her emergence from one scene to another and the animals and people she meets are reminiscent of the pantomime. A favourite device at the time was the transformation scene of which Percy Fitzgerald gave a vivid account in his *The World Behind the Scenes* (1881):

> All will recall in some elaborate transformation scene how quietly and gradually it is evolved. First the 'gauzes' lift slowly one behind the other – perhaps the most pleasing of all scenic effects – giving glimpses of 'the Realms of Bliss', seen beyond in tantalising fashion. (p. 52)

Insubstantial walls, animals that talk, outsize heads, riddles and puns were all features of the pantomime. Frankie Morris reproduces the montage 'What I saw in the Fire' and 'Preparing for the Pantomime' (*Illustrated London News* 31 December 1861 and 13 December 1870 respectively), both of which illustrate large heads in the style of the Duchess and the Cook. As Morris says, the kitchen location is traditional for pantomimes. Playing cards coming to life and conversing find their counterpart in *The Children in the Wood, or Harlequin Queen Mab and the World of Dreams* by Carroll's favourite pantomime author E. L. Blanchard:

> Ebony cabinet suddenly closes, and the Twelve Tavern Signs simultaneously enter, six on each side. These signs are represented by personation of the signs themselves, so as to produce a thoroughly pantomimic effect, but each bears the signboard on a standard. The Brown Bear...The Eagle...The Mother Redcap. (1872, p. 15)

Court of law scenes were not associated with pantomimes, but there had been two celebrated examples in plays that Carroll had seen: Boucicault's *Janet Pride*, which he saw twice (Adelphi 13 December 1856 and 16 July 1864), and the same author's *The Trial of Effie Deans* (from Scott) at Astley's (Theatre Royal, Westminster) on 9 February 1863, of which Michael Booth writes:

> For Boucicault's *Janet Pride* at the Adelphi in 1855 the entire Central Criminal Court at the Old Bailey was reproduced for the last act; so praised was this scene that Boucicault repeated it at the Westminster in 1864 with *The Trial of Effie Deans*. (1981, p. 15)

At *The Trial of Effie Deans* on 9 February 1864 Carroll was particularly impressed by 'the speech of Boucicault in the trial'. Given Carroll's own

56   *Lewis Carroll and the Victorian Stage*

description of *Alice in Wonderland* as 'made up almost wholly of bits and scraps', this seems to be a likely example of his method.

By the time *Through the Looking-Glass* was published in 1871 Carroll had seen a couple more pantomimes (Blanchard's *Faw, Fee, Fo, Fum; or, Jack the Giant Killer* at Drury Lane on 16 January 1868 and H. J. Byron's *The Yellow Dwarf* at Covent Garden on 22 January 1870), but there is no record of him having attended the Surrey Theatre where the 1865-6 pantomime was *Harlequin King Chess; or Tom the Piper's Son and See-saw Margery Daw*. The Surrey Theatre (see Knight, 1997) was a 'transpontine' playhouse, catering for the local principally working-class clientele, so it is not surprising that Carroll ventured there only once, on 17 January 1877 because his friend Lizzie Coote was appearing in the pantomime. However, Carroll did not need to go to the Surrey to be aware of the pantomime. *The Times* (27 December 1865) and the *Illustrated London News* (30 December 1865) both carried a review, which in the latter was accompanied by an illustration, 'Surrey Theatre: King Chess Giving Check to the Queen, 1865'. *The Times* described one scene 'of an entirely novel character', the Palace of the 'evilly-disposed' King Chess 'in which an actual game, following the rules of that ancient pastime, is played out upon the stage by living figures so costumed that Chang might do duty among them as a pawn.' Furthermore, as the *Illustrated London News* observed, the Standard pantomime, *Pat-a-Cake, Pat-a-Cake, Baker's Man; or, Harlequin Bah! Bah! Black Sheep*, also took up the chess theme: 'Here, again. We have a magic chessboard with living chessmen. They play for the title of the pantomime, and the King (Mr. Gardiner) gains.' By way of variety at Astley's: 'We have next scenes at Card Castle, and are introduced to the Knave of Hearts (Mr. Templeton) and Pope Joan (Mr. Atkins). Then comes the Palace of Diamonds'. Chess, cards and dominoes were clearly popular features of pantomimes in the 1860s.

Morris also detected other pantomimic elements in *Through the Looking-Glass*. The fireside, which Thackeray used in his 'Fireside Pantomime' *The Rose and the Ring* (1855) and the idea of seeing 'amidst the glowing coal…strange faces – stern, fantastic, droll' ('What I Saw in the Fire', *Illustrated London News* 21 December 1861):

> It was important that Alice did not go through just any looking-glass, but through the looking-glass of the chimney…Alice's passage through the large mirror…combines elements of a transformation scene and of a harlequinade…The essence of the harlequinade was the comic chase during which Harlequin, followed by Clown, would dive headlong through concealed traps in the scenery which closed after their passage to present an unbroken surface. (Morris, 1983, pp. 76-8)

4. Surrey Theatre *Harlequin King Chess*

Henry Savile Clarke incorporated these features into his dramatisation. Act II Scene I ends as Alice 'climbs on to the mantelpiece, and goes through Looking-glass'. Scene II is 'Looking-glass Land. The Garden of Live Flowers. Chessmen discovered on stage. CHESS CHORUS ["Here ranged in due order of battle we stand"]' (Lovett, 1990, pp.174-5).

Morris reproduces an illustration of the first of these techniques in the form of one of John Tenniel's *Punch* cartoons: 'Initial T' showing a clown disappearing head first through (what had seemed to be) a wall. That Carroll was a keen reader of *Punch* is apparent from references in his diaries and scrapbook items such as the cartoon of Charles Kean as Cardinal Wolsey holding on to a large (animal) seal, with the caption 'render up the *Great Seal* presently' (*Punch* 8 September 1855). As *Punch*'s own historian, M. H. Spielmann, has pointed out, the magazine's association with the theatre has been long and productive, with '*Punch* writers from first to last' contributing 'no fewer than five hundred plays to the stage' (1895, p. 129). The 1850s and 1860s were particularly active, with the likes of Douglas Jerrold, Shirley Brooks, F. C. Burnand and Tom Taylor. The benefit performances for the widow of Charles H. Bennett at the Adelphi Theatre on 11 May and the Theatre Royal, Manchester on 29 July 1867 might be regarded as the high point of this era, with the participation of Shirley Brooks, Mark Lemon, Arthur Sullivan, George du Maurier and Tom Taylor in *Cox and Box*, Burnand's operatic version of J. M. Morton's *Box and Cox* and Taylor's *A Sheep in Wolf's Clothing*. Carroll attended the Adelphi performance (see Chapter 6).

Tenniel's interest in the theatre began early, as his 'Pencillings in the Pit',[2] dated 1835, when he was only fifteen, shows. This volume comprises fifty-six drawings, the subjects of which include Macready, Helen Faucit, Van Ambrugh and T. P. Cook. Engen describes how, when he was working for *Punch*, Tenniel 'made quick sketches' during performances, befriended 'actors like Charles Kean and William Macready', treasured the theatre as a 'means of escape' from personal problems and continued to attend 'until blindness and old age prevented him' (1991, p. 28)

Their enthusiasm for the theatre was more than just a common interest for Carroll and Tenniel. It influenced and informed the former's writing and the latter's illustrations. Tenniel's '*Punch*'s Illustrations to Shakespeare' (Simpson, 1994, p. 122 *et seq.*), which ran through 1855-6, show his brilliance at capturing what is essentially a moment in a play, a technique which he was to employ in his illustrations for the 'Alice' books. Despite his justifiable comment about the absence of 'real dramatic coherency' in the 'Alice' books, Lovett goes on to claim that this

Alice 59

...undramatic aspect of *Alice* is one of the chief elements which has attracted dramatists to the story, for here is a group of characters, well known and loved by youngsters and adults, upon whom the dramatist can hang his own ideas and interpretations.

This is borne out by 'Appendix A A Checklist of Dramatic Adaptations of The Works of Lewis Carroll', which runs to over 400 items, of which Savile Clarke's is the sixth. Lovett chronicles the 'Early Attempts' at adapting 'Alice' for the stage in considerable detail, compared with which the following is a brief summary.

Though on 25 January 1866 Carroll sent dramatist Tom Taylor a lengthy letter and scene by scene summary for a domestic drama which he had been prompted to start by seeing 'the performance of Percy Roselle in the Pantomime the other day' (17 January), he does not seem to have considered the possibility of a stage version of his book until 2 March 1867 when he attended a performance of the child troupe the *Living Miniatures*, whom he had already seen in the company of two of George MacDonald's daughters on 24 January. Taylor's response to Carroll's proposed domestic drama *Morning Clouds* had not been such as to encourage his aspirations to dramatic authorship, but Carroll wrote to his brother Edwin on 11 March 1867 that he had presented Thomas Coe, the manager of the *Living Miniatures*,

...as an appropriate return for his entertainment, with a copy of *my* 'juvenile entertainment', *Alice*. I have vague hopes (though I haven't suggested the idea to him) that it may occur to him to turn it into a pantomime. I fancy it would work well in that form.

In view of Carroll's use of pantomime in the 'Alice' books, it is not surprising that that was the form he had in mind, but when eventually the 'Alice' books were dramatised it was not as a pantomime. Carroll's next approach – on 18 October 1872 – was to Percy Fitzgerald, whose book on *Principles of Comedy and Dramatic Effect* he had read:

...the idea has been suggested to me of making one or other [of the two books] into a drama (or extravaganza) for children...The *books* have been so wonderfully popular among children that I am encouraged to hope they would be popular as an 'entertainment'.

The realisation of this potential may have prompted Carroll a few weeks later to ask his publishers Macmillan to arrange 'to have all the speeches from the *Alice* books copied out so that Dodgson could register them as dramas' (Cohen and Gandolpho eds., 1982, p. 22), though, as

60   *Lewis Carroll and the Victorian Stage*

Lovett points out, this proved to be ineffective (1990, p. 22). On 1 February 1873 Carroll wrote to A. W. Dubourg, a clerk in the House of Lords who was also playwright: 'Don't trouble yourself to broach the subject of a dramatised 'Alice' to Mr. Blunt, as I have myself done so with Mr. German Reed'. Over the years Carroll had attended several of the genteel drawing-room entertainments by the German Reeds, with whom actor Arthur Cecil [Blunt] appeared.

Carroll also addressed the matter of music. In March (24 and 31) 1877 he wrote two letters to Arthur Sullivan enquiring whether he would set '2 or 3 of the songs…to be kept for the occasion (if that should arrive) of its being dramatised'. Sullivan replied: 'I have often thought that "Alice" might be dramatised, but to my thinking it would have to be done with much aid from scenery and music. I could not afford to write a song and part with it outright.'[3] The two men, though basically in sympathy with one another, were at cross-purposes about the way to proceed. Carroll wanted Sullivan to compose the songs so that they would be ready as and when a suitable dramatisation was available. Sullivan, understandably, did not want to expend the effort unless the prospect of performance was imminent and realistic. Six years later on 6 August 1883 Carroll wrote to the composer Alexander Campbell Mackenzie on the subject, but still with a protracted timescale: 'Is there any chance, say within 2 or 3 years, that you would be willing to entertain such a proposal at all?' By 1883 there had been some small-scale productions of the 'Alice' books, beginning with the Arnold sisters in *The Mad Tea-Party* at their home in Oxford on 7 December 1874. In 1876 Mr Buckland presented an 'Entertainment' at the Royal Polytechnic in London of which Carroll wrote:

> Ap: 18. (Tu). Went to the Polytechnic with Caroline and Henrietta to see Mr. Buckland's Entertainment *Alice's Adventures*. It lasted about 1¼ hours. A good deal of it was done by dissolving views, extracts from the story being read, or sung to Mr. Boyd's music; but the latter part had a real scene and five performers (Alice, Queen, Knave, Hatter, Rabbit) who acted in dumb show, the speeches being read by Mr. Buckland. The 'Alice' was a rather pretty child of about 10 (Martha Wooldridge) who acted simply and gracefully. An interpolated song for the Cat, about a footman and housemaid, was so out of place, that I wrote afterwards to ask Mr. Buckland to omit it.

With some revisions being introduced on 29 May, Buckland's 'Entertainment' ran from 17 April to 19 August (Lovett, 1990, p. 107). Altogether inferior was *Alice in Fairy-Land*, performed by the Elliston family at Diplock's Assembly Rooms in Eastbourne, where Carroll saw it on 28 September 1878 and pronounced it 'very third rate'. The Ellistons'

Alice 61

inadequacies were compounded by their total disregard for Carroll's action in registering his books as dramas. In contrast Kate Freiligrath-Kroeker showed more deference to the author with her version, which was published in *Alice and Other Fairy Plays for Children* in 1880.

At last in August 1886 Carroll received a request from Henry Savile Clarke to adapt the '*Alice*' books for the stage. In his letter of reply dated 30 August 1886, Carroll made

> one, and only, one condition, which I should regard as absolutely *essential* before allowing my name to appear as 'sanctioning' any dramatic version of *Alice in Wonderland* or *Through the Looking-Glass*...that I should have your written guarantee that, neither in the libretto nor in any of the stage business, shall any coarseness, or anything suggestive of coarseness, be admitted.

In addition he had 'two wishes', the first being that 'it should not have a harlequinade tacked on to it' and second that 'only *one* of the two stories should be dramatised'. There was a further 'request' that for songs that were parodies 'the *old* air should be used'. Carroll also asked for his real name not to be used in any publicity and added a postscript: 'P.S. Kindly tell me what plays, etc., you are author of. I am very ignorant of names of dramatic authors.'

Generally Carroll was well informed about the theatre so his protestation of general ignorance may have been to spare Savile Clarke's feelings, for he was by no means a household name. Born in 1841 he and his wife Helen had a satisfactory complement of three daughters, Katherine, Clara and Margaret, with the eldest of whom, known as Kitty, Carroll was corresponding by November. Her father had in fact contributed to the *Theatre*, a journal which Carroll read and also contributed to, in September 1885. His article, which was entitled 'The Stage and Society', quoted one of Carroll's favourite entertainers, Corney Grain, as saying 'the position of the artist is very much what he makes it'. In other words the stage did not confer the same status on all its members, instead 'the position of the artist is very much what he makes it, and if he happens to be a gentleman he is treated like one'. Carroll himself recurrently made the distinction between actors who were members of theatrical families and the genteel recruits who were being attracted to careers on the stage.

At least when he wrote for the *Theatre* Savile Clarke's articles carried his name, which was not the case with *Punch*: 'he [Savile Clarke] was not enthusiastic about writing for the paper, as the chance of gaining reputation by unsigned contributions was very small' (Spielmann, 1895, p. 371). Nevertheless, especially after F. C. Burnand's appointment as editor

62 *Lewis Carroll and the Victorian Stage*

in 1880, Clarke specialised in 'Society verse, mostly bearing on medical and scientific subjects, for he was brought up a doctor'. As the biographical piece about Savile Clarke in the *Theatre* on 1 May 1889 (which also carried a photograph of him) revealed, he had practised as a doctor in Scotland before taking up journalism and still maintained his northern link as dramatic critic of the *Scotsman*. Nicoll lists fourteen plays by Savile Clarke in a variety of genres: comedy, drama, farce, burlesque and comic opera (1946, vol. II, pp. 312–13), but with none of them to date had he scored a substantial success. In agreeing to Savile Clarke's request to dramatise the 'Alice' books, Carroll was committing himself to not only an unknown, but an unproven quantity.

Whatever the merits of the resulting adaptation, the co-operation between the two men produced an extended correspondence, of which Carroll's side (over ninety letters) has survived, providing an insight not only into the project in hand but also into Carroll's views on the theatre generally.[4] Through September 1886, whilst he was staying at his customary holiday address (7, Lushington Road, Eastbourne), Carroll was dispatching his ideas to Clarke: using adult actors as well as children, retaining old tunes for parody songs and developing his plan for a children's theatre (17 September), a preoccupation since his marionette theatre at Croft. On 22 September he discussed the music, which was entrusted to Walter Slaughter, with whom Clarke was to work on other projects, including Thackeray's *The Rose and the Ring* in 1890. On 26 October Carroll recommended his 'dear little friend of the stage – Phoebe Carlo, now playing in "The Governess"' and on 31 October had her very much in mind, proposing that the second of three acts should be taken up with 'The Hunting of the Snark', his 'main reason for wishing for this interlude' being 'to give a rest to Phoebe', whom he proposed 'to dress...at my own expense' and have coached by Mrs Arthur Lewis. Carroll wrote some new verses (the Panther and the Owl) and lines for the Cook. 'Throughout November', as Charles Lovett records, 'Dodgson continued to express concern about the use of original airs upon which some of his poems had been based' (1990, p. 42). In the end two were retained: 'Beautiful Star' for 'Beautiful Soup' and 'Will you walk into my parlour?' for 'Will you walk...?'

The theatre chosen for *Alice in Wonderland*, as Savile Clarke's dramatisation was called, though it comprised both 'Alice' books, was the Prince of Wales, not to be confused with the Prince of Wales's (in Tottenham Court Street) where Carroll had seen several productions of Tom Robertson plays under the management of Squire and Marie Bancroft, who transferred to the Haymarket in 1880. The actor-manager Edgar Bruce took over the theatre, but within two years it was 'condemned by the Metropolitan Board of Works' and in 1884 Bruce opened the Prince's Theatre (in Coventry Street, Piccadilly), which in 1886 changed its name to the Prince of Wales (Mander and Mitchenson, 1963, p. 138). Designed by C. J. Phipps in the Moorish style, the Prince of Wales had a capacity of between 960 (Howard, 1970, p. 184) and 1062 (Mander and Mitchenson, 1963, p. 138).

5. Phoebe Carlo as Alice with the Dormouse

64   *Lewis Carroll and the Victorian Stage*

Savile Clarke's comic opera *Alice in Wonderland* opened on 23 December 1887, but Carroll was as usual spending Christmas with his sisters in Guildford and did not make the first of his five visits until 30 December when he wrote in his diary:

> *Dec: 30. (Th).* The first act ('Wonderland') goes well, specially the Mad Tea Party, Mr. Sydney Harcourt is a capital "Hatter", and little Dorothy d'Alcourt (aet. 6½) a delicious Dormouse. Phoebe Carlo is a splendid 'Alice'. Her song and dance with the Cheshire Cat (Master C. Adeson, who played the Pirate King in *Pirates of Penzance*) was a gem. The second act [*Through the Looking-Glass*] was flat. The two queens (two of the Rosa Troupe) were *very* bad (as they were also in the First Act as Queen and Cook): and the 'Walrus etc.' had no definite finale. But, as a whole, the play seems a success.

In a letter to Savile Clarke the next day Carroll reiterated his praise for Phoebe ('*very good indeed*') and little Dorothy ('a genius!'), but continued:

> I should like to have a long talk with you over the whole thing, and possibly might make a useful suggestion or two: but I hope you would feel *perfectly* free (and it won't wound my vanity a bit) to reject every suggestion I may make.

Fortunately for posterity, Carroll made most of his suggestions to Savile Clarke in writing. The first topic (on 4 January 1887) was author's royalties, which in his case amounted to £12.11s.9d for the first week instead of 'about £100' as he said he was expecting. For a professional mathematician Carroll seems to have been rather vague about the terms to which he had agreed, but which he eventually recorded in a letter on 12 April 1889 showing the distribution of profits to be: 9/10 to Mr Bruce, 1/24 each to Savile Clarke and his composer Walter Slaughter and 1/60 to Carroll himself. The rationale was that Bruce had put up the capital and taken on the risk of loss. His reward was £6,375, Clarke's £295 and Carroll's £118. Not that Carroll was particularly concerned about the money for himself, though he evidently was for Clarke: 'I don't care whether my profits are large or small...but, for you, I am really sorry that dramatic authors get so little out of what has cost them work and worry beyond calculation' (4 January 1887).

The attraction for Carroll was getting his work staged and being involved in the process, albeit, as he was at pains to point out, as an amateur. Nevertheless his attention to detail and his feel for theatrical effect come through time and time again. He was particularly concerned about the final fall of the curtain on Alice's line 'Oh, I've had such a curious dream!' suggesting that

> she [should] not begin her 7-word speech till it [the curtain] is (say) about a third of the way down, and she might easily time it so as just to say the words before she disappears from view – That would, I believe, be a more effective end than it is now. (6 January 1887)

Carroll was insistent on where stresses were made, to the extent that in the revised 1888 version 'words which should be emphasised were printed in italics' and for Isa Bowman, Phoebe Carlo's successor as Alice, he underlined words in her script (Lovett, 1990, p. 85). He bombarded Savile Clarke with examples of the cast's deficiency in this respect. The White Queen 'seemed to try her best to lay the emphasis on the wrong word in every sentence' (2 February 1887) and her partner in crime the Red Queen compounded this fault by 'making utter nonsense of dialogue, by putting the pause after "compared" instead of before it' (8 January 1887). Others offended by substituting a wrong word, in the Gryphon's case 'any sorrow' instead of 'no sorrow' (8 January 1887) and by distasteful and/or poorly executed business such as that between Tweedledum and Tweedledee in the quarrel about the rattle in which

> they have now a lot of rough horse-play bringing the thing down to the level of Clown and Pantaloon, or 2 Clowns in a circus – I won't go so far as to say it's actually 'coarse and vulgar' (which I think were the 2 things I barred in giving my sanction), but it certainly is not refined: it is not the least in the spirit of my book and I don't like it. (8 January 1887)

There is an echo of the young Carroll who 'ran' his own marionette theatre in his concern for every aspect on stage and in the auditorium and foyers (advertising, programmes, copies of the book of the play, the duration of the performance) and his suggestions for an improved new version:

> The play needs besides better acting, more changes of scene to give it light and interest. Instead of spending £700 only in putting it on the stage, I would say 'spend £1500', and be prepared to give £100 more a week in salaries, than the present company receive. Then you might get some of the best comic talent of the day. Suppose I were to join in the speculation, and advance (say) £1000, would that make the idea more feasible? (9 January 1887)

On 26 June 1888 Carroll enquired if Savile Clarke was 'still cherishing any idea of reviving "Alice in Wonderland"? And if so have you considered, as possible representatives of "Alice", Minnie Terry or Vera Beringer?' He had expressed his admiration for Phoebe Carlo's acting in an article '"Alice" on the Stage' in the *Theatre*, which he had discussed with its editor Clement Scott in a letter on 18 February 1887. Of Phoebe Carlo's performance he wrote 'it would be difficult to speak too highly', not least as a feat of memory, but

> what I admired most, as realising most nearly my ideal heroine, was her perfect assumption of the high spirits, and readiness to enjoy *everything*, of a child out for a holiday. I doubt if any grown actress, however experienced, could have worn this air so perfectly. (*Theatre* 1 April 1887)

6. Isa Bowman as Alice

Alice 67

Whenever Carroll wrote of child actors he insisted that they thoroughly enjoyed their work. He had first seen Phoebe Carlo on New Year's Day 1883, when, aged nine, she was at the Avenue Theatre in Joseph Cave's pantomime *Whittington and his Cat*, to which Carroll twice returned. Phoebe played Ned in H. A. Jones's *The Silver King*, which Carroll also saw three times.When Carroll wrote again (4 July 1888) to Savile Clarke on the subject of a replacement for Phoebe Carlo, Minnie Terry and Vera Beringer had been overtaken by Isa Bowman: 'I very much *hope* you may find Isa good enough'. Isa and Phoebe were both born in 1874, but Carroll now considered the latter 'too old and too tall' and that 'in its latter stages Phoebe was beginning to play mechanically'. Furthermore 'Isa's "English" is better than Phoebe's. In one special and important point, the use of the "H", she is altogether better' and 'Isa looks more of a lady than Phoebe' (16 July 1888). Given Carroll's comments about misplaced emphasis by actors, his underlining of 'looks' is obviously significant. Clearly neither Phoebe nor Isa actually was a 'lady', but in appearance and voice Isa looked more like one. This reflected the two girls' family background. Phoebe Carlo was 'the daughter of William Carlo, a packer and his wife' (Cohen ed., 1979 a, vol. I, pp. 581-2, n. 1), whereas Isa, and her sisters Maggie and Nellie, were daughters of 'Charles Andrew Bowman, professor of music' and had been educated 'at convent and private schools' (*The Green Room Book*, 1906, p. 39). Further up the social scale were the Vanbrugh sisters Violet and Irene: 'As to Miss Irene Vanbrugh, I do hope you will be able to include her in the company. She can sing. And she is so sweet and ladylike, and her enunciation is so perfect' (13 October 1888). Violet, the daughter of Carroll's Oxford contemporary Reginald Barnes, Prebendary of Exeter Cathedral, had been educated at the 'High School, Exeter, France, and Germany, and for the stage by the late Sarah Thorne' (*The Green Room Book*, 1906, p. 344). Both Vanbrugh sisters were given parts at 'a guinea a week' (Vanbrugh, 1949, p. 19). Thus the casting for *Alice in Wonderland* was indicative of the social composition of the theatrical profession, with three young actresses from different backgrounds: Phoebe Carlo was rising from her modest origins by going on the stage; Isa Bowman was maintaining an honourable family tradition; Violet and Irene Vanbrugh were bringing their superior social and educational credentials with them. As for Carroll, although he was aware of these nuances he seems to have treated them all similarly, including invitations to Eastbourne.

The new production of *Alice in Wonderland* opened on 26 December 1888 at the Globe Theatre in Newcastle Street, Strand. Although on 3 January 1889 Carroll wrote to Savile Clark that the 'new version, as a whole, [is] very successful...in many respects it is quite superior to the old

68   *Lewis Carroll and the Victorian Stage*

one', it was in fact less successful, to the extent that when Carroll learnt how much Savile Clarke had lost he sent him his own profits from the first production (16 June 1889).

His involvement in the staging of the 'Alice' books reveals certain features in Carroll's character. To create the books in the first place he had drawn on some of his theatrical experiences. With Savile Clarke he seems to have been genuinely modest, constructive and generous. He was interested in all aspects of the venture. His attention to the details of what was happening on the stage was very close. Although he took the opportunity to promote the careers of his young actress friends he was a shrewd judge of their strengths and weaknesses.

Notes

1   Hugues Lebailly, 'Charles Lutwidge Dodgson et la Vie Artistique Victorienne. Thése Doctorat présentée et soutenue publiquement Hugues Lebailly. Université des Sciences Humaines de Strasbourg', 1997.
2   In the Harvard Theatre Collection.
3   AAH 489 in The Pierpoint Morgan Library, New York.
4   Series 1 Box 3 207-297 Lewis Carroll letters to Henry Savile Clarke in the Berol Collection, The Fales Library, New York University, New York.

5 Home Entertainments

'...nor do the grave or the gay of riper years disdain to join the merry actors'

Anne Bowman, *Acting Charades and Proverbs*

As Kathleen Blake has written:

> Consider that the Victorians enjoyed the product of a much-expanded toy-and-game industry that backgammon and charades flourished in the parlour, archery and croquet in the garden, football and cricket in the public schools and universities, field sports in the country. (1974, p. 17)

The conditions were absolutely right for the expansion of family leisure pursuits. In the increasingly numerous well-off middles classes the father of the house was the sole breadwinner, servants were plentiful, the wife-and-mother was relieved of most domestic duties and certainly not expected to undertake paid work, several children in rapid succession were the norm. It was not surprising that market forces responded to this situation by producing many games and other pastimes, but this would have been to no avail had there not been a widespread disposition towards enjoyment.

Two nineteenth-century schools of thought on the subject of leisure can be represented by Jeremy Bentham and Edward Bulwer Lytton. Bentham, whose interests encompassed ethics, jurisprudence, logic and political economy, is best remembered as one of the ablest champions of utilitarianism. Edward Bulwer Lytton was a Liberal politician, novelist and playwright. Bentham died in 1832, the year of the Reform Bill and of the Select Committee appointed to Inquire into the Laws affecting Dramatic Literature, of which Bulwer Lytton was a key member. The Select Committee recommended establishing copyright for dramatic authors and abolishing the metropolitan monopoly on the performance of 'legitimate' drama enjoyed by Covent Garden and Drury Lane since King Charles II granted them patents in 1660. The second recommendation was not approved until 1843, but its objective remained as stated:

> While, as regards the Public, equally benefited by these advantages, it is probable that the ordinary consequences of competition, freed from the possibility of licentiousness by the confirmed control and authority of the Chamberlain, will afford convenience in the number and situation of

70 Lewis Carroll and the Victorian Stage

> Theatres, and cheap and good entertainment in the performance usually exhibited. (*British Parliamentary Papers, Stage and Theatre I*, 1968, pp. 5-6)

This was a huge advance towards free trade and expansion, even though the public theatres were still circumscribed by 'the confirmed control and authority of the [Lord] Chamberlain' through his Examiner of Plays, who ensured that theatres remained 'freed from the possibility of licentiousness'. Opposition to the continuing role of the Lord Chamberlain as licenser (censor) of plays strengthened towards the end of the century, but playgoers such as Lewis Carroll would no doubt have favoured more rigour from him as they found plays that he had passed fell far below the standards (subject matter, language) that they regarded as acceptable. The existence of censorship may very well have been an important factor in reassuring the respectable middle classes and attracting them to the theatre during Queen Victoria's reign.

Bulwer Lytton envisaged a far more proactive role for the state, not merely ensuring safeguards in a free market, but providing certain types of leisure activities for the lower orders, as he advocated in *England and the English*, first published in 1833:

> In proportion as the poor are enlightened, they will have higher and purer resources than mere amusement to preserve them from drunkenness and vice...In short, with the lower orders, as education advances, it will be as with the higher, – the more intellectual of whom do not indulge in frivolous amusements, solely because *it amuses them less* than intellectual pursuits. (1971, vol. II, p. 327)

Bulwer Lytton's self-improving agenda was at odds with Bentham who, in the tradition of Adam Smith's *The Wealth of Nations*, had written:

> The utility of all these arts and sciences, – I speak both of those of amusement and curiosity, – the value which they possess, is exactly in proportion to the pleasure they yield...Prejudice apart, the game of push-pin is of equal value with the arts and sciences of music and poetry. If the game of push-pin furnish more pleasure, it is more valuable than either. Everybody can play at push-pin: poetry and music are relished only by a few. The game of push-pin is always innocent: it were well the same be always asserted of poetry. (Bowring ed., 1962, vol. II, p. 253)

As far as we know Lewis Carroll did not indulge in push-pin, but neither did he conform to Bulwer Lytton's belief that 'the higher, – the more intellectual...do not indulge generally in frivolous entertainments'. Carroll's enthusiasm for play-acting, charades and his marionette theatre continued, as we have seen, well into his twenties, but by no means ended then. Kathleen Blake has compiled 'a list of some of his published games and treatises on games' which encompasses croquet, charades, doublets, lawn tennis, *The Game of Logic*, circular billiards, syzygies [word-puzzle] and rules for 'Co-operative Backgammon'. As she says: 'These games reached the public; others were invented for private use.' (1974, p. 57) The publication of compendia such as *Cassell's Book of Sports and Pastimes* reflected the level of interest which prompted the author of 'The Gospel of Amusement' to ask: 'Is not the theory that amusement is an indispensable part of life getting pushed nowadays a little too far?' (*Spectator* 26 October 1889).

In 'They Taught the World to Play' Sir Charles Tennyson wrote: 'One achievement of Victorian England has, I think, not been adequately appreciated. She was the world's game-master.' (1959, p. 211). Sir Charles is mainly concerned with ball games, amongst which the 'most significant of all was the development at Rugby School of the practice of catching and running with the ball said to have been due to William Webb Ellis' (p. 212). Though Carroll had himself attended Rugby he evidently succeeded in avoiding not only the game which took its name from the school but other ball games: 'Charles enjoyed watching cricket and tennis, but never played either.'[1] Indeed Carroll's preferences did not really lie in the section of *Cassell's Book of Sports and Pastimes* covering 'Manly Games and Exercises'. The games and pastimes that Carroll preferred were those that mostly appealed to little girls.

Whereas public entertainments required official surveillance to keep them free of 'the possibility of licentiousness', the middle classes could be relied upon to maintain suitable standards in their own homes. In fact these were the very people who were still deeply uneasy about attending public theatres and regarded home entertainments as a safer alternative, though unwittingly they were often fostering their children's appetite for theatregoing and in some cases an inclination to become a professional actor. As Mrs Alec Tweedie reported, her father's response to her revelation that she wanted to go on the stage was: 'So this is the result of allowing you to play in private theatricals. What folly.' (1904, p. 2)

However, resistance would probably have been as futile for Dr George Harley FRS (Tweedie's father), as for most parents, as enthusiasm for charades and other forms of home entertainment swept through middle-class drawing-rooms during the 1850s and 1860s. As Anne Bowman wrote in her preface to *Acting Charades and Proverbs Arranged for Representation in the Drawing-Room*, first published in 1856:

72 *Lewis Carroll and the Victorian Stage*

> Among the many pleasant and harmless fireside recreations of the present day, perhaps the most popular is Charade-acting. Even children have their little performances for Christmas pastime, nor do the grave or the gay of riper years disdain to join the merry actors. (1891, p. 5)

With the passage of time Carroll increasingly qualified as one of 'the grave or the gay of riper years', but he was of course perfectly well able to devise charades himself, as numerous entries in his diaries and published examples such as 'Four Riddles' in *Phantasmagoria* show. Typical is IV in which each of the six verses gives clues to the three syllables forming I-Magi-nation:

> My First is singular at best:
> More plural is my Second:
> My Third is far the pluralist –
> So plural-plural, I protest
> It scarcely can be reckoned! (Woollcott ed., 1997, pp. 806-7)

Anne Bowman was catering for those without such powers of invention, but doing so in dramatic form, colouring her 'sketches so far as to form complete though slight pieces, the performance of which would be a mere act of memory to the idle; yet leaving scope for the brilliant and ready actor to extend and improve the dramas by adding the finishing touches of the accomplished artist' (Bowman, 1891, p. 6). Each charade is made up of three scenes with between three and five characters and an answer of two or three syllables (e.g. Mend-i-cant). A variation on the charade was the 'Acting Proverb', 'a fresh, though kindred pastime…full of homely truth, of wholesome application, and of racy humour' (p. 225), as in 'A bird in the hand is worth two in the bush', featuring King Charles II and Oliver Cromwell, and 'Penny Wise and Pound Foolish' with the Graspington family (p. 224). Yet for all the reassurance of 'racy humour', 'Acting Proverbs' stray beyond amusement into moralising.

Families in need of a 'pleasant and harmless fireside entertainment' did not need to go to the expense of buying a special book. On 21 December 1861 the *Illustrated London News* followed an article on 'Christmas Mummers' with a selection of 'Christmas Games':

> As it is ordained that no pleasure – scarcely a sorrow – should be enduring, it is not to be wondered at that even 'Christmas holidays' should have their hours of tedium, and that little people should often desire 'something to do, mamma.'

Home Entertainments

73

As it is the pleasant mission of the ILLUSTRATED LONDON NEWS to supply amusement and instruction to the family circle, we, in our Christmas Supplement, always endeavour to interest the youngest of our readers, and to aid them in making the holiday time pass cheerfully...

The first game we call a Doll drama, to be played by young children after the preparation of stage characters and scenery by older heads and hands.

An illustration depicting a successful performance in progress was followed by directions for achieving this result: a diagram and instruction for constructing the stage, the scenery ('painted upon pasteboard'), the characters ('wooden cones...dolls' heads, dressed to represent the Dramatis Personae. They are placed on flat-guide-sticks, which have a wire pin about an inch long') and the text of *Little Red Riding Hood*, which reached this dramatic conclusion:

> *They* [Little Red Riding Hood and the Wolf] *are now both hidden from view*
> *Red Riding Hood.* How large your mouth has grown my dear grandmother!
> *Wolf.* Your fancy, child!
> *Red Riding Hood.* Your teeth! How sharp and long!
>   Don't hug me so!
> *Wolf.* I must! I've grown so strong.
>   My appetite requires some dainty dish:
>   A daintier one than you no wolf could wish.
> [*A Noise. The fairy landscape is let down and*
> *Enter* MOTHER BUNCH,
> *Mother Bunch.* Her mother's warning having disobeyed,
>   The cruel wolf Red Riding Hood betrayed,
>   And thus we see that little faults in time
>   May lead to sorrow and incite to crime.
> [*The stage curtain is drawn, and so ends*
> LITTLE RED RIDING HOOD.

The enduring and socially diverse appeal of toy theatres is reflected in an item which appeared near the end of the decade showing 'An Entertainment for the Children at Arundel Castle', the home of the Duke of Norfolk (*Illustrated London News* 9 January 1869).

Three Christmases later the seasonal obligation to entertain children was honoured in the form of a *tableau vivant* of 'Una and the Lion' showing a decidedly imperious girl (called Susie, almost an 'Alice' look-alike) of eight or nine, grasping a stick with one hand and tweaking the ear of a bearded gentleman (Uncle Jack) crouched on all fours. The accompanying narrative sets the scene at Drayton Court:

74   *Lewis Carroll and the Victorian Stage*

7. Una and the Lion

Home Entertainments   75

The children of whom there is a host, hold high revel, you may be sure, and look at all adults as their sworn vassals, born for the express purpose of doing their bidding and attending to all their whims and caprices...

Susie [pointing to a print of 'Una and the Lion' on the wall]...clapped her hands and screamed with delight, 'O, I know! Look there! Uncle Jack, you shall be the lion and I will be Una...Mind, uncle, that you go properly on all fours, and please don't be too tame, but ramp and roar like a real live lion, while I hold you by the ear.'

This brief episode over, other sports and pastimes rapidly followed – there were conjuring-tricks, magic lanterns, Punch-and-Judy shows – and the fun waxed furious till breaking-up time came. (*Illustrated London News* 28 December 1872)

For families aspiring to something better than 'the impromptu charade, or the frequently-discussed and often ill-rehearsed comedy', there was *Drawing-Room Plays and Parlour Pantomimes Collected by Clement Scott* (1870, p. iii). This consisted of fourteen 'entirely new plays' in a variety of genres (burlesque, extravaganza etc.) by the likes of W. S. Gilbert (*A Medical Man*, A Comedietta), Tom Hood, E. L. Blanchard, Alfred Thompson and Scott himself. That such successful and well-established professional dramatists should write a play specifically for amateur drawing-room performance is a measure of the status and popularity of these entertainments. Blanchard, whose pantomimes were Carroll's preferred choice, had written an all-purpose induction 'to take the place of an occasional Prologue at Private Theatricals' with the scene set in 'The Factory of Fun in the World of Waggery', where 'Joketta, Witticisma, Punarena and Whimwag [are] discovered' (p. ix). Tom Hood contributed *Harlequin Little Red Riding-Hood; or The Wicked Wolf and The Virtuous Woodcutter A Juvenile Pantomime...Period, uncertain. The Scene is laid near Ware?* With the main characters reappearing in the harlequinade (Red Riding Hood as Columbine), costumes were clearly important and Hood offered suggestions for these and for the transformation scene: 'The best means of managing the transformation is to wear the dresses of the opening over the pantomime costumes.' (p. 52). In contrast to this traditional pantomime, Alfred Thompson's contribution was *The Happy Despatch A Japanese Opéra-Bouffe...Music by Ducenozoo* with its principal character Kongoutwankakami (otherwise Jeremiah Twankey). *Opéra bouffe*, originating in Paris, was very much in vogue and the Japanese craze was to peak with *The Mikado* in 1885, but Thompson reassured his readers that the setting could be easily realised: 'Scene: Interior of a Japanese shop looking on to a public road (NB with

76   *Lewis Carroll and the Victorian Stage*

the help of a screen or two, some Oriental vases, and a few lanterns, much interesting local colour may be given to this scene)' (p. 135).

It is clear from the above examples that entertainments for and by children were a seasonal feature in middle-class Victorian homes. The prevailing attitude towards children (particularly at Christmas) was indulgence and some young girls, such as Susie, would appear to have been adept at capitalising on this. As for grown-ups ('the grave or the gay of riper years'), some were required to do more than allow the children to indulge in their performance and were expected to indulge in it themselves, by joining in as Uncle Jack, roaring on all fours, had done. Any family gathering graced by Lewis Carroll's presence would no doubt have found him willing to enter into the spirit of pastimes such as these.

Following the death of their father in June 1868 the Dodgson family had to vacate the Croft rectory. On a preliminary visit to Guildford in August Lewis Carroll inspected The Chestnuts, where his sisters took up residence that autumn. Whatever its other attractions Guildford did not possess a theatre, though it was near to London where Carroll often broke his journey to and from Oxford. Within a year of his sisters settling in Guildford Carroll had befriended the Synge family. As Edward Wakeling has noted, William Webb Follett Synge had held various diplomatic postings before retiring to Guildford in 1868. Carroll was the Synge's guest at dinner on 5 October 1869 when the party included Anne Isabella Thackeray, the daughter of the novelist (Wakeling ed., vol. 6, p. 100, n. 156). On 27 December Carroll returned to the Synge dwelling for an evening of home entertainments:

> Dec: 27.(Tu). Theatrical performance at Mr. Synge's, very enjoyable. *The* treat of the evening, to me was the 'Dirge over Dundee', sung by Alice Shute, to the tune of 'Ye banks and braes', unaccompanied, and with a perfectly true and deliciously sweet voice. There was a good scene from *King Lear*, for Mr. Synge, *Kenilworth*, versified in which Miss Synge acted capitally as Queen Elizabeth, *Old Poz*, in which Eva Shute acted the child very sweetly and simply, a few charades in dumb show [including one on the word Killiecrankie], in which I took part as an M. D., ending with *Poor Pillicoddy* [by John Maddison Morton], very fairly acted by Wilfred, Mr. Synge and Miss Synge. Mr. and Mrs. Trollope were present. I am going to commemorate the evening in print, *The Guildford Gazette Extraordinary*.

The Guildford Gazette Extraordinary was dated 29 December 1869 and numbered as issue 9999. It ran to sixteen pages in which Carroll reproduced the various items that had been performed, adding linking passages and an introduction:

Home Entertainments

THE GUILDFORD GAZETTE EXTRAORDINARY
'If I chance to talk a little wild, forgive me.' – *Shakespeare*.
No.9999.   Dec. 29, 1869
OPENING OF THE NEW THEATRE
(*From our Special Correspondent, Mr Lewis Carroll*)
It was towards the close of one of those days of dreamy and delicious languor
for which Guildford is so justly celebrated...the mellow shades of Evening
were fast deepening into the brilliant obscurity of Night. At such a moment
might have been observed (had there been light enough for the purpose, and
any one present to observe) a small but resolute band of wayfarers (they
numbered a thousand at most) wending their way in the direction of the new
and spacious Theatre, just about to be opened for its great and long-to-be-
remembered Inaugural Entertainment...

The fact that the Inaugural Entertainment was to be given solely by amateurs
lent an additional zest to the evening, and even if the enterprising Manager
had not, with his usual liberality, given away orders of admission in almost
reckless profusion, the house would still have been filled to overflowing. The
reporters of the Press were alone excluded on this occasion, the Manager
tersely remarking, that there would be 'press enough without them'.

Time would fail us to describe the decorations, and many of the contrivances
for the comfort of the audience, and we must content ourselves by briefly
mentioning a most original feature in the arrangements – the abolition of pit,
gallery and boxes; so that the whole house constituted one magnificent dress-
circle. We append the programme of the performance.[2]

The first and most obvious observation is that Carroll signed the piece as
'Lewis Carroll', as he did his articles, which were published in the
Theatre and his letters on theatrical topics to the *St. James's Gazette*. In
private life he generally insisted upon being Charles Dodgson, but on this
occasion felt that the use of celebrated *nom de plume* was appropriate.
Synge himself was an author and friend of authors (the late William
Makepeace Thackeray, after whom Synge's youngest son – the novelist's
godson – was christened; Anthony Trollope who was present on 27
December), so Carroll was presumably disinclined to shroud his own
literary success in false modesty. The presence of the author of *Alice's
Adventures in Wonderland* must have been a considerable coup for the
Synges, especially when he not only joined in with the charades, but went
on to write and have printed a sixteen page pamphlet recording the
occasion. Carroll's own enthusiasm for the whole business of theatrical
performance comes across: the crowds outside, the features of the
auditorium and of course the performance itself. In *The Guildford Gazette*

78   *Lewis Carroll and the Victorian Stage*

Extraordinary Carroll combined two youthful enthusiasms: home entertainments and the production of a magazine.

The entertainment at the Synges's was the only performance that Carroll attended in 1869. He did not set foot inside a professional theatre from the death of his father in June 1868 until he went to H. J. Byron's *The Yellow Dwarf* at Covent Garden on 22 January 1870. There is a clear change in mood from Christmas-New Year 1868-9 to the same period in 1869-70. On 15 December 1868 Carroll recorded that he had bought tickets for the Christ Church theatricals: 'I treated the Donkin party with tickets, but did not go myself' and on 7 January 1869 he wrote of his visit to the painter Millais: '[I] had a short talk with him under trying circumstances, in the room where Effie, Mary and Carrie (who have all increased rather than diminished in beauty), with two friends, were playing a particularly noisy version of "Puss in the Corner"'. For Carroll to describe being in a room with five young girls, who were playing 'Puss in the Corner', as 'trying circumstances' suggests that he was very out-of-sorts. In contrast, following his whole-hearted participation in the Synges's evening, Carroll made a succession of visits which included home entertainments: teaching 'my three little friends to act their parts' on 3 January 1870; 'a bran-pie, and charades in the evening...I took the word "Carte-ill-age"' on 11 January; 'a magic-lantern exhibited by the vicar, and various round games, ending with some extremely simple (almost dumb-show) charades, acted at my suggestion' on 12 January; 'an amateur concert' on 17 January, leading to his return to a professional theatre on 22 January: 'The Pantomime [*The Yellow Dwarf*] was splendid and fairly amusing. Nellie Power and the brothers Payne sustaining the principal parts. Back to Guildford.' Anyone suffering from a close bereavement is likely to desist from light-hearted pastimes for a while, but in Carroll's case it is difficult not to link his abstinence from theatregoing of any kind directly to his late father's disapproval of it. By Christmas 1869 eighteen months had passed since the Revd Charles Dodgson's death and Carroll entered into what might almost be described as a frenzy of home entertainments, such as he had done during his vacations at Croft in the mid-1850s, which had possibly incurred his father's displeasure. Interestingly these home entertainments seem to have eased Carroll's return to the professional theatre, about his father's hostile attitude to which there had never been any doubt.

Copies of *The Guildford Gazette Extraordinary* probably got into the hands of some of Carroll's Oxford acquaintances, who shared his enthusiasm for home theatricals. Amongst these were the Bartholomew Prices, at whose house, Myddleton Hall, Carroll watched 'some tableaux and theatricals' on the evening of Tuesday 29 November 1870, having

Home Entertainments

seen the *tableaux vivants* rehearsed the day before, which suggests the family's recognition of his expertise. The *tableaux* 'were done by the children only, with the children of Mr. Hatch. Mrs. Hatch acted remarkably well for an amateur'. The parents of the five Hatch children were Dr Edwin Hatch, Vice-Principal of St Mary's Hall, and his wife Bessie, who was a talented amateur actress. In certain quarters the attitude towards adults taking part in amateur theatricals would not have been as indulgent as that towards children in *tableaux* and suchlike. Fred. B. De Sausmarez recounted that:

> it required some courage to brave the disapproval of a certain section of the University, and it was in these circumstances that Mrs. Hatch, the wife of the Vice-Principal of St. Mary Hall, approached the Rev. C. L. Dodgson (Lewis Carroll) with the request that he would write a prologue for some private theatricals which she proposed giving at Clevedon House on November 1 and 2, 1871. With this request he complied. The plays were *The Loan of a Lover* [J. R. Planché] and *Whitebait at Greenwich*, and the prologue was spoken by Mr. Maxwell-Lyte, of Magdalen. (1932)

This was not the first prologue Carroll had penned, fifteen years earlier he had shown his skill in the form and his knowledge of the theatre with *La Guida di Bragia*, but in the interim he had honed his literary talents:

> PROLOGUE (by C. L. Dodgson, spoken at Oxford, November 1 and 2, 1871)
> (*Curtain rises and discovers the SPEAKER, who comes forward thinking aloud.*)
> 'Ladies and gentlemen' seems stiff and cold,
> There's something personal in 'Young and old',
> I'll try 'Dear friends' (*to audience*) – Oh! Let me call you so! –
> Dear friends look kindly on our little show;
> Contrast us not with giants in the art,
> Nor say 'You should see Sothern in that part';
> Nor yet, unkindest cut of all in fact,
> Condemn the actors while you praise the act;
> Having by coming proved you find a charm in it,
> Don't go away and hint there may be harm in it.

This is precisely what follows in dialogue between Miss Verjuice ('You showed your wisdom when you stayed away') and Miss Crabb ('...Theatricals in *our* quiet town! / I've always said "The law should put them down."'). The 'comedy of manners' style is reinforced by the use of fans and continues in the Speaker's concluding speech:

80 *Lewis Carroll and the Victorian Stage*

What! *Acting* love!! And has that ne'er been seen
Save with a row of footlights placed between?
My gentle censors, let me roundly ask
Do none but actors ever wear a mask?
Or have we reached at last that golden age
That finds deception only on the stage?
(*Bell rings*)
But hark! The bell to summon me away:
They're anxious to begin their little Play.
One word before I go; we'll do our best,
And crave your kind indulgence for the rest;
Own that at least we've striven to succeed,
And take the good intention for the deed. (De Sausmarez, 1932)

Carroll makes no reference in his diaries to attending either performance at Clevedon House, but his services were again in demand by Mrs Hatch in 1873 when on 14 February he recorded: 'Feb: 14. (F). To Mrs. Hatch, to see rehearsal of *Checkmate* [by Andrew Halliday], a Mr. Bainbrigg [*sic*] acted very well, as also De Sausmarez, Tylee, and Arthur Hatch as page. After returning, I wrote a prologue for Wilfred and Beatrice to speak.' The prologue is reproduced in facsimile in an article by Beatrice Hatch in which she recalled Carroll's 'strict views of morality, and refined taste', which meant that 'the plays that he cared to go to were very limited in number', but 'he particularly enjoyed seeing children act...he did once favour us years ago with a tiny Prologue, for our own special use, at some private theatricals which our elders were to perform' (Hatch, 1898). The prologue is between Beatrice and Wilfred, whose 'Mamma's been trying on a funny dress' in preparation for a performance to the audience at which Wilfred appeals:

Wilfred. (*to audience.*)You'll praise them, won't you, when they've done
their Play?
Just say (*clapping his hands*) 'How nice!' before
you go away.

Carroll's growing reputation as the author of the 'Alice' books must have made him a sought-after guest even in the highest ranks of society. Thus on 31 December 1872 he arrived at Hatfield House to stay with the Marquess of Salisbury, the Chancellor of Oxford University and future Prime Minister, and his family. Carroll meticulously listed those present, including nineteen children, in his diary, but this aristocratic gathering's taste for amusements was much the same as the Synges's, the Hatchs's and other middle-class families:

Home Entertainments

a charade on 'Chance-sell-law', acted with plenty of spirit, but not much power of assumption of character. Afterwards I told some of the children the story of the Pixies, and the Russian one (which I heard at Ralston) of the 'Blacksmith and Hobgoblin'.

In the evening there was 'dancing, and I tried Gwenny etc., with some puzzles'. On New Year's Day '100 or more children came' in the evening for 'dancing in the gallery, then conjuring'. On the morning of 2 January 1873 there was more story telling, this time of Carroll's own 'new chapter of *Sylvie and Bruno*'. In the afternoon he 'went up to town, to the Simpsons (Cornwall Gardens), and witnessed far the best amateur juvenile acting I have ever seen' in *Cinderella* and, far less conventionally, Ben Jonson's *Epicoene, or, The Silent Woman*, but was back at Hatfield for dessert. Carroll spent the morning of 3 January regaling his listeners with 'a few more incidents for *Sylvie and Bruno*', having already 'helped the children to act a few proverbs etc. in dumb show'. He rounded off the day with '*The School for Scandal* (poorly done) and the Pantomime of *Goody Two Shoes*' at the Princess's Theatre in Oxford Street.

Though the delights of Christmas were devised primarily for the benefit of children, Carroll seemed to be enthusiastically throwing himself into them, if not to recapture the pleasures of his own childhood, then in recompense for what he had missed. The close identification of the principal Christian festival with childhood reflected Victorian attitudes to the young, but it was weighted more to girls than boys. In *Men in Wonderland: The Lost Girlhood of the Victorian Gentleman*, Catherine Robson examines accounts of childhood in the works of William Wordsworth, Thomas De Quincy, John Ruskin and Lewis Carroll to explore the 'myth of feminized origin' in which 'men only become masculine after an initial feminine stage' (p. 3). She characterises the Romantic and the Puritan attitudes towards childhood as the 'pure point of origin' and the 'primary corruption of human nature' (p. 6) respectively, or original sin and what Nina Auerbach has called 'original innocence' (1985, p. 131). As photographs and other representations show, Victorian boys (of the middle classes and above) were clothed like girls in their early years, but 'an initial period of feminine happiness comes to an abrupt and definite end and is succeeded by a harsh and competitive masculine world' (Robson, 2001, p. 40). Less robust and masculine males, such as De Quincy (of whom Robson is writing above) and Carroll engage in

> an essentially nostalgic construction, associated with the past...Simply through their presence, children offer the best possibility for adults to

82   *Lewis Carroll and the Victorian Stage*

reconnect to their imaginary pasts, to the fantasy era of their own idyllic childhoods. A girl, furthermore, radically distant from an adult male by virtue of her physical difference, more perfectly represents the safe, feminized, time of the nursery from which he has been irrevocably banished. (p. 136)

Robson is of course writing with the benefit of hindsight and late twentieth-century psychological theorising, but one of Carroll's closest friends, George MacDonald, provides some contemporary insights in his *Unspoken Sermons*,[3] in particular 'The Child in the Midst' based on Mark IX. 33-37:

And he took a child, and set him in the midst of them: and when he had taken him in his arms, he said unto them, Whosoever shall receive one of such children in my name, receiveth me; and whosoever shall receive me, receiveth not me, but him that sent me.

Running through MacDonald's sermon is 'the divine idea of childhood, which moved in the heart of God when he made that child after his own image' (1867, p. 5) and the 'special sense, a lofty knowledge of blessedness' which

belongs to the act of embracing a child as the visible likeness of the Lord himself. For the blessedness is the perceiving of the truth – the blessing is the truth itself – the God-known truth, that the Lord has the heart of a child. The man who perceives this knows in himself that he is blessed – blessed because that is true. (pp. 11-12)

Thus, viewing Carroll through the eyes of MacDonald, his attentiveness to young children imbued him with 'a lofty knowledge of blessedness' rather than raising suspicions of paedophilia.

George MacDonald was eight years older than Carroll and, having moved south after an unsuccessful spell as a Congregationalist minister, supported his growing family (eleven children in total) by writing numerous novels from *Phantastes* (1858) to *The Princess and the Goblin* (1872), which Arthur Hughes illustrated, and *Lilith* (1895) an allegorical fantasy for adults. The actor Johnston Forbes-Robertson testified to MacDonald's own commitment to and enthusiasm for child-centred activities:

Many children's parties were given, and a child with us all was the lovable George MacDonald, who entered into the games with naïve enthusiasm, to the joy of us youngsters...MacDonald was a saintly character and literally worshipped by his friends. (1925, p. 19)

Home Entertainments
83

Greville MacDonald, the eldest son, incorporated an account of Christmas Day 1857 in his memoirs: 'games of scampering', the arrival of 'thirteen poor children...with clean frocks and bright faces, to see the Christmas tree', MacDonald telling 'the story of the Ugly Duckling', lighting the tree, diving into 'the mysterious bran-cake' and a performance of Punch and Judy by 'Papa' who displayed 'his elocutionary talents in giving it to our party' (1924, pp. 286-7). Greville MacDonald quotes a letter from Johnston Forbes-Robertson recalling how MacDonald 'used to cover himself with a skin rug, and pretend to be a bear to the great delight of us all!' in what Greville MacDonald himself described as 'a charade representing the *Story of the Three Bears*, my two elder sisters as the little child and the Little Bear, my father the Big Bear, and perhaps, I am not sure, Arthur Hughes the Mother Bear' (p. 312). It is apparent from Carroll's photographs of George MacDonald (Taylor and Wakeling, 2002, p. 86) that he bore a striking resemblance to 'Uncle Jack' in the *Illustrated London News* drawing of 'Una and the Lion'.

The home entertainments at the MacDonald household were more ambitious than most. Forbes-Robertson reproduced a photograph of George MacDonald as Macbeth in his autobiography, in which he describes Mrs MacDonald as 'his brilliant and witty wife'. Mrs MacDonald was herself the author of *Chamber Dramas for Children*, published in 1870, which comprised *Cinderella or The Glass Slipper*, *Beauty and the Beast* and *Snowdrop*. Cinderella is described by Arabella (an Ugly Sister) in the first scene as 'only staring at herself in the glass' and sure enough the stage direction at the beginning of the second scene reads: '(Cinderella goes to the glass and looks at herself)' after which she sweeps the hearth (1870, p. 6). The similarity with the opening of Carroll's *Through the Looking-Glass*, published the next year, holds even though, unlike Alice, Cinderella remains on the hearth side of the looking-glass. Mrs MacDonald's pantomimes were performed some time before they were published and Carroll records seeing *Cinderella* (rather unseasonably) on 4 July 1864 with the numerous children in roles which their mother may well have created for them, 'but Lily was far the best'.

As R. B. Shaberman observed, 'Carroll's friendship with the MacDonalds...extended for more than twenty years' (1976, p. 73). The two men had much in common, not least a speech impediment, for which they both consulted Dr James Hunt of Hastings, where they met for the first time in 1859, but clearly neither man was prevented by his malady from taking full, *vocal* part in home theatricals. The MacDonalds and Carroll attended the chapel of St Peter's, Vere Street (just off Oxford Street) where the Revd Frederick Denison Maurice was incumbent from 1860 to 1869: 'Ap: 7. (Sun) [1867]. Went as usual to Vere Street Chapel,

84   *Lewis Carroll and the Victorian Stage*

where I met Mr. and Mrs. MacDonald...As a great many staid [*sic*] for the Communion I offered my help: even with three it took a long time.'

As a staunch Tory, Carroll did not share the politics of F. D. Maurice, who was one of the founders of Christian Socialism, but he was in sympathy with Maurice's revisionist ideas on the afterlife, which he had expressed in *Theological Essays* (1853), as a result of which he was dismissed from his chair in theology at King's College, London. Like Maurice, Carroll could not accept the idea that a merciful God would inflict eternal punishment on his creation. He set up his dilemma in an essay on 'Eternal Punishment' posing '*three* incompatible Propositions...I. God is perfectly good. II. To inflict Eternal Punishment on certain human beings, and in certain circumstances, would be wrong. III. God is capable of acting thus.' (Collingwood, 1899, p. 250) Although he described his 'object' as '*not* to indicate one course rather than another' (p. 257), readers are left in little doubt about Carroll's own opinion. The debate could not be confined to adults who could be held responsible for their own actions; it inevitably extended to babies, infants and children and raised the question whether for them baptism was an essential pre-requisite for salvation. To subscribe to hard-line beliefs in the afterlife would have been as difficult for Carroll as for the author of 'The Child in the Midst'. Indeed, their disposition to treat all God's creatures well is reflected in Carroll's and MacDonald's declared opposition to animal vivisection.

Greville MacDonald recollected the many treats which 'Uncle Dodgson' provided:

> Our annual treat was Uncle Dodgson taking us to the Polytechnic for the entrancing 'dissolving views' of fairy-tales, or to go down in the diving bell, or watch the mechanical athlete *Leotard*. There was also the Coliseum in Albany Street, with its storms by land and sea on a wonderful stage, and its great panorama of London. And there was Cremer's toy-shop in Regent Street – not to mention bath-buns and ginger-beer – all associated in my memory with the adorable writer of *Alice*.' (1924, p. 343)

Of the eleven MacDonald children it was Lilia Scott MacDonald, whose talent in *Cinderella* Carroll noted, who showed the greatest disposition towards the theatre. In 1875, aged only twenty-three, she played Lady Macbeth to her father's Thane and was warmly received by friends who travelled from near and far to see it. The MacDonalds' greatest and most enduring success was *The Pilgrim's Progress*. George MacDonald played Mr Greatheart and over the years most members of the family were involved in some capacity as they took the play on successive summer tours. Lilia MacDonald's performance as Christiana was the centrepiece of the whole thing, its *raison d'être* even, for in Greville MacDonald's account his father's 'whole-hearted endorsement of it [was because]...it gave an outlet for my eldest sister's genius: she played Christiana – a near presentment of her own person and character' (1924, p. 503). MacDonald's endorsement was important not just because his family was appearing in a play, but because it was on a religious subject, albeit not actually biblical. Greville MacDonald refers to his mother 'circumventing' the Lord Chamberlain's refusal 'to license a religious play' (p. 502) and the 'profound impression' it created 'upon everyone susceptible to such spiritual art' including Dean Stanley and Burne-Jones (p. 504). Carroll's attitude to the Oberammergau Passion Play indicated his disinclination to mix religion and the theatre, but he seems to have overcome his reservations with *The Pilgrim's Progress*, which he saw four times: 17 and 25 June 1879, 23 July 1879 and 26 June 1880. On each occasion he took friends and felt able to recommend it to others such as Mrs Blakemore, to whom he wrote on 14 October 1879:

Dear Mrs. Blakemore,
The MacDonalds are old and dear friends of mine (I have known them nearly 20 years) and *The Pilgrim's Progress* is a most graceful, refined, and reverential performance. Unless you object on general principles to *all* dramatic performances, I do hope you will be able to go, and to take Edith, and that you will allow me the pleasure of paying for her ticket, so that it may be my treat to her.

Somewhat later (in the 1880s and 1890s) Carroll actively helped aspiring actresses from the middle classes. Despite his enthusiasm for Lilia in *Cinderella*, Carroll's considered judgement on the MacDonalds, expressed in a letter to Edith Lucy on 15 January 1894, was that although 'they spoke slowly and clearly...the family had but little dramatic talent'. It emerges from the same letter that performances were given 'in their garden, to poor people'. Nowadays marshalling the poor to provide an audience for their theatricals may not seem quite such an act of philanthropy as the MacDonalds no doubt considered it to be. Greville MacDonald records that Lilia was deterred from taking up acting professionally by the response of Mrs Arthur Lewis, Ellen Terry's sister Kate, who had given up her acting career when she married Arthur Lewis, who 'gave so repugnant a picture of the stage that my sister's hopes were disallowed' (1932, p. 308). It is of course quite possible that Carroll had facilitated an opportunity for Lilia to seek his friend Kate's advice. In any case Lilia faced a second obstacle, that of an unidentified, impoverished

86 *Lewis Carroll and the Victorian Stage*

suitor who deferred to a 'relative whose probable heir he was...[who] refused to sanction their marriage unless she undertook never to act in public again' (1924, p. 516). Lilia rejected this condition, which she regarded as 'an insult to her own gifts and art'. Carroll's last sight of her was on 22 September 1882 when he travelled from Eastbourne to Brighton where he saw her in Corneille's *Polyeuctus*. In practice Lilia had fallen between two stools by turning down the opportunity to marry, but not having the resolve to go on stage professionally. Her brother describes hers as a life 'devoted – I dare not say *wasted* – to the interminable demands at home' (1932, p. 309).

It would be inappropriate to conclude a chapter on a subject that was the source of as much delight, fun and laughter as home entertainments on a melancholy note. Greville MacDonald took up a career in medicine and became an eminent nose and throat specialist with many actors and singers, including Sir Henry Irving, Sir John Hare and Sir Charles Wyndham, amongst his clients. As well as his two volumes of memoirs he contributed articles to journals. In 'The Spirit of Play' (1923) MacDonald discussed the nature and function of play, insisting that 'joy...is at once the incentive and outcome of play', 'the essence of play is...imaginative', but 'play is not morality perhaps: but it is the hunger for higher things than the chase or the dinner, and so it is the beginning of religion'. The idea that though play is not morality it is nevertheless spiritual in that it refreshes and re-creates would surely have struck a chord with Carroll (who figured prominently in MacDonald's childhood memories), as also would his emphasis on joy.

Carroll's enthusiastic and wholehearted involvement in home entertainments was very much what was expected of adults, from the pages of the *Illustrated London News* to Anne Bowman's drawing-room plays, from Hatfield House to the more modest Synge, Hatch and MacDonald dwellings. Nearly all these activities were designed to give pleasure to children and the more an adult contributed to the children's enjoyment the better. If in doing so he (or she) was upholding an ideal of innocence and recreating or recompensing for his own childhood that was hardly likely to be obvious or a matter of concern.

Notes

1   Typescript of talk given to Leamington Literary Society by Miss Violet Dodgson on 17 October 1849. DFC/C/1/1-15.

Home Entertainments

2   Few copies of *The Guildford Gazette Extraordinary* have survived. Derek Hudson reproduces the introduction (1995, pp. 327-30) from the copy in Christ Church library.

3   Another of MacDonald's sermons has a Carroll connection. 'The New Name' takes as its text: 'To him that overcometh, I will give a white stone, and in the stone a new name written, which no man knoweth saving he that receiveth it. – Revelations II 27.' Carroll awarded a 'white stone' to days that he had particularly enjoyed. MacDonald wrote: 'And the writer thought of it mystically, a mode far more likely to involve a reference to nature than to political custom. What his mystic meaning may be, must be taken differently by different minds. I think he sees in its whiteness purity, and in its substance indestructibility.' (1867, p. 104)

6 The Terrys

> 'He was as fond of me as he could be of any one over the age of ten'
> Ellen Terry, *Memoirs*

Lewis Carroll's first reference to a member of the Terry family occurred in his diary entry for 16 June 1856 when he attended a performance of *The Winter's Tale* at the Princess's Theatre and 'especially admired the acting of Mamillius, Ellen Terry, a beautiful little creature, who played with remarkable spirit and ease'. On 16 December he recorded: '"Puck" was cleverly acted by the little Ellen Terry, who was "Mamillius" in *The Winter's Tale* exactly six months ago'. Since Ellen Terry was aged nine at the time and Carroll was twenty-eight it is tempting to see her as an early example of the theatrical child-friend and he does indeed describe her as 'a beautiful little creature'. However, the most striking thing about these two brief entries is Carroll's judgement of Ellen Terry's acting ability: 'especially admired the acting of Mamillius...played with remarkable spirit and ease', 'Puck was cleverly acted'. Carroll was then only in his second year of theatre-going, but he singled out the nine-year-old and particularly commended her 'remarkable spirit and ease', qualities which were to be hallmarks of Ellen Terry's lengthy and distinguished career and which he also used as a benchmark for his acting protégées decades later.

By the standards of her family Ellen Terry was a late developer. As Christopher St. John observed:

> [her] sister Kate, four years older, had long before this begun a very successful stage career by dancing a hornpipe in a diminutive sailor's jumper and white ducks at the Amphitheatre, Liverpool, and in 1851, when Ellen was only three years old, was playing Robin at the Princess's Theatre, London, in Charles Kean's revival of 'Merry Wives of Windsor.' Mrs. Terry accompanied her elder child to London, and left Nelly in the provinces with her father. Two or three years later Mr. Terry was also engaged by Kean, and the family were reunited. (1907, pp. 3-4)

But for their talented offspring Benjamin Terry and his wife Sarah (*née* Ballard), though themselves both actors, would barely register in the annals of the nineteenth-century stage, nevertheless they do deserve credit for their children's success. In *Nicholas Nickleby* Dickens portrays Vincent Crummles as a parent eager to exploit the supposed acting gifts of his daughter 'The Infant Prodigy', but in the theatre a parent fortunate enough to have a child with genuine talent had an asset which, as the future Dame Madge Kendal's father and the future Adelaide Calvert's father realised, could be beneficially developed in the short term for the family as a whole as well as that child's longer term prospects. Thus Mrs Terry devoted herself to Kate's career as a little later did her husband to Ellen's and significantly Terry's own engagement at the Princess's followed his children's. As Carroll's early awareness of the Terrys developed into acquaintance and friendship, his understanding of how theatrical families functioned informed his encounters with other such units and in due course his contribution to the debate about the employment of children in the theatre. Though he died ten years before Ellen Terry published her memoirs, Carroll can hardly have been unaware of the debt she owed to her father, in whose charge she was left aged three whilst her mother was in London with her sister Kate:

> He never ceased teaching me to be useful, alert, and quick. Sometimes he hastened my perceptive powers with a slipper, and always he corrected me if I pronounced any word in a slipshod fashion. He himself was a beautiful elocutionist, and if I now speak my language well it is in no small degree due to my early training. (1908, p. 8)

This stood her in good stead when she auditioned for Mamillius:

> Several children were tried, Nelly Terry...among them. She was chosen, it is instructive to remember, because she *spoke* better than the others. Mr. Terry's lessons in elocution had not been thrown away. (St John, 1907, p. 5)

Although Carroll did not remark specifically on the young actress's elocution, it was something upon which he always placed the utmost importance and no doubt her skill in it contributed significantly to the favourable impression he formed. It also contributed – certainly no less significantly – to the Terry family finances 'as the child's salary at the Princess's, which began at fifteen shillings a week, was of course handed over to her parents' (pp. 6-7), but there seems to be no reason to suppose that Terry or Carroll would have dissented from her biographer's opinion that 'she was stronger in the experience of life than children whom good fortune had protected from the cradle' (p. 4).

Certainly none of the Terrys' surviving nine children (two died in infancy) was in danger from that particular form of good fortune (see Pemberton, 1902 and Steen, 1962). Carroll continued to admire the sisters

90 *Lewis Carroll and the Victorian Stage*

on stage, taking particular delight in seeing them both in *A Midsummer Night's Dream* on 22 January 1857 when:

> As some of the actors were at Windsor [performing at the Royal Theatricals], their places were taken by others...Miss Kate Terry for Miss C. Leclerque [*sic*]...[she] made a beautiful 'Titania', and her little sister as good a 'Puck' as ever.

It was on a night when her 'sister Kate was playing Titania...as understudy to Carlotta Leclercq' that 'the man shut the trap-door too soon and caught my toe', but if it was this particular performance, such was Ellen Terry's professionalism (urged on by Mrs Kean: 'Finish the play, dear, and I'll double your salary!' Terry, 1908, p. 17) that her predicament passed unnoticed by Carroll. Not that she would have indulged herself in the audience's sympathy. There is not a trace of self-pity in her recollection of the incident fifty years later, when:

> It is argued now that stage life is bad for a young child, and children are not allowed by law to go on the stage until they are ten years old – quite a mature age in my younger days! I cannot discuss the whole question here, and must content myself with saying that at the Princess's I was a very strong, happy, and healthy child. I was never out of the bill except during the run of 'A Midsummer Night's Dream', when, through an unfortunate accident, I broke my toe. (pp. 16-17)

As Ariel in *The Tempest* Kate's performance relied on the theatre's flying apparatus rather than the trap-door:

> July 3. (F) [1857] the gem of the piece was the exquisitely graceful and beautiful Ariel, acted by Miss Kate Terry. Her appearance as a sea-nymph was one of the most beautiful living pictures I ever saw, but this, and every other one in my recollection (except Queen Katherine's dream), were all outdone by the concluding scene, where Ariel is left alone, hovering over the wide ocean, watching the retreating ship. It is an innovation on Shakespeare, but a worthy one, and the conception of a true poet.

As well as expressing his admiration for Kate Terry as Ariel, Carroll also shows himself to be a typical mid-nineteenth-century playgoer delighting in the scenic accomplishments of the age untroubled by any scruples about Shakespearian authenticity. Not surprisingly he returned to the Princess's for the final performance of Charles Kean's revival of *The Tempest* on 28 November 1857 when he found 'the whole better acted than when I saw it in the summer, and the scenic effects as beautiful as ever. Prospero and

The Terrys 91

the inimitably graceful Ariel (Miss K. Terry) were both called before the curtain.'

Although Ellen Terry went on to play Prince Arthur in *King John* and Fleance in *Macbeth*, neither part offered such good opportunities as those that she and Kate had so successfully grasped and the conclusion of Kean's management of the Princess's in 1859 coincided with the sisters' progression from child performers to actresses. Whereas during the 1850s the Princess's Theatre had been *the* theatre for playgoers of Carroll's social and educational ilk, during the 1860s there was no such locus. Similarly Kean's company dispersed in many directions. Benjamin Terry's initial response was to 'exploit the fame of his daughters by going on the road with a "Drawing-room Entertainment" – so-called no doubt to catch the public still fearful of the theatre (that "devil's hot-bed") but curious to see what its performances were like' (Manvell, 1968, p. 21). Terry, who was working in a vein that the German Reeds were to make their own, enjoyed some success, but nurtured on full-bloodied theatre from infancy his daughters 'demanded sterner stuff than this' (p. 22). Carroll caught up with Kate Terry ('a perfect treat') as Ophelia to Charles Fechter's Hamlet at the Lyceum Theatre on 21 June 1864 and at the Olympic where she partnered Henry Neville ('an ideal hero of romance', Pemberton, 1902, p. 109) in a succession of plays by Tom Taylor. Following its reconstruction in 1861 Ellen Terry appeared at the Royalty Theatre in Dean Street, Soho, where her experience bore out Mander and Mitchenson's description of it as 'the unlucky little playhouse' (1968, p. 414). The Royalty was not a theatre that Carroll attended save for F. C. Burnand's *Rumplestiltskin and the Maid* and *Ixion* (twice) in June 1864 and a couple of later visits. It was at the Theatre Royal, Bristol, under the management of James Henry Chute, that Ellen Terry enjoyed a succession of personal successes in 1862 and 1863, but Carroll did not venture there to see her. Someone who did see and admire her performances was the architect E. W. Godwin, but the next year 'when she was almost seventeen, she married the forty-six-year-old neurasthenic painter George Frederick Watts and became his wife in art' (Auerbach, 1987, p. 76). Watts was ten years older than Carroll. Auerbach describes Ellen Terry at the time as 'a magically beautiful and vigorous child, brimming with disruptive power' (p. 78) and this is very much the motif of Lynn Truss's fictional character in her novel *Tennyson's Gift* set on the Isle of Wight in the summer of 1864:

> The sad thing was that when he [Watts] married Ellen, he assumed she wanted the same release from her own career. After all, her career was the *theatre*. But he had learned that while you can take the child out of the

92 *Lewis Carroll and the Victorian Stage*

theatre, it is a more difficult matter to extract the theatre from the child. She still dressed up quite often. She danced in pink tights. A couple of times she had sat next to him at dinner, dressed as a young man, and he had talked to her for two hours without in any way piercing her disguise, or noticing the absence of his wife. (1997, pp. 24-5)

Truss, through the eyes of the Tennysons at least, sees Carroll as 'this treacherous Oxford stammerer' (p. 11). Although she changes his university allegiance from Oxford to Cambridge, Anne Thackeray's portrayal of Carroll as George Hexham, 'A photographer', 'travelling gypsy fashion, in search of subjects for his camera', in *From an Island* (1877, reprinted 1996, p. 23) is little more appealing. Carroll's pursuit of the Tennysons as photographic subjects had resulted in their distrust of him, but, as Morton N. Cohen has observed, Carroll had made 'numerous efforts to photograph the Terrys...Getting them to sit for him on four successive days in July 1865 was indeed a triumph' (Cohen ed., 1979, vol. I, p. 78, n. 1). Carroll's diary entries record his persistent attempts to meet and photograph the Terrys, beginning on 22 June 1864 when dramatist Tom Taylor, who was his intermediary, told him that 'Miss [sic] Terry and the children are all away ill'. On 14 July he 'at last found my way to "Little Holland House"', where he was 'received most kindly' by Watts, who 'nearly promised to come with her [his wife], on Saturday to be photographed'. Not a man to be contented with the mere prospect of a favour, Carroll took the initiative and proposed 'to Mr. Watts, to bring my camera to Little Holland House, and take pictures there', but nothing came of that. After his marriage Watts had continued to live with the Prinseps at Little Holland House rather than set up a home with his new bride.

On 26 July Carroll left for the Isle of Wight, the time and place of Lynn Truss's novel *Tennyson's Gift* in which Carroll and Ellen Terry meet, though in fact this did not happen there and then. Back in London on 13 August Carroll received a note of introduction to the Terrys from Tom Taylor and on 20 August at 'about one went with Mr. Tom Taylor's note of introduction to 92, Stanhope Street'. Michael Baker has traced the residential patterns of Victorian actors, identifying 'the move to Bloomsbury' as 'a natural one for the wealthier actor' (1978, p. 68). Although Stanhope Street abutted North Gower Street it lay beyond Euston Road to the east of Regent's Park. In the absence of her husband Mrs Terry, whom he 'thought...particularly pleasant and ladylike', invited Carroll into what he described as 'the little sitting room'. Devout Wesleyans, the Terrys were highly respectable members of their profession, but a sense of social uncertainty underlies Carroll's account. His description of Mrs Terry as 'ladylike', the term he later applied to

Irene Vanbrugh (who as a cleric's daughter was indisputably the real thing), implied that she genuinely had the bearing and manners of a lady and was not merely giving the appearance of being ladylike, which, as an accomplished actress, she was no doubt capable of doing. When Carroll returned on Sunday 21 he offered to take two of the Terry children 'on to Hampstead Heath with me, but Mrs. Terry did not like to let them go in Mr. Terry's absence'. Whether her response was general or particular to Carroll, it shows that a mother who had no qualms about her children appearing on the professional stage from three upwards was none the less highly protective of them. Carroll eventually met Mr Terry in October on 12, 13 and 28 after which he could write that: 'I have now met all the party except Miss Terry and Mrs Watts'. When he returned on Tuesday 20 December 1864 Carroll noted several features of the Terry household: the front door was opened by Benjamin, the eldest son, who took him 'up into the drawing room, telling me that his sister Kate was just having lunch in the sitting room', where he had previously been entertained by Mrs Terry. First Polly (Marion) then Kate (Miss Terry) joined him 'and introduced herself, as the other two did not attempt any introduction'. Carroll's concern about the niceties of introductions and where meals were taken continued:

> She [Kate] took us down into the dining room, where was a young friend of hers, whom she did not introduce, and there we had to wait a good while before Mr. Terry made his appearance. She did the honours of the house with ease and grace, and I thought her very ladylike and natural in manner, not an atom of shyness: that however one would expect.

Thus despite her failure to observe the social niceties of introductions, Carroll judged Kate Terry to be 'very ladylike' and 'left, well pleased in having at last accomplished my wish of meeting one I have so long admired from a distance'. Frustratingly Mrs Watts (Ellen Terry), though on a visit to Stanhope Street, was out, but the following day Carroll went 'once more to Stanhope Street' and met 'the one I have always most wished to meet of her family, Mrs. Watts'. Their first face to face encounter matched Carroll's expectations: 'I was very pleased with what I saw of Mrs. Watts, lively and pleasant, almost childish in her face, but perfectly ladylike'. In contrast Kate 'seemed ill and out of spirits' and though he found 'both sisters...charming', Carroll fancied that 'their gaiety' (Ellen's that day, Kate's the day before) was 'partly assumed'. Nevertheless nothing could mar his happiness at having at last met Kate and Ellen: 'I think it a piece of rare good fortune to have made two such acquaintances in two days. I mark this day also with a white stone.'

94 Lewis Carroll and the Victorian Stage

Carroll emerges from his accounts of visiting the Terrys like one of the theatrical Bliss family's guests in Noël Coward's *Hay Fever*: the awed admirer who nevertheless cannot help but hold on to his more conventional standards.

Unfortunately for Carroll he had to endure a lengthy wait before the photographing season began and by then the Terrys had moved to Kentish Town: 'Their new house is much larger than the old, and has a garden behind, which I hope to use for photography in the summer.' That preliminary visit on 7 April 1865 seems to have been more relaxed, with Carroll joining the family for lunch after which he heard 'Mrs. Watts play and sing and Florence sing two songs, one being "Pretty Polly Perkins".'

The Terrys' progress to 24 Caversham Road, Kentish Town, illustrates 'the move to the suburbs...among well-to-do actors and actresses' (Baker, 1978, p. 70). In late June Benjamin Terry agreed to the photographic session, requesting notice of Carroll's approach, and on 10 July Kate Terry alerted Carroll that her sisters 'Polly and Flo are leaving soon'. Carroll 'packed up the photography' and left for London the next day. After a night at the Old Hummuns Hotel he 'drove over to the Terrys with the camera etc.'. That day Wednesday 13 July it rained and Carroll 'took only three pictures', but the next day was much more productive with photographs of most of the family. On his way back to Kentish Town on Saturday 15 July Carroll was delayed at his publishers, Macmillan's, signing copies of *Alice's Adventures in Wonderland*, an important reminder that he too was now a celebrity.

That afternoon and on the following Monday Carroll took more than twenty photographs of members of the Terry family in various permutations in the garden of 24 Caversham Road.[1] Carroll's own account is bland: 'took a large one of Miss Terry in fancy costume', which presumably was of Kate Terry as Andromeda with her wrists in chains (Taylor and Wakeling, 2002, p. 259). This is the one really dramatic photograph in the group which principally consists of family portraits. Carroll's most theatrical studies of members of the Terry family were those taken of the younger sisters Marion (Polly) and Florence a decade later (see Chapter 8). For a few hours during those summer days in Kentish Town Carroll realised what must have been the summit of his ambition by combining his twin passions for photography and the theatre, and thereby defying the innately ephemeral nature of the stage and leaving behind a permanent record of a theatrical family thanks to the invention of photography.

Carroll combined his photography of the Terry family with seeing Kate on stage in Tom Taylor's *The Serf*, which he attended at the Olympic Theatre on the evening of 15 July when he and Marion (Polly) had 'good places in the dress circle' courtesy of 'Miss Terry's season ticket'. He had already seen *The Serf* on 3 July when he had ordered several photographs of the Terrys at Southwell's shop and he returned to the Olympic on 19 and 24 of July:

> July 19. (W) Hume joined me in the evening and we went to the Olympic. We were to have had Miss Terry's admission-ticket, but she forgot to bring it. I met her at the stage-door, and by her direction we simply mentioned her name, and were admitted. I like *The Serf* better every time I see it.

Carroll considered 'the moral' of Taylor's 'Russian' play, in which Miss Terry as the Countess falls in love with a serf (Henry Neville) who turns out to be a prince, to be 'very hazy', but it was 'acted well'. The strength of the mid-nineteenth-century theatre lay much more in its acting and production (scenery, lighting, costumes) than in its new plays, and like most other playgoers Carroll accepted the reality of the situation. In this case it was undoubtedly the acting of Miss Terry in a play, the sub-title of which was *Love Levels All*, that attracted him and there must surely have been some synergy between repeatedly seeing her on stage and photographing her all within the compass of little over a week. The suggestion that Carroll fell in love with Ellen Terry has been fairly widely considered (Cohen, 1982, p.1), but at this time anyway it seems that Kate Terry exercised a potent attraction for him. The age gap between them was only five years, much less than that between her sister Ellen and Watts, and above all she was unmarried. With his fame as an author, his skill as a photographer and his status as an Oxford don Carroll was not without his credentials as a potential husband and it is clear that Kate, having been on stage since the age of three, was tiring of it and ready to settle for a comfortable married life, but Carroll's references to her 'assumed' gaiety and forgetfulness over the admission ticket hardly suggest that she took him as seriously as he might have wished.

The impression given by Marguerite Steen is that there was a degree of calculation in Kate's attitude towards matrimony: 'There was no glimmer of bohemianism in Katie; she liked rich, successful people' and amongst 'her many swains', Arthur Lewis 'handsome and kindly, wealthy and influential...was emphatically a *parti* – even for a theatrical star of the magnitude of Kate Terry' (1962, pp. 104-5). The magnitude of Kate Terry's theatrical stardom was apparent at her farewell performance (as Juliet to Henry Neville's Romeo) at the Adelphi Theatre on 2 September 1867 of which *The Times* wrote:

96 *Lewis Carroll and the Victorian Stage*

> Successes, demonstrations, and ovations of a kind may be made to order; but the scene of Saturday was one of those genuine, spontaneous, and irrepressible outbursts of public recognition which carry their credentials of sincerity along with them. The widespread feeling that the stage is losing one of its chosen ornaments had been manifested by the full houses, more and more crowded on each successive night. (Pemberton, 1902, p. 115)

The scene evokes A. W. Pinero's *Trelawny of the 'Wells'*, but unlike Rose Trelawny Kate Terry exhibited no regrets at leaving the stage and though Arthur James Lewis may have shared his namesake's (Arthur Gower) fascination with the theatre, he had no intention of pursuing it professionally. For several years before his marriage Lewis, whose substantial family wealth was derived from Lewis and Allenby 'By warrant silk mercers to Her Majesty Queen Victoria', had been the moving spirit behind gatherings of 'artists, authors, journalists and singers who came to smoke, to eat oysters (at 6d. a dozen) and to make music' initially at his apartment in Jermyn Street, when they were known as the 'Jermyn Band', and after 1862 at Moray Lodge on Campden Hill in Kensington when they became 'The Moray Minstrels' (Terry Gielgud, 1953, p. 15). Amongst those present were 'Dickens, Thackeray, Richard Doyle, Landseer, Frith, Millais, Leighton and Keene, as well as royalty and sportsmen' (Engen, 1991, p. 58). Tenniel was a regular visitor as was Arthur Sullivan whose *Cox and Box* with a libretto by F. C. Burnand 'was given by the Moray Minstrels in Lewis's house on 26 May 1866' (Jacobs, 1986, p. 51). It was repeated on 11 May 1867 at the Adelphi Theatre as a benefit in aid of the widow of the *Punch* artist Charles Bennett. Carroll attended and found it 'a great treat' with so many familiar faces on stage including Quintin Twiss as Box. After the first piece Carroll 'went round to the Terry party, who were in the stage-box...[including] Mr. Lewis (Miss Terry's intended) to whom I was introduced'. Tom Taylor's *Sheep in Wolf's Clothing* followed with the author, Mark Lemon, Shirley Brooks, F. C. Burnand, 'John Tenniel "Colonel Churchill." Miss Terry, Mrs Watts, and Flo...Tenniel seemed nervous, and was hardly audible. Miss Terry was, in parts, very pathetic, and reduced Polly to floods of tears'. Happily the cast was captured for posterity by a camera, albeit not Carroll's (Terry Gielgud, 1953. opp. p. 32; Engen, 1991, p. 59).

Although his acquaintance with Arthur Lewis had begun with a proper introduction (something the Terrys could not always be relied upon to provide), Carroll experienced considerable difficulty over the correct form of address between them. On 23 December 1870 he began his letter 'My dear Lewis', but pointed out that in recent correspondence Lewis had changed from 'My dear Dodgson...Yours sincerely' to 'My dear

The Terrys 97

sir...Yours faithfully', but instead of following suit 'I prefer, as you see, to assume that our friendship remains at its former temperature', but nine years later on 8 May 1879 Carroll wrote 'My dear Lewis, (We oscillate between surname terms and "Mr." terms: I am glad we have swung back to the former)'. The Terry sisters and their marital status were a source of considerable anxiety to Carroll. In the view of herself, her family and the world generally, Kate Terry had married very well, but, whereas he tended to regard theatre folk as a special case socially, Carroll could not entirely overlook the fact that Lewis was fundamentally 'trade'. This was negligible compared with the problems caused by Kate's wayward sister Ellen.

Recalling her childhood at Moray Lodge, Kate Terry Gielgud (Sir John Gielgud's mother) wrote 'he [Carroll] would come (often to lunch) when the need for some photographic material brought him to London' (1953, p. 26) and in his letter of 8 May 1879 Carroll wrote to Lewis 'it is one of my special treats, when I have a day in town, to pay a visit to Moray Lodge'. One of the most memorable of these was on Wednesday 24 January 1883 when *Lady Barbara's Birthday* (a comedietta by a 'Miss Barker') was

> acted by the six children. It was a great treat. Janet [Terry Lewis] and Lucy [Terry Lewis] looked charming in male attire, but were not specially good: but Edith [Craig] was clever (though not very articulate) and Katie [Terry Lewis] distinctly good: then Teddie [Craig] was *very* good, though a little given to rant: but Mabel [Terry Lewis] was the gem of the whole thing. I never saw her equal among children, except Ellen Terry herself. She is a born actress. We met all four of the Terry sisters – Mrs Lewis, Mrs Wardell, Polly and Flossie.

By way of a bonus the dramatist W. S. Gilbert was also present.

Ellen Terry's personal life had inevitably placed a strain on family relationships, not least with 'the rather starchy' (Steen, 1962, p. 105) Kate, whose own courtship by Lewis was conducted against the background of her sister's estrangement from Watts and liaison with the architect E. W. Godwin, the father of Edith and Teddie. That they and their mother were now back in the bosom of the family and accepted in society was largely thanks to Ellen's status as Mrs Wardell. But for this Carroll would almost certainly not have taken Ethel Arnold along to the performance at which 'Ethel was actually introduced to Miss E. T. *three* times' each of which Carroll, with his customary concern for that ritual, described in detail to Agnes Hull in a letter dated 26 January 1883, it made a 'Terryble Tale'. For Carroll such a gathering of Terrys must have recalled those July days

98 Lewis Carroll and the Victorian Stage

at Kentish Town, but this time: 'All the 4 sisters were there: I never met all four at once before.'

The previous year Florence, at the age of twenty-seven, had followed Kate's example and left the stage to marry William Morris, a solicitor, and set up home near the Lewis family on Campden Hill. On 21 June 1882, in the best family tradition, she gave a farewell performance at the Savoy Theatre of W. S. Gilbert's *Broken Hearts*, Act IV of *The Merchant of Venice* as Nerissa with her sisters Ellen (Portia) and Marion (the Clerk) to Henry Irving's Shylock, and *Trying a Magistrate* with J. L. Toole. Though the occasion fell short of that for Kate Carroll pronounced: 'The whole thing...quite first-rate'. This left just two Terry sisters as professional actresses, Ellen and her younger (by six years) sister Marion (Polly). Though overshadowed by her more famous sister Marion enjoyed a highly successful career from her debut in Leeds in 1873 onwards. Carroll saw her at the Haymarket Theatre in Gilbert's *Dan'l Druce, Blacksmith* on 10 October 1876 and found her acting 'as tender and graceful as possible'. On 10 March 1877 at the same theatre in the same author's *Pygmalion and Galatea* he thought her 'very sweet and charming, though perhaps a little wanting in *vis*', a quality not particularly needed as 'Dearest' (Mrs Erroll) in *The Real Little Lord Fauntleroy* which Carroll saw on 26 June 1889: 'Marion Terry is now "Mrs Erroll", and does it very sweetly and pathetically.' Carroll avoided *Lady Windermere's Fan* in which Marion Terry played Mrs Erlynne and H. A. Jones's short-lived *Michael and his Lost Angel* in which she had replaced Mrs Patrick Campbell at the last minute as the *femme fatale* Audrie Lesden. These were not Carroll's type of play even with a Terry in the cast. In contrast he attended R. C. Carton's *Liberty Hall* at the St James's Theatre, three times. On the first occasion (4 March 1893) 'Edie Wardell' (as Carroll persisted in calling Edith Craig) stood in for Maude Millett and 'did *well*, barring her unfortunate lisp. Her mother was in the stage-box close to us, so we had a little talk with her'.

Apart from anything else they had in common, Ellen Terry and Lewis Carroll were natural letter writers and their correspondence, whilst it falls far short (in volume and *vis*) of hers with George Bernard Shaw, is an invaluable source of information for their relationship and Carroll's views on the theatre of the day. The connection between Carroll and Ellen Terry manifested itself in three principal ways: exchanges on specific roles that she was playing, her personal life, and favours for his young protégées.

The plays about which Carroll wrote most fully to Ellen Terry were *The Merchant of Venice, Much Ado About Nothing* and *Faust* by W. G. Wills. All three remained in the Lyceum repertoire for many years and Carroll saw the first two six times each and *Faust* twice. The Lyceum production of *The Merchant of Venice* opened on 1 November 1879 and Carroll attended for the first time on 10 January 1880 when he pronounced it 'a real treat...The trial-scene was about the best thing I ever saw.' Within a couple of days (12? January 1880) Carroll wrote very appreciatively to Ellen Terry:

> You gave me a treat on Saturday such as I have very seldom had in my life. You must be weary by this time of hearing your own praises, so I will only say that Portia was all I could have imagined, and more. And Shylock is superb – especially in the trial-scene.

Though he had no criticisms of the leading performers Carroll objected strongly to one clause in the play: 'That, for this favour, / He presently become a Christian' (IV, I, 382-3). His objection was twofold: religious and artistic. He considered that to 'all Christians now (except perhaps extreme Calvinists) the idea of forcing a man to abjure his religion, whatever that religion may be, is...simply horrible.' This clearly places Carroll of the liberal, tolerant wing of the church in line with F. D. Maurice and their mutual friend George MacDonald who had been 'banished' from a living in Arundel 'for his unorthodox opinions, among which was the hope that mercy might be shown to the heathen in the after world' (Moore, 1974, p. 98). Clearly in the era of colonialism the question of whether followers of non-Christian religions could attain an afterlife was widely considered, but the case of the Jews was of course complicated by their role in the death of Christ. Irving undoubtedly based his cosmopolitan and sympathetic Shylock on prominent contemporary Jews such as the Rothschilds and Disraeli (Foulkes, 1972), whom Carroll described on his death as 'quite the greatest statesman of our time' in a letter to Mrs Blakemore on 25 April 1881. Carroll also objected to the lines because 'we are suddenly called on to see in him [Shylock] the victim of a cruelty a thousand times worse than his own, and to honour him as martyr. This, I am sure, Shakespeare never meant.' Thus although Carroll regarded Antonio's demand as 'simply horrible', he was no apologist for Shylock for whom in his view Shakespeare allowed 'two touches only of sympathy..."I will not pray with you"; "I had it of Leah, when I was a bachelor."'

Of *The Merchant of Venice* Carroll protested to Ellen Terry that 'I should not like to suggest putting in a single word that is not Shakespeare's', but with *Much Ado About Nothing* he actually wrote six new lines for Beatrice, which would have provided an alibi for Hero, but would also of course have drastically foreshortened the play:

100 *Lewis Carroll and the Victorian Stage*

> But, good my lord, sweet Hero slept not there:
> She had another chamber for the nonce.
> 'Twas sure some counterfeit that did present
> Her person at the window, aped her voice,
> Her mien, her manners, and hath thus deceived
> My good lord Pedro and this company?

Carroll included these lines in his letter to Ellen Terry of 20 March 1883 in which he expressed Lucy Arnold's great pleasure at seeing the play (with him), it being 'her first visit to the theatre'. This (15 March 1883) was Carroll's third visit and immediately before it Ellen Terry wrote to him: 'Look out for new business in the Church scene. I'm sure it's much better now. Also...you are right about some other things you said one day at Kate's about the same Church scene'[2] Carroll had in fact described to Agnes Hull 'Miss E.T. ...talking, in a very excited way, to me about *Much Ado*' when he attended *Lady Barbara's Birthday* at Moray Lodge on 24 January 1883. It seems from Carroll's diary entry for 15 March that originally Hero had fainted twice and he had sent a note to Ellen Terry suggesting that: 'Hero fainting *twice* is awkward, and that she had better fall, once for all, where she means to be: this was done tonight, but whether owing to me or not, Miss Terry did not say.' In his letter of 20 March to Ellen Terry Carroll wrote:

> By the way, I must not forget to say that I thought the change in the fainting business a *great* improvement. I presume the change was made owing to some one else having suggested it, before *I* did (as you do not say it was owing to me), but even so I am glad to have my opinion thus confirmed.

It would certainly be gratifying (not only to him) if Carroll was the direct cause of this change, but even if he was not his advice was clearly sound and his comments are a wonderfully characteristic blend of humility and reproach.

Carroll expressed his major objection to the Lyceum *Much Ado About Nothing* in his article 'The Stage and the Spirit of Reverence' in the *Theatre* (1 June 1888) in which he 'heartily wish[ed] Mr. Irving could see his way to transfer it [the Church scene] to the *outside* of the church', but that was beyond his or anyone's else's powers of direct or indirect persuasion.

In that case Carroll did express himself unequivocally in print, but in a (lost) personal letter to Ellen Terry about her performance as Marguerite/ Margaret in *Faust* he offended the actress, as she recalled in her memoirs:

8. Ellen Terry as Marguerite [Margaret] in *Faust*

102 *Lewis Carroll and the Victorian Stage*

> Mr Dodgson (Lewis Carroll, of the immortal 'Alice in Wonderland') once brought a girl to see me in 'Faust'. He wrote and told me that she had said (where Margaret begins to undress): 'Where is it going to stop?' and, perhaps in consideration of the fact that it could affect a mere child disagreeably, I ought to alter my business!

> I had known dear Mr Dodgson for years and years. He was as fond of me as he could be of any one over the age of ten, but I was *furious*. 'I thought you only knew *nice* children', was all the answer I gave him. 'It would have seemed awful for a *child* to see harm where harm is; how much more so when she sees it where harm is not.' (1933, pp. 141-2)

It seems likely that the child in question was Ethel Arnold from whom Carroll learnt of Ellen Terry's annoyance, writing to her on 9 June 1887 (over a year after the performance in question):

> just to tell you how sorry I was to learn...that I had given you pain by what I wrote to you about *Faust*. I cannot say more without needlessly re-opening a painful subject, than that I am very very sorry to have given you pain.

Carroll did not revisit *Faust* until 26 May 1894 when he took Dolly Baird and spent five or ten minutes with Ellen Terry backstage at the end of Act III watching the elaborate set for the 'Brocken' scene being set up: 'Coming back, we encountered a stream of witches and demons going onto the stage. Norah [his cousin Menella, 'Minna', Quin] among them.' A few days later (7 June) Carroll wrote expressing his thanks for Ellen Terry's help in securing employment for Norah, but also taking the opportunity to set the record straight:

> Once I wrote to you about *Faust*, and was so unfortunate, I fear, as to vex you a little, by a remonstrance (probably very unskilfully worded) about the 'business' in the chamber scene. I only allude to it again because I noticed the other day, that you have altered the 'business', and now wholly omit what I had feared might make some of the audience uneasy. Would you mind telling me, some time, whether the alteration is a permanent one, or merely an accidental difference that day; and, if permanent, whether the change is concerned at all with my letter?

The change might not have been permanent; Ellen Terry, aware of Carroll's presence, may have made it for that performance only.

A subsidiary theme to these visits to the Lyceum was the special favours accorded to Carroll and his companions by Ellen Terry. On 15 January 1880, shortly after the first of his six visits to *The Merchant of Venice*, he sent Agnes Hull, whom he had taken with him, a copy of his letter to 'Portia', promising: 'If I get any answer, you shall hear about it.' Prior to the aforementioned visit with Lucy Arnold to *Much Ado About Nothing* on 15 March 1883 Carroll 'had hinted to "Beatrice" how much she would add to Lucy's pleasure by sending round a "carte" of herself: she sent a "cabinet" – besides one for Ethel: she is certainly an adept in giving gifts that gratify!' For another visit on 18 June 1887 he 'telegraphed to Miss E. Terry to get us stalls: failing that, she gave us a box, where "Edie" joined us for a while'. On his second visit to *Faust*, despite having offended Ellen Terry with his remarks after his first visit, Carroll had no compunction in taking Dolly Baird 'with a vague hope of being able to introduce, or get introduced, Dolly to Miss Ellen Terry', which he eventually succeeded in doing: 'She was most kind and stood talking with us for five or ten minutes'. It was on that occasion that Carroll spotted his cousin Menella 'Minna' Quin, who initially adopted the stage name Norah O'Neill and on whose behalf he had petitioned Ellen Terry, who as he put it in a letter of 11 April 1894: 'did a very kind and Christian deed on Friday, in *inventing* a vacancy (as I feel pretty sure you did) for my cousin Minna Quin'. Such interventions were not unusual at the time and Carroll made them on behalf of his brothers to possible employers.

As to Carroll's solicitation of gifts or other favours to his young companions, he wrote to Ellen Terry on 20 March 1883 of 'the amount of happiness' she had conferred on Lucy Arnold 'not only by your acting, which was for all the others as well, but by your special kindness to herself. I think you have learned a piece of philosophy which many never learn in a long life – that, while it is hopelessly difficult to secure *for oneself* even the smallest bit of happiness, and the more trouble we take the more certain we are to fail, there is nothing so easy as to secure it *for somebody else*'. Presumably Ellen Terry was expected to be suitably grateful for the (unending) opportunities that Carroll afforded her in this respect. In fact the actress was contributing greatly to Carroll's happiness since her willingness to engage in various acts that showed his young companions that a degree of friendship existed between them greatly increased the esteem in which they held their host and thereby his pleasure in the occasion. A sense that such gratification might besmirch the avowed aim of giving happiness to others underlies a lengthy paragraph in a later letter (13 November 1890) to Ellen Terry thanking her for helping Isa Bowman:

> And so you have found out that secret – one of the deep secrets of Life – that all, that is really *worth* doing, is what we do for *others*? Even as the old adage tells us, 'What I spent, that I lost; what I gave that I had.' Casuists

104   *Lewis Carroll and the Victorian Stage*

have tried to twist 'doing good' into another form of 'doing evil,' and have said 'you get pleasure yourself by giving this pleasure to another: so it is merely a refined kind of selfishness, as your own pleasure is a motive for what you do.' I say 'it is *not* selfishness, that my own pleasure should be *a* motive so long as it is not *the* motive that would outweigh the other, if the two came into collision. The "selfish man" is he who would do the thing, even if it harmed others, so long as it gave *him* pleasure: the "unselfish man" is *still* the unselfish man, even though his own pleasure *is* one of his motives! I am very sure that God takes real *pleasure* in seeing his children happy!'

Carroll's argument stumbles when the recipient of the supposed pleasure takes little or no delight in it, but is obliged to indulge because the 'unselfish man' persists in the (genuine?) belief that real pleasure is being experienced. This appears to have been precisely the case with Ellen Terry's son Edward Gordon Craig, who in *Index to the Story of My Days* recalls a visit from Carroll in January 1879, when at the age of seven he was experiencing frustration at not being 'put on the stage' (1957, p. 32). Carroll and Craig would have been in sympathy about that at least, but Craig remained resistant to Carroll's usual guiles:

> Here it was I saw Lewis Carroll once. He had called to see E.T. at about six o'clock. She was asleep – but about to get up, so as to go to act at the theatre. I can see him now, on one side of the heavy mahogany table – dressed in black, with a face which made no impression on me at all. I on the other side of the heavy mahogany table, and he describing in detail an event in which I had not the slightest interest – 'How five sheep were taken across a river in one boat, two each time – first two, second two – that leaves one – yet two must go over' – ah – he did this with matches and a matchbox – I was not amused – so I have forgotten how the sheep did their trick. (p. 32)

In fact the date appears to have been 2 April 1880 when Carroll recorded spending 'half an hour or more with Mr. Wardell, Edie, and Eddie: Mrs Wardell was in bed, resting for the evening performance'. This was only Carroll's second visit to 'the Wardells', since he had resumed contact with Ellen Terry on 18 June 1879 when he 'called on the Wardells, to renew the friendship with Ellen Terry, which has now been broken off for 12 years (we last met May 11, 1867). She was as charming as ever, and I was much pleased with her husband (Mr. C. Kelly on the stage). I also liked her two children, Edith and Eddie.'

Intriguingly Ellen Terry had evidently extended an olive branch to Carroll much earlier when she had offered him tickets to see *The Merchant of Venice*, in which she played Portia, at the Prince of Wales's Theatre in May 1875. Furthermore Carroll not only contemplated

The Terrys

accepting, but wrote to the Marquis of Salisbury on 9 May reporting Ellen Terry's offer of 'the best box in the house' and asking 'if Gwenny and Jem [Salisbury's daughters] may come'. The visit never happened – the run of *The Merchant of Venice* was cut short after only thirty-six performances because of poor houses – but if it had Carroll would presumably not have extended it to any personal encounter with the actress, whose relationship with Godwin (whose 'valuable aid in archaeological research' for their production the Bancrofts had acknowledged, Bancroft, 1889, p. 211) was then still continuing (Manvell, 1968, p. 94).

Carroll cast Ellen Terry's (actually very doughty) children by Godwin in the roles of victims, as he wrote to Tom Taylor on 24 February 1880: 'And I also saw the 2 children. Poor little things! I hope they will never know their own sad history'. This was a pious wish since Carroll himself was well aware of the gossip surrounding their mother, Watts and Godwin. He made his views clear in a letter to Mrs. H. A. Feilden dated 16 March 1880 to whom he confided that he had 'consulted, a friend here, Canon King', when Ellen Terry had made overtures to resume their friendship and he had advised him that with Ellen Terry now (since 1877) 'a legally married wife..."yes: it would be the right thing to do"'. Carroll then proceeded to give an essentially sympathetic account of Ellen Terry's personal relationships with Watts. Taking the axiom 'No human law is binding unless it embody a principle of divine right' his view was that 'in a case like hers' the law '*ought*' to grant a divorce, 'but it does not'. He found Watts at fault 'how could she keep her marriage vows?' Carroll's position was much the same when he wrote to Mrs Baird fourteen years later. He described the match with Watts as 'pushed by well meaning friends, who thought it a grand thing for her', but Watts never provided 'her a home of her own' and after the separation he 'cynically told his friends that he found he had never *loved* her'. Then Godwin came along and Carroll said that he [Carroll] 'honestly believe[d] her position from her point of view' was:

> I am tied by *human* law to a man who disowns his share of what ought to be a *mutual* contract. He never loved me and I do not believe, in God's sight, we are man and wife. Society expects me to live...as if I were single...This other man loves me as truly and faithfully as any lawful husband. If a marriage ceremony were *possible* I would insist on it before living with him. It is *not* possible and I will do without it.

Carroll maintained that such women '*are*, I believe, married in God's sight though not in Man's' and that once divorced by Watts she would

106   *Lewis Carroll and the Victorian Stage*

have married Godwin had he remained steadfast 'and it would have gradually been forgotten that the children were born before the ceremony'. In the event it was Wardell (Charles Kelly), the son of a clergyman, who provided respectability by marrying Ellen Terry in 1877, but he drank and in 1885 left her a widow. By then of course Terry's professional relationship with Henry Irving was well established and on 27 June 1893 Carroll wrote to his cousin Dorothea Wilcox of 'the story...that I am constantly hearing, of the (alleged) immoral life of Miss E. T. and Mr. Irving':

> It is to me simply *astounding*, the wicked recklessness with which people repeat scandalous reports about actresses, without taking the *slightest* trouble to verify them...

> If the lady *did* tell you this story, will you kindly accept *me* as decidedly a more competent witness on the subject than she is: and if you hear the story told again, will you kindly say that you have reliable authority for declaring it to be *absolutely* false?

> I know all Miss Terry's history, and, knowing it, am proud to still regard her as my *friend*. I have introduced to her several girl-friends – always telling the *mother* of the girl the whole history, and asking leave to introduce the daughter; and in every case, leave was given.

Carroll's connection with the Terrys stretched over five decades and reveals different aspects of his personality. They were the quintessential acting family and as such undoubtedly informed his attitude towards child performers. In their company there is little of the outgoing Carroll to be detected, even in the early years when elsewhere he was an extrovert performer. Instead he was star-struck if not love-lorn. After Kate's marriage Moray Lodge became one of his favourite visiting places and though he cut off Ellen for twelve years his was not an exceptional response and he later showed himself to hold liberal views on marriage. Similar liberal views are to be found in his attitude towards Shylock. On the other hand there is a persistent staidness in his preoccupation with formalities such as introductions and forms of address and prissiness in his dealings with Ellen Terry over his child-friends. Not for the first time there are contradictions even within a single aspect of Carroll's life.

The Terrys

Notes

1   There has been some divergence of opinion about where Carroll took these photographs, at Stanhope Street or Caversham Road, but his own diary account makes it clear that it was at the latter address.

2   Letter dated 15 March 1883 from Ellen Terry to Lewis Carroll No 453 in the Berol Collection (The Fales Library, New York University).

7 Minors and Protégées

> '...a taste for *acting* is one of the strongest passions of human nature...they
> simply *rejoice* in their work.'
> Lewis Carroll, *St James's Gazette*

Carroll's rebuttal of allegations about the 'immoral life of Miss E. T. and Mr. Irving', quoted at the end of the preceding chapter, was accompanied by a spirited defence of other (unnamed) actresses who were the subject of 'scandalous reports...I have more than once investigated such stories, and have found them to be (as I *know*, on perfectly good evidence, *this* one to be) simply *false*'. Carroll needed to convince himself as well as others of the morality of the stage if his conscience was to be clear about children working there and young women from respectable non-theatrical families embarking on acting careers.

The first full-scale performance that Carroll saw in a professional theatre was *Henry VIII* at the Princess's on 22 June 1855 with Charles Kean 'magnificent as Cardinal Wolsey' and Mrs Kean 'a worthy successor to Mrs. Siddons in Queen Catherine'. At the same theatre on 16 January 1856 Carroll had 'five hours of unmixed enjoyment', beginning with *Hamlet* and ending with John W. Howard Payne's *The Maid and the Magpie, or the Fairy Paradisa and Hanky Panky the enchanter* into which 'some really wonderful performing dogs were introduced' leading to:

> [the] concluding scene, where the dance in *Henry VIII* is acted in dumb show entirely by children...the prettiest thing I ever saw on the stage, and the pretty little Anne Boleyn went through her part in a manner quite worthy of an older actor. The little queen Catherine (A. Smith) was a merry little creature of about five years old, and pulled the ears of Anne Boleyn (Emily Edmonds) in anything but a malicious spirit. The little creatures enacted a second transformation, and Henry VIII became a tiny Harlequin, with Anne Boleyn as Columbine. The whole scene was a picture not to be forgotten.

The Maid and the Magpie was evidently a seasonal piece, the conclusion of which had been fashioned to introduce the *Henry VIII* theme into the harlequinade with child performers. Thus the children, presumably most of them 'about five years old' like A. Smith as Catherine, had to wait until the very end of a long evening before their services were required, with the result that they would not have left the stage until 11pm after which

Minors and Protégées 109

they would have needed to change their clothes before returning to their homes (probably at some distance from Oxford Street). There is no suggestion of concern for their welfare in Carroll's account, but in this he was typical of that and many other audiences who enthusiastically attended performances by child actors.

Tracy Davis cites evidence that in '1887 it was estimated that approximately 1,000 children were hired yearly as supernumeraries and dancers in London pantomimes' (1986, p. 117). However children were not confined to the ranks of 'supernumeraries and dancers', especially not in performances which were given entirely by a child company. Carroll attended many such, including the *Living Miniatures* at the Haymarket Theatre to which a brief reference has already been made in Chapter 4. Collectively Carroll's two diary entries for 24 January and 2 March 1867 and his letter of 11 March to his brother Edwin constitute a wonderfully vivid and detailed picture of the young performers backstage. The plays were a comedy *Littletop's Christmas Party* and a burlesque *Sylvius* and on his first visit Carroll acclaimed the 'whole performance' as 'far beyond anything I have yet seen done by children'.

When Carroll returned on 2 March for what was the final performance of the run he had secured and accepted an invitation from the manager Thomas Coe and presented himself at '7 Jermyn Street, to join Mr. Coe', who seemed 'to have a very pleasant lively manner' and his wife whom he thought 'particularly nice', though she was in fact Coe's 'common-law wife, Ellen Blanch Hanson' (Wakeling ed., vol. 5, p. 205, n. 328). From the company of twenty-seven children several particularly caught Carroll's eye. No less than four belonged to the same Jewish family: Solomon, aged 5½, his two brothers who appeared in the bill as F. Charles and C. Lewis and their sister Annette Tinytoe. He judged the three boys about the best in the company and took a particular shine to Annette, aged four, who seemed to be 'a general pet' and was carried into the prompter's box by Mrs Coe, presumably, Carroll supposed, to keep her (and her costume) free from dust. He found her 'a very conversational little creature, not a bit shy', who aspired to progress from merely dancing an Irish jig to playing the part of Mrs Mite (who had a violent scene with her ill-tempered husband), which she had learnt 'quite perfect, from her own accord' and in which she assured Mr Coe: 'I'd get an encore for every word!' She trotted around the backstage area without getting in anyone's way and was last seen by Carroll 'carrying a heap of things, almost as big as herself, to the green-room'. According to Carroll Annette was paid 'five shillings a time for her performance, which consists of dancing an Irish jig, and the others earn sums varying from that to about 10 shillings'. This does seem high, compared with Ellen Terry's 15s a week in the

110   *Lewis Carroll and the Victorian Stage*

1850s and Tracy Davis cites 'between 6d and 1s' a night for children dancing at London theatres (1986, p. 124), so the amount quoted by Carroll may have been per week rather than per performance. Nevertheless as Tracy Davis observes these rates were higher than those for most other forms of child labour, though theatre work was more seasonal. Carroll insisted that 'all the children seemed to regard the whole thing as a treat', but for their parents the wages they earned were no doubt a significant contribution to the family budget, particularly since, as Carroll implied clearly enough, the children all came from humble backgrounds.

The children of certain families became attractions, most notably the Vokes family and the Cootes. Carroll saw E. L. Blanchard's *The Children in the Wood* at Drury Lane on 18 January 1873 and praised 'the dancing of the Vokes family. I have never seen any thing more graceful than Miss Victoria Vokes as the boy', but by then she was aged twenty. Carroll's interest in the Coote family was sustained over a considerable period. He saw and admired Lizzie in Frank W. Green's pantomime *Hop-o'-my-Thumb* at the Theatre Royal, Brighton on 6 January 1874 when he described her as 'a clever little American girl' and the following year (7 January 1875) she 'made a charming little sprite' in the same author's *Froggy would a-wooing go* at the same theatre.

In Lizzie Coote's case he wrote to several of his friends (Tom Taylor, A. W. Dubourg and Marion Terry) enlisting their support and encouragement for her. The Coote family was also represented (by Bertie and Carrie) when Carroll's enthusiasm for child-only pantomimes reached its height with E. L. Blanchard's *Robin Hood and his Merry Little Men* 'performed by children' (*Illustrated London News* 29 December 1877) which he saw at the Adelphi Theatre six times between 31 December 1877 and 17 January 1878. Carroll took at least three child friends to each performance. It was probably no more likely that the social divide between the children on the stage and those watching in the auditorium ever crossed Carroll's mind than it did Henry James's when in Christmas week 1877 he 'went religiously to see...the great, gorgeous pantomime given at Drury Lane', where 'the best of the entertainment...was seeing the line of rosy child faces in the boxes, all turned towards the stage in one round-eyed fascination' (Wade ed., 1957, p. 111).

In all probability most of the children in the audience were receiving full-time education, whereas the provisions of the 1876 Education Act permitted considerable latitude for those employed in theatres. In Carroll's view far from being deprived the stage children had the better deal as he argued in his letter published in the *St James's Gazette* on 19 July 1887 in response to what he described in his diary for 16 July 1887 as 'an account

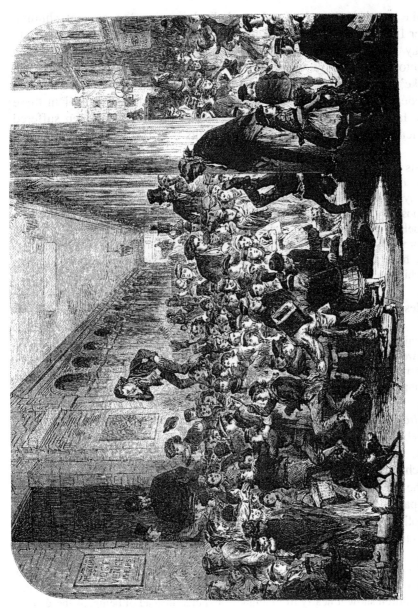

9. Engaging children for the Drury Lane pantomime

112 *Lewis Carroll and the Victorian Stage*

[in the previous issue] of a large ladies' meeting "to prevent children under 10 acting in theatres"'. Carroll based his letter on how he had spent Friday 15 July with Phoebe Carlo, Dorothy d'Alcourt and Lizzie Carlo in Brighton where they were appearing at the Theatre Royal in Savile Clarke's dramatisation of *Alice in Wonderland*, which Carroll had attended on Thursday 14. Carroll challenged the ladies' claim ('in these days, ladies know everything') that child performers under ten suffered physical strain which 'had led to fatal results':

> As to her assertion that 'the physical strain is exceedingly heavy', I demur to it altogether as a matter of fact. The 'cases' of children 'personally known to' myself, some in schools and some in theatres, are very many – as many, possibly, as those known to the speaker whose words I have quoted: and I deliberately assert that, while I have known several cases of complete breakdown in health, due to the physical strain of competitive examinations, I have met none, where the strain could even be called 'heavy', among children employed in drama or pantomime.

He described the five hours during which he had

> enjoyed the society of three exceedingly happy and healthy little girls, aged twelve, ten, and seven…all three are on the stage – the eldest having acted for five years at least, and even the tiny creature of seven having already appeared in four dramas!

In *Alice* she (Lizzie Carlo) had a non-speaking part, whereas her sister (Phoebe) had 'quite the heaviest part in the whole play, and, I should think, the heaviest ever undertaken by a child: she has no less than 215 speeches'. Nevertheless despite 'acting every night this week, and *twice* on the day before I met them, the second performance lasting till after half-past ten at night', they got up 'at seven next morning to bathe'. Carroll explained the co-existence of 'severe work…with blooming health and buoyant spirits' as an example of working *con amore*:

> And I believe the apparent paradox is to be explained by the fact that a taste for *acting* is one of the strongest passions of human nature, that stage-children show it nearly from infancy, and that, instead of being, as these good ladies imagine, miserable drudges who ought to be celebrated in a new 'Cry of Children' they simply *rejoice* in their work, 'even as a giant rejoiceth to run his course.'

Children who went on the stage under the age of ten were bound to be either from theatrical families or families for whom the stage offered the

Minors and Protégées 113

prospect of at least short-term financial gain and possible long-term social improvement. The father of Phoebe and Lizzie Carlo was, as has already been noted, a packer; Dorothy D'Alcourt's (D'Albuquerque) was a hotel-keeper (Cohen ed., 1979, vol. II, p. 657, n. 2). In encouraging them in their stage aspirations Carroll was helping them improve their lot financially and socially, but it is clear from his contributions to the public debate in the late 1880s that he believed that the theatre was a perfectly suitable, indeed beneficial, place for such young girls. This most certainly was not the view of the pressure groups, such as the one Carroll had rebuffed in the *St James's Gazette* in July 1887, and as Tracy Davis explains, they agitated 'throughout the winter and spring of 1889, until the Cruelty Bill was introduced. The theatrical clauses were the most contentious, particularly the attempt to disallow employment of all children under the age of ten in all entertainment capacities.' (1986, p. 131) The House of Commons approved the measure, but when the House of Lords debated the bill on Thursday 8 August 1889 various amendments were proposed and passed (*Hansard's Parliamentary Debates Seventh Volume of Session 1889*, vol. VII, 715-21) including one permitting children over seven to be employed by special licence.

Carroll's possible influence on this debate emerges from this diary entry:

> Aug: 4. (Sun). Mr. J. Coleman, who is bringing out a book on 'Stage-Children', and the new law passed by the Commons forbidding them to appear under ten, has asked for my [*St. James's Gazette*] letter about 'Brighton Pier'. I sent it and a new one, which he has printed in today's *Sunday Times*, of which he has sent a copy to every member of the Lords!

Writing (on 3 December) to Clement Scott, editor of the *Theatre*, the September 1889 issue of which had reprinted the *Sunday Times* letter as part of his article 'Stage Children', Carroll explained:

> I did *not* contribute [the letter] to the *Sunday Times*. On the contrary, I wrote it for publication in a pamphlet (which never appeared) projected by Mr. J. Coleman. *He* sent it to the *Sunday Times* (not even having time to consult me on the subject – I should have demurred at it appearing in such a paper) in order to be able to send copies to the members of the House of Lords... – little thinking that he has now ruined my reputation with that august body, who will say in future 'Mr. Lewis Carroll? Ah, yes. *One of the writers in the* Sunday Times!'

Carroll was already well known to one member of the House of Lords who intervened in the debate: 'The Prime Minister and Secretary of State

114   *Lewis Carroll and the Victorian Stage*

for Foreign Affairs (The Marquess of Salisbury).' (*Hansard's*, 1889, vol. VII, 716)

Carroll began his letter by disclaiming any vested interest in the subject to which he wished to 'be allowed to add that I have given some attention to logic and mathematics, which help so largely in the *orderly* arrangements of topics of controversy – an art much needed when so many controversialists are ladies'. Carroll presents his case very methodically indeed, setting out his contention:

> I. That the employment, in theatres, of children under the age of ten is *not* harmful.
> II. That it *is* beneficial.
> III. That, while this practice needs certain safeguards not yet provided by law, it does *not* call for absolute prohibition. The harm attributed to this practice may be classed under three headings – (1) physical; (2) intellectual; (3) moral.

Under 'Physical harm' Carroll rebuffed the charge of 'excessive bodily fatigue', asserting that 'the work is well within healthy limits, and the children enjoy it with an intensity difficult to convey by mere words'. Next he answered such charges as 'late hours, impure air, draughts, exposure to night air etc.' in terms that showed his awareness of the social conditions of the class from which child actors were drawn:

> The good people who raise these cries seem to think that the homes of these little ones are perfect models of regular habits and good sanitary arrangements, and that such a sight as a child outside its house after 9pm would thrill the neighbourhood with horror! Let them visit a few London alleys, and judge for themselves.

Under 'Intellectual harm' Carroll rejected the notion that 'the heaviest child parts' placed an unacceptable strain on the performer and dismissed the objection that these children were missing 'other studies' with an attack on

> the present craze for teaching everybody everything, so many little minds are compelled, not to *digest*, for that is impossible, but merely to swallow, we may hope that the stage child is all the better for escaping much of this.

As for 'Moral harm' Carroll first addressed 'immorality, whether of general tone or particular passage in the play itself', arguing that 'ignorance of the ways of the world, and of the meaning of most of the words they hear, is a protection enjoyed by young children, and by them

Minors and Protégées

only'. After briefly dismissing 'the encouragement of vanity, love of dress', Carroll turned to the 'gravest and most real of all the dangers that come under the category of "moral harm," viz., "the society of profligate men"'. He asserted that 'for adult actresses this danger is, I believe, in well-conducted theatres, distinctly less than it would be in most of the lines open to them' and proceeded to show, as he had done with 'sanitary arrangements', an awareness of contemporary life:

> Here again the good people, who see such peril in the life of the actress, seem to be living in a fool's paradise, and to fancy they are legislating for young ladies who, if they did not go on stage, would be secluded in drawing-rooms where none but respectable guests are admitted. Do they suppose that attractive-looking young women, in the class from which the stage is chiefly recruited, would be safer as barmaids or shopwomen from the insidious attention of the wealthy voluptuary than they are as actresses?

Carroll went on to argue that 'young women of this class may choose a stage life with as fair a chance of living a reputable life as they would have in any other profession open to them' and that being the case 'it is surely desirable to begin learning their business as soon as they are competent, unless it can be shown that they are in greater danger as children than as young women'. This of course broaches issues, which have come into greater prominence in the late twentieth and early twenty-first century and have been discussed with reference to Carroll, but his view was:

> I believe the danger is distinctly less. Their extreme youth is a powerful safeguard. To plot evil against a child, in all its innocence and sweet trustfulness and ignorance of the world, needs no common voluptuary; it needs one so selfish, so pitiless, and so abject a coward as to be beneath one calling himself a man.

There seems to be no reason to doubt the genuineness of Carroll's condemnation of what would now be called a paedophile.

Carroll structured his second contention 'that stage life is beneficial to children, even the youngest' under the same three headings as his first. Physically stage children had the benefit of training in deportment and were less susceptible to curvature of the spine than their peers. Intellectually 'stage life distinctly *brightens* the mind of a child' whereas a lot of school work 'is intensely fatiguing and depressing to spirits and intellect alike'. And then:

116 *Lewis Carroll and the Victorian Stage*

3. Morally. I believe that stage life, in a well-conducted theatre, is valuable moral training for young children. They learn –
a) Submission to discipline.
b) Habits of order and punctuality.
c) Usefulness (this on the principle on which you always find children in large families less selfish than only children).
d) Humility. This because, however clever they may think themselves, they soon find that others are cleverer.

So far Carroll had presented his case not only with the order and clarity of one who had 'given some attention to logic and mathematics', but he had also shown his awareness of the conditions in which stage children worked and *lived*. He had voiced the Victorian ideal of the child's 'innocence and sweet trustfulness and ignorance of the world'.

In his third contention he went on to show his sense of the role of the state in such matters:

III. My third contention is that, though it is desirable to provide, by law, certain safeguards for the employment of children in theatres, there is no need for its absolute prohibition. The legislation that seems to me desirable would take some such form as this:-
That every child under sixteen (ten is too low a limit), employed in a theatre, should hold a licence, annually renewable.
That such licence should only be granted on condition of the child having passed the examination for a certain 'standard', adapted to the age of the child.
That a limit should be fixed for the number of weeks in the year that the child may be engaged, and for the number of hours in the day that he or she may be at the theatre. (This rule to be relaxed during rehearsals.)
That, during a theatrical engagement, the child shall attend a specified number of hours, during the afternoons, at some school; at other times in the year during the usual hours, if attending a Board school. (High schools would probably adopt the same principle, and allow half-day attendance during engagements.)
That some guarantee be required that girls under sixteen are provided with sufficient escort to and from a theatre.
I do not believe that the law can absolutely prohibit children under ten from acting in theatres without doing a cruel wrong to many a poor struggling family, to whom the child's stage salary is a godsend, and making many poor children miserable by debarring them from a healthy and innocent occupation which they dearly love.

As already noted the House of Lords amended the bill to permit employment of children over seven with a special licence. Carroll's other proposal that all performers under the age of sixteen should be licensed was modified slightly by a reduction of the age to fourteen for boys. Perhaps most important was Carroll's common sense, challenging the vigilantes who sought prohibition and arguing instead for sensible regulation. In this he showed himself to be a typical Victorian Tory.

Carroll's attitude towards women ranged from his condescension towards 'the ladies' behind the proposed reduction in the minimum age for actors to his down-to-earth assessment of the prospects of 'young women, in the class from which the stage is chiefly recruited' and his protectiveness towards girls of his own class who went on the stage. The latter in particular were beneficiaries of the increasing provision of education for women at The Queen's College in Harley Street, Cheltenham Ladies' College, Oxford High School and the like. Carroll, who taught some classes at Oxford High School, was clearly not unsympathetic towards women's education. Two letters written early in 1882 reflect Carroll's interest and concern. On 30 January 1882 he sent a copy of a prospectus for a School of Dramatic Art to Lord Salisbury:

> may I venture to call your attention to an object which seems to me of quite first-class importance? It needs no words of mine to tell you, what you no doubt know better than I do, what a low ebb the modern stage has reached in *quality* of acting, and what good might be done to the theatre, and through it to society, by raising it.
>
> Your *name*, as a patron, would indeed be a tower of strength to the cause.

And on 13 March 1882 to Mrs F. W. Richards:

> Are you a Shakespeare reader? I have a dream of Bowdlerising Bowdler, i.e. of editing a Shakespeare which shall be absolutely fit for *girls*. For this I need the advice of *mothers*, as to which plays they would like to be included.

Neither scheme (see Ziegler, 2003) came to fruition but they still serve as illustrations of Carroll's outlook: girls needed special protection, but they should not be deprived of opportunities. As the census returns show, the acting profession expanded hugely between 1841 and 1911, the number of men increasing from 1153 to 9076 and women from 310 to 9171 (Davis, 1991, p. 10). Inevitably much of this increase consisted of new members who were not from theatrical families. Some of them, including virtually all stage-children, came from similar or lower social classes, but other, older, recruits were from the better-off, well-educated, 'professional' middle-class families. Thus whereas only 5.8% of actresses making their

118   *Lewis Carroll and the Victorian Stage*

debut pre-1880 had parents in the professions, from 1880–89 it had risen to 34% and in 1890-1913 to 46% (p. 15).

In the absence of a training institution for acting (the – Royal – Academy of Dramatic Art was not founded until 1904), aspiring actresses had to secure a place with a respectable theatre company. Carroll was unfailingly helpful in giving introductions and guidance to one in particular member of his own family, the daughters of friends and even strangers. The father of Violet and Irene Vanbrugh (their stage name) was Carroll's Christ Church contemporary the Revd Reginald Barnes, who became Prebendary of Exeter Cathedral. When he learnt that one of his daughters wanted to go on the stage ('entering the profession at that time was unheard of') Barnes 'felt the situation poignantly and was tormented by his convictions of the dangers Violet would encounter in entering such an unknown world' (Vanbrugh, 1949, p.12). His attempts to discourage his daughter failed. He and his family moved to London in 1887, living in Earls Court Road, near to Ellen Terry whom they knew. Kenneth Barnes, Violet and Irene's brother, who was to become principal of RADA, recalled Carroll as a frequent visitor: 'a shy, grey-haired man in a semi-clerical grey suit, fresh complexioned and with keen grey eyes' (1958, p. 9).

On 14 May Carroll saw Violet in *The Butler* at Toole's Theatre where the small part of Lady Anne Babbicombe, 'a rather haughty young lady...gave her no chance of *acting* but she did well all that she had to do'. Then as her sister Irene related 'one morning a letter came from Miss Sarah Thorne, who ran a stock season at the Theatre Royal Margate, suggesting that Violet should go and play there for a few weeks' (p. 16) and thanks to the contribution of £2 from 'a sympathetic friend, Miss Audrey Campbell' both sisters could go to Margate. They shared a room in Miss Thorne's house, The Towers in Hawley Square. Miss Thorne 'advertised for "Ladies and Gentlemen wishing to enter the theatrical profession." And she satisfied herself that they were Ladies and Gentlemen. She was a severe chaperone' (Morley, 1966, p. 109). Fees for tuition (covering voice production, gesture, mime, dialect and accents, make-up and so on) were '£20 for three months or £30 for six months', but 'if a pupil showed sufficient merit he was enlisted in the company at the theatre and given a salary in the neighbourhood of thirty shillings a week'. On September 25 Violet Vanbrugh 'made her debut at Margate in Frank Harvey's drama *The Ring of Iron...*A beginner, she was seeking experience under the tutelage of Sarah' (p. 111); in the summer of 1888 she played Portia, Helena (in *A Midsummer Night's Dream*), Rosalind and Ophelia. Carroll went down to Margate to see her as Rosalind (on 20 August) and Ophelia (on 14 September) writing of her performances:

Minors and Protégées 119

Violet was an astonishing *Rosalind* – I had no idea she could do one tenth part as well. And dear Irene was the sweetest of Phoebes: her recitation (for it *was* a recitation: she cannot yet get *out* of herself) was lovely.

Violet was really very successful, and so was Mr. Gould [Nutcombe Gould] as 'Hamlet': the rest of the cast was weak.

As usual Carroll was judging each performance, including those by his protégées, on its merits and it is evident that Violet Vanbrugh had benefited greatly from Sarah Thorne's tutelage. Even during their father's lifetime it was not easy to fund this, but when Reginald Barnes died the following year the family's financial circumstance must have been further straitened.

On the death of his father Carroll had assumed responsibility for his seven sisters, only one of whom married, so he was fully aware of the economic plight affecting unmarried daughters of clergymen. None of Carroll's sisters ever earned her own living, but a generation later circumstances and expectations were different. The Revd Barnes had equipped his daughters with a good education at the High School, Exeter and in France and Germany and they clearly intended to put it to good use, in the theatre.

The Barnes sisters' experience at Margate was successful not only professionally but also for Violet personally since she met and married Arthur Bourchier (Eton and Christ Church) and founding luminary of OUDS. In addition to its other attractions Miss Thorne's School of Acting held out the prospect of a good marriage.

These factors may have influenced Carroll when early in 1892 he set about helping a distant cousin, Menella 'Minna' Quin, whom he had in fact not even met, in her theatrical aspirations. She was one of five sisters 'all grown-up', but 'their means are scanty' and 'the eldest, Minna' had written to him

about her idea of trying to *earn* some money. She believed she had talent for acting: and, by my advice, she has placed herself under Miss S. Thorne, who takes pupils for the Stage, and forms them into a Company, and sometimes goes on tour with them. They are now on tour, acting a Pantomime called *Mother Goose.*

The purpose of this letter of 7 February 1892 to Mary Manners and others like it to friends who lived 'at the places they play at' was 'to tell them

120 *Lewis Carroll and the Victorian Stage*

about her, and to suggest how it would cheer and please her to have a little change in her life by being asked to friends' houses'.

To his credit Carroll did what he asked of others:

> March 18. (F). Went over to Banbury, to see Minna Quin as Miss Thorne's company are now there playing *Mother Goose*...Minna met me at the station, and we seemed to become intimate friends at once. Minna's companions on the tour are Miss Temple and Miss Ellen Thorne: both were very pleasant and ladylike – the latter is only 16 and looks hardly out of childhood. Also a Mr. Beaumont came in for tea (he played 'Robert Macaire' in the dumb-show act, and seems a fairly good actor). Minnie had only one chance of showing what she can do – as the wife of Robert, it is a *very* small part, but I think she shows talent. Little 'Nellie' (as Minna calls her) was principal boy ('Colin' a shepherd) and played very prettily, and not in music-hall style. A very clever little actress, Miss Ada Barry, played 'Jack Horner' very well. It was a very inoffensive, and altogether good pantomime.

Carroll's letter of 3 April 1892 to Marion Terry reveals some further details: Minna had 'long experience in amateur acting' and Carroll himself 'wrote, about her, to Miss S. Thorne'. Now that Minna was about to leave Miss Thorne's she 'would be very glad to get taken on (no doubt it would be as an unpaid "super" at first) in some respectable theatre'.

On the basis of her performance in the pantomime Carroll 'fancied' he 'saw evidence of real talent for acting'. As usual for him an important criterion was that 'she seems able to throw herself *into* her part and to forget the audience'. He then drew attention to two other qualities: 'she is distinctly pretty. Also she is a *lady*, and can look and *speak* like one: which is surely an advantage, when one sees how many actresses are spoiled, for *that* line of work, by their cockney accent. She is about 24, I believe.' Further letters followed to Clement Scott (15 May 1892), to Mrs Beerbohm Tree (9 June 1892) and to Ellen Terry (4 April 1894, 11 April 1894, 7 April 1894), who as we have seen '*invented*' a vacancy for her, and to Wilson Barrett on 28 August 1896 by which time Minna's '*stage-name*' was 'Desmond O'Neill'. Carroll had seen Barrett on stage many times and particularly admired him in *The Silver King*. Minna was evidently not the first protégée in whom Carroll had sought to interest Barrett, but it seems unlikely that he was any more encouraging to her than he had been to her predecessor(s). As with his letter to Marion Terry Carroll based his advocacy of his cousin on her social class:

> There is, of course, great difficulty in finding work in these crowded days. But I think real *ladies*, even if of less dramatic ability than some who come

Minors and Protégées 121

from a lower rank, deserve consideration from the fact that a play often needs an actress who can *look* like, and *talk* like, a lady.

Carroll's point about the social composition of plays reflected the change to drawing-room and 'Society' dramas in the late nineteenth century and his appeal for positive discrimination for his cousin and other '*real* ladies' equally reflected changes in the acting profession. The two were not, of course, unconnected. The reaction to this influx of gentility amongst more dynastic professionals was articulated by Mrs Charles Calvert, whose father James Biddles had managed the Bower Saloon in the late 1840s and whose husband Charles produced Shakespeare revivals of great distinction at the Prince's Theatre, Manchester, for a decade from 1864 (see Foulkes, 1992), in her aptly titled memoirs *Sixty-Eight Years on the Stage.* Surveying changes during her long career under the heading 'An Invasion of Amateurs' she wrote of how the long run and the touring system had reduced 'the labour of study and rehearsals…actors found that one part lasted for many weeks, no study, no rehearsals, their lives became comparatively easy':

> The stage then became very attractive to young ladies and gentlemen, not only those who were anxious to do something for a living, but to many who simply desired to while away the time, so dramatic schools came into existence, of which they became dramatic pupils. And they came in shoals – with their refinement, their education and, very often, their indifference to remuneration. (1911, pp. 269-70)

The young women whose aspiration to the stage Carroll encouraged very much fit Mrs Calvert's description, though it has to be said that amongst the shoals he generally, Minna Quin notwithstanding, backed genuine talent. This was certainly true of the Vanbrugh sisters and Dorothea Baird, whom he saw in a production of *The Taming of the Shrew* by the Christmas Dramatic Wanderers at the Holywell Music Rooms on 12 January 1894 as a spirited Petruchio. In two letters (13 and 15 January) to Edith Lucy, who had attended Carroll's logic classes at Oxford High School and played Bianca, Carroll candidly described

> the performance…as a whole *very* poor…it was simply and solely the fault of bad *delivery*…With one (or perhaps two) exceptions, you have *all* to learn the elements of stage elocution. Such things as to pronounce *every* letter, to make all the *consonants* audible…and those who lisp (and most people lisp a little) must give *special* sharpness and force to the 's', and (above all) *never* to go quicker than is consistent with perfect articulation.

122   *Lewis Carroll and the Victorian Stage*

In this respect Dorothea Baird was particularly culpable:

> Petruchio was played with real spirit. Miss Dolly Baird is *good* in action, and in stage-business: and, if ever she learns to speak at about *half* that rate, and to recognise that she has a decided *lisp*, so as to give extra force to the 's', she would do well. I liked her conception of the character.

Carroll's own speech impediment and 'deafness in his right ear, which his mother ascribed to "Infantile fever"' (Cohen, 1995, p. 8) may have been factors in his emphasis on clear pronunciation, but it was of course very sound advice. As for Dolly Baird, Carroll, after explaining the actress's marital problems in the letter to Mrs Baird already quoted, introduced her to Ellen Terry. Dolly Baird made a sensational professional debut in the title role in *Trilby* with Beerbohm Tree as Svengali at the Haymarket Theatre on 30 October 1895 and subsequently married H. B. Irving (see L. Irving, 1967) who had been actively involved in OUDS as an undergraduate at New College.

Oxford had a high proportion of families who attached importance to the education of their daughters. Constance Featherstonhaugh and her widowed mother lived for a short time in Oxford and recalled Carroll as 'another friend of my childhood' (Benson, 1926, p. 23). Constance married Frank Benson, a prominent OUDS actor, and ran her own acting school as well as appearing in her husband's productions. Angelita Helena de Silva, who married John Martin-Harvey, had a distinctly dramatic encounter with Lewis Carroll in her childhood, as her husband recounted. The eight-year old Angelita, who was staying at Sandown on the Isle of Wight, had become angry at 'the way in which Bates, the man who kept the bathing-machines, treated the old horse'. First she fed the horse Bates's packed lunch and then smashed the bathing-machine windows:

> The culprit was held up to popular indignation and Bates demanded full recompense for the damage done to his property. Then, from the crowd which had gathered upon the sands a meek little gentleman stepped forward, paid for the damage and, lifting the naughty little girl on his shoulder, bore her away. (1933, p. 129)

In his diary entry for 6 September 1876 Carroll merely recorded meeting 'Nellie De Silva Ferro', but made no mention of the incident and when they met at the Lyceum in 1894 'she and her name had quite passed out on my life' as he wrote to Mrs Wilcox on 8 July 1894. Presumably the occasion was Carroll's attempt (already alluded to) to take Dolly Baird, who was evidently already a friend of Nellie's, behind the scenes at the

Minors and Protégées 123

Lyceum Theatre during the performance of *Faust* on 26 May 1894, when he also recorded seeing Minna Quin. No doubt this was the basis for Carroll's description of Mrs Martin-Harvey as 'a friend of Minna Quin'.

The acquaintance re-established, the Martin-Harveys met Carroll in Eastbourne during their summer tour of 1894 when he attended their triple bill at the Devonshire Park Theatre, though Martin-Harvey unaccountably wrote: 'We could not induce him to visit the theatre, for which he had an intense aversion.' (1933, p. 129) Carroll saw the Martin-Harveys at the Court Theatre on 30 October 1897 in *The Children of the King* with Minna Quin still a 'super' on what was to be his last but one theatre visit. The existence of 'respectable' theatre companies such as those run by the Bensons, the Martin-Harveys and Philip Ben Greet gave the likes of Minna Quin the opportunity to pursue a stage career, which though it never scaled professional heights could at least be undertaken amongst those whom she would have regarded as her social equals.

Carroll's encouragement of aspiring actresses falls into two distinct categories. As he candidly stated in a letter (12 February 1894) to Beatrice Hatch 'some of my little *actress*-friends are of a *rather* lower status than myself'. His attitude to these was that the theatre offered them an opportunity to improve their position (and to help their families), a case which he made effectively and in all probability influentially on the eve of the House of Lords debate in 1889. Towards the other category, 'ladies', Carroll showed a snobbish protectiveness. Nevertheless in both categories he encouraged female employment and generally showed sound judgement about the abilities of the young women in question. His positive endorsement of acting as a profession must also have stemmed from his own delight in performing in his youth. He knew from his own experience that 'a taste for *acting* is one of the strongest passions of human nature'.

8 Photography

'...a lot of dresses, which the A. A. M. kept in a cupboard, to dress up children in, when they come to be photographed.'
'Isa's Visit to Oxford'

As Violet Dodgson pointed out in her lecture to the Leamington Spa Literary Society on 17 October 1949, 'in his 24th year four notable things happened to him [Carroll]': he met the Liddell girls, went to the theatre for the first time, took up photography and began to write.[1] That an interest in the theatre should coincide with one in photography was not particularly surprising or unusual at that time. Indeed the next fifty years could be seen as a progression towards the unification of the two arts in the 'moving pictures' of early film. Roland Barthes, the leading French authority on structuralism and semiology, has argued that the connection between the theatre and photography goes far beyond shared technology and techniques. In *Camera Lucida Reflections on Photography* Barthes wrote:

> Yet it is not (it seems to me) by Painting that Photography touches art, but by Theater. Niepce and Daguerre are always put at the origin of Photography (even if the latter has somewhat usurped the former's place); now Daguerre, when he took over Niepce's invention, was running a panorama theatre animated by light shows and movements in the Place du Chateau. The *camera obscura*, in short, has generated at one and the same time perspective painting, photography, and the diorama, which are all three arts of the stage; but if photography seems to me closer to the Theater, it is by way of a singular intermediary (and perhaps I am the only one who sees it): by way of Death...Photography is a kind of primitive theatre, a kind of *Tableau Vivant*, a figuration of the motionless and made-up face beneath which we see the dead. (1982, pp. 31-2)

For Barthes there is 'nothing Proustian in a photograph', the effect of which on him 'is not to restore what has been abolished (by time, by distance) but to attest that what I see has actually existed' (p. 82). He describes what he sees in the photograph as 'reality in a past state: at once the past and real...not a memory, an imagination, a reconstruction...Every photograph is a certificate of presence.' (pp. 86-7)

As Carol Mavor observes it is significant that for Barthes 'the most meaningful (performative) photograph in *Camera Lucida* is one of his

Photography 125

mother as a little girl: the famous Winter Garden Photograph...taken when she was five...[in] 1898'. The brevity of the moment captured by the camera, the speed of the aging process and the inevitability of death combine to imbue these images with immense poignancy: 'Their [of the Liddell sisters and the Llewelyn Davies boys] pictures are no more and no less than a keepsake of a golden splash.' (Mavor, 1995, pp. 5-6)

At the time when he embarked on his passions for theatre and photography Carroll was at his most carefree, developing his skills as a home entertainer in various ways including the marionette theatre, a magic lantern and his one-man performances for which he practised several voices. It is apparent from his diary entry for 29 January 1856 that Carroll was thinking of a way in which these different elements could be combined: 'I think it would be a very good idea to have slides of a magic lantern painted to represent characters in some play, which might be read aloud, a sort of Marionette performance.' On 13 December 1856 Carroll 'chose a Magic Lantern and slides at Watkin and Hills for the Croft school', where on 31 December he gave his 'first exhibition of the Magic Lantern' to an audience of 'about 80 children'. He 'divided it into two parts, of 24 and 23 pictures, with a rest of about half an hour between. I introduced 13 songs in the course of the performance, six for myself, and seven for the children; and employed seven different voices'.

More information about the slides Carroll bought at Watkin and Hill would be fascinating. Another supplier, Carpenter and Wesley, included 'Mr. Punch landing his horse' on their list (Francis, 1968, no. 244). Carpenter and Hall were particularly renowned for the 'exquisitely painted transparencies' which they produced 'between 1826 and 1850', but thereafter, as Olive Cook explained, images were sometimes

> transferred to slides and horribly coloured in bright blue and crimson by girls specially employed for that purpose, who were usually wholly ignorant of the originals of the subjects they were called upon to paint. They worked in the Toy Theatre tradition, which was delightfully appropriate in the case of trick slides and fairy-tale subjects, but often disastrous and sometimes comic when applied to old masters or views of foreign parts. (1963, p. 90)

Quality deteriorated further in 'many of the later mass-produced glasses' in which 'the Toy Theatre tradition was abandoned in favour of the most repellently anaemic colour range the lantern-slide painter's palette could muster'. Whatever his choice of slides (the Toy Theatre tradition seems the most likely) Carroll clearly used them very imaginatively with his thirteen songs and numerous different voices.

126 *Lewis Carroll and the Victorian Stage*

As well as running dioramas in Paris, Daguerre expanded his activities to London at the Regent's Park Diorama, which opened in 1823 behind Nash's elegant façade at the centre of Park Square East (Cook, 1963, p. 38). Not that there was a lack of home grown talent with Clarkson Stanfield's 'Grand Local Drama' attracting great attention at Drury Lane Theatre in 1830. Richard Altick presents many other examples in *The Shows of London* (1978) and his inclusion of the Great Exhibition is a reminder that in 1851 visitors (of whom Carroll was one) were treated to an unprecedented global display of culture and technology. The Princess's Theatre in Oxford Street where Carroll saw his first professionally performed play on 22 June 1855 had originally opened in 1829 as the Royal Bazaar, British Diorama and Exhibition of Works of Art, with works by Clarkson Stanfield and David Wright depicting 'Lake Maggiore in Italy', the 'Interior of St. George's Chapel, Windsor', the 'Wreck of an Indiaman and Storm on the Coast' and the 'Ruins of Tintern Abbey'. On 27 May 1829 the Bazaar fell victim to a fire that 'originated in the Diorama gallery, and was supposed to have been caused by the flame of some turpentine communicating with a transparency near which it was placed' (Mander and Mitchenson, 1968, pp. 336-7). It was rebuilt and opened with a new diorama in 1830 and in 1833 Charles Mathews's collection of theatrical paintings was displayed there, but it failed to prosper and underwent conversion to a theatre, opening as the Royal Princess's on 28 September 1850. Not that the delights of the diorama disappeared. In Kean's *A Midsummer Night's Dream* Act II:

> there is a dream-like moving of the wood, beautifully managed...Oberon stands before the scene waving his wand, as if he were exhibitor of the diorama, or a fairy conjuror causing the rocks and trees to move...This change leads to the disclosure of a fairy ring, a beautiful scenic effect, and what is called in large letters upon the playbills, 'Titania's Shadow Dance'. Of all things in the world, a shadow dance of fairies! (Morley, 1891, p. 134)

Henry Morley's (understandable) scorn notwithstanding, the prominence of 'Titania's Shadow Dance' on the playbill reflected the effort that had gone into its preparation and its appeal to audiences. Kean was very adroit at merchandising his productions not only in terms of tickets but also in the sale of souvenirs in particular photographs. Examples of two photographs of *A Midsummer Night's Dream* survive, one of Carlotta Leclerq as Titania and the other of her and four attendant fairies entitled: 'Shadow Dance of Fairies'. In all a total of fifty-two different photographs covering eleven of Charles Kean's Shakespeare revivals in the 1850s have been identified as the work of his Oxford Street neighbour, Martin

Photography 127

Laroche, born William Henry Silvester, who lived with his wife, five children and a servant girl at 65, Oxford Street, separated by just seven premises from the Princess's Theatre at no 73.[2] Martin Laroche's place in the history of photography rests not with his work with Kean, but as the defendant in a celebrated legal case, Talbot v. Laroche in December 1854 (see R. Derek Wood, 1975). Briefly, in layman's terms, the case revolved around the patent, which W. H. Fox Talbot held for the calotype process of producing photographs on paper from negatives (an important advance on the earlier Daguerrotype) and his claim that it extended to the collodion process introduced by F. Scott Archer in the early 1850s. The outcome of the case was of personal concern to the burgeoning number of professional and amateur photographers, including Carroll's Uncle Skeffington. As Donald Thomas has remarked 'by 1855 it [the wet collodion process] was in the hands of amateurs and professionals alike. The camera which was to effect this change in Dodgson's life was purchased on 18 March 1856' (1996, p. 119). In other words Carroll's ability to use the process he preferred was facilitated by Laroche's legal success.

Being both an aspiring photographer and an enthusiastic attender at the Princess's Theatre, Carroll had two reasons to be aware of Laroche. It is clear from Carroll's diaries that he bought photographic prints of actors by other photographers, and Edward Wakeling has suggested that those of Frederick Robson to which Carroll refers in his diary entries for 22 January and 16 February 1857 (as Medea and the Wandering Minstrel) were by Laroche (Wakeling ed., vol. 3, p. 13, n. 11 and p. 26, n. 36). Laroche produced photographs of twelve Shakespeare productions at the Princess's of which Carroll saw: *Henry VIII*, *The Winter's Tale* (including a portrait of Ellen Terry as Mamillius and Charles Kean as Leontes), *A Midsummer Night's Dream*, *Richard II*, *The Tempest* and *Henry V*. If Carroll bought Laroche photographs of performers at the Princess's Theatre he had the choice of ordinary prints, stereo-photographs or hand-tinted prints. Laroche's customers included the highest in the land. For Christmas 1857 the Prince Consort ordered (through his librarian Dr Ernst Becker, a founder member of the Photographic Society) photographs of Kean's *Richard II* to the value of £126, of which a set of eighteen 'slightly coloured' photographs accounted for £54. 14s. The prince himself paid £91. 7s.; the other £34. 13s was debited to the Privy Purse.[3] The photographs themselves were photographed by Dr Becker and can be seen on prominent display amongst other gifts at the base of the queen's Christmas tree (Dimond and Taylor, 1987, p. 80).

10. Charles Kean as Leontes and Ellen Terry as Mamillius in *The Winter's Tale* at the Princess's Theatre

Laroche was not the only photographer to take photographs of the Keans; there are also examples by H. N. King of Bath and Brady of New York. The proximity of the Princess's Theatre to Laroche's premises inevitably raises the question of *where* the photographs were taken: in the theatre or in the studio? As Terence Rees (1978) has shown there were huge advances in stage lighting in the mid-nineteenth century, but the prevailing view as expressed by Helmut Gernsheim is that there were 'some notable early experiments with different forms of artificial lighting, which in progressive stages laid the groundwork for its application after 1880' (1968, p. 314). In the Laroche photographs Kean and the rest of his company appear fully costumed and surrounded with props, but it would

Photography   129

have been relatively easy to achieve this effect in the – conveniently near – photographer's studio, which was of course sited and constructed to make maximum use of natural light. What is most revealing is what is left out. As Carroll noted of Kean's *Richard II*: 'The entry into London was marvellous.' This is an allusion to the celebrated interpolated episode of Richard and Bolingbroke entering London on horseback with crowds of onlookers dispersed at different levels about the architectural set. The subject of a well-known illustration (*Illustrated London News* 28 March 1857) it seems inconceivable that Kean would not have had this scene and others like it photographed in some form had Laroche been able to work inside the theatre.

Always on the lookout for suitably worthy subjects for his lens, Carroll evidently did not actively pursue Charles Kean until late 1860, by which time he had concluded his management at the Princess's Theatre. Interceding on Carroll's behalf was the Revd Alfred Gatty, whose wife Margaret Scott Gatty enjoyed considerable success as an author with her graceful *mélange* of fanciful stories *The Fairy Godmother, and other Tales* and numerous volumes under her *nom de plume* of 'Aunt Judy'. On 7 January 1861 Gatty wrote to Carroll as follows:

> I wrote about you to Charles Kean about a fortnight ago but have received no answer, and I am always obliged to bide his time, for when employed as now in a professional tour, he cannot be expected to answer letters but when it suits him. He has been for some time in Ireland and acts in London at the beginning of February, but whether he would *at once* consent may be doubtful, as he will probably be much engaged, and his temperament from the long strain of intense study is very sensitive, and he can only do things his own way, and in his own time. (Wakeling ed., vol.4, p. 46)

In fact given the enthusiasm with which the theatre espoused photography, both as a method of publicity and a means of capturing its fleeting art, and Carroll's own enthusiasm for the stage and his persistence in securing sitters, it is surprising how very few actors feature in his photographs. Indeed with the exception of the Terrys, in July 1865 and (Marion and Florence) July 1875, adult professional actors are notable by their absence from Edward Wakeling's 'Register of All Known Photographs by Charles Lutwidge Dodgson' (Taylor and Wakeling, 2002, pp. 240-75). University restrictions about the theatre may have been a factor in discouraging Carroll from taking such opportunities as he might have seized to photograph visiting actors when he had a studio in Babcock's Yard and later Christ Church itself, and as we have already noted he rarely attended

130 *Lewis Carroll and the Victorian Stage*

plays in Oxford and those that he did attend at the New Theatre were long after he gave up photography.

Even the photographs of the Terry family, or those of them in theatrical costume at any rate, have not been well regarded as examples of Carroll's photographic skills. Helmut Gernsheim runs through such compositions as Kate Terry as Andromeda, Rose Wood as Jeannie Campbell, Xie Kitchen as Joshua Reynolds's Penelope Boothby, Holman Hunt's nephew as the King of Hearts and Quintin Twiss as the Artful Dodger and delivers his verdict:

> It goes without saying that most of these costume pictures have to be condemned as errors of taste. Whereas Lewis Carroll's other photographic work shows a remarkable independence of contemporary photography, the sentiment of these pictures is a lamentable concession to Victorian taste. As a producer of costume pictures Lewis Carroll is almost always banal, as a photographer of children he achieves an excellence which in its way can find no peer. (1969, pp. 21-2)

The images of the two younger Terry sisters Marion (Polly) and Florence taken at Henry Holiday's Oak Tree House, Hampstead, on 12 July 1875 are unusual examples of adult (twenty-one and nineteen respectively) subjects in costume. Marion appears as 'Fitz-James' clad in chain mail and holding a sword (Taylor and Wakeling, 2002, p. 271) in a solo pose and kneeling to Florence (in vaguely oriental female clothes) who is dubbing her knight in another. Marion Terry's female curves are if anything accentuated by her masculine attire and there is a directness in her gaze at the camera rarely seen in Carroll's photographs of adults. Untrimmed prints of this and the other Oak Tree House photographs in the Fales Library at New York University reveal the wider context of a platform and backdrop of a drape covering part of the wall of the house. In effect Carroll had created his own small stage for the purpose.

Any consideration of Carroll as a photographer inevitably invites comparison with that other renowned Victorian amateur photographer Julia Margaret Cameron. The two knew each other's work and met several times during Carroll's holiday on the Isle of Wight in 1864. As Carroll explained to his sister Louisa in his letter of 3 August 1864, he and Mrs Cameron had rather different photographic styles:

> In the evening Mrs. Cameron and I had a mutual exhibition of photographs. Hers are taken purposely out of focus – some are very picturesque – some are merely hideous. However she talks of them all as if they were triumphs in art. *She* wished she could have some of *my* subjects to take *out* of focus – and *I* expressed an analogous wish with regard to some of *her* subjects.

Photography 131

Though Carroll and Mrs Cameron differed on the important matter of focus, they shared an enthusiasm for home entertainments such as recitations, charades and theatricals. At Dimbola Lodge, her home on the Isle of Wight, Mrs Cameron eventually erected a small theatre: 'Amateur Theatricals. At Mrs. Cameron's Thatched House' as the playbills were headed (Melville, 2003, p. 97). Hallam Tennyson recalled in his memoir of his father that:

> From 1869 to 1880 my brother, myself and the younger members of the Cameron family spent many of our evenings during the Christmas and Easter holidays in Mrs Cameron's little theatre. Here we acted plays by Sheridan, Gilbert, Robertson and Tom Taylor, and my father was seldom absent, for he loved the stage. He was a careful critic and never missed a point. (1897, vol. II, pp. 85-6)

Neither, it seems, did Mrs Cameron, being in Joy Melville's words 'as critical in her role of producer as photographer, she once demolished her son's performance with the words, "Oh heavens, Henry, do you call that making love? Here let *me* show you how to do it."' (2003, p. 97) Nevertheless Henry Cameron did attempt, none too successfully, to become an actor, his credits including the Carpenter in a production of *Alice in Wonderland* (Hill, 1973, p.174). By birth Mrs Cameron was one of the celebrated Pattle sisters of whom Sarah married H. Thoby Prinsep. G. F. Watts made their home Little Holland House his and it was there that Ellen Terry endured her brief marriage to 'the Seigneur' as the Prinseps called him. Their son Valentine Cameron Prinsep wrote a couple of plays, including *Cousin Dick* which Carroll saw in a triple-bill at the Court Theatre on 3 July 1879, but his real accomplishment was as a painter, in which capacity he was greatly influenced by Watts, which may have been evident in the new act-drop which he painted 'at his own wish' (Pemberton, 1895, p. 5) for the Court. Val Prinsep's son Anthony became a theatre manager.

Helmut Gersheim makes the link between the theatrical activities that Mrs Cameron and her family indulged in so enthusiastically and her photography: 'It was not a big step from the amateur theatricals at Dimbola to Julia Margaret Cameron's illustrations to *The Idylls of the King*, which were conceived in the same spirit.' (1975, p. 42) Whilst married to him, Ellen Terry was the subject of paintings by Watts (*Choosing, Ophelia, Joan of Arc*) and photographs by Mrs Cameron taken during their visit to Dimbola Lodge in the summer of 1864. These photographs ranged from conventional portraits, to costume subjects such as Cordelia (with the poet-playwright Sir Henry Taylor as King Lear) and

132   *Lewis Carroll and the Victorian Stage*

the extraordinary and atmospheric 'The South West Wind from Life' of which Nina Auerbach has written:

> in 1865, when Julia Cameron photographed Ellen Terry as child and woman, *Alice's Adventures in Wonderland* appeared. Like the Nelly Terry who is also 'The South West Wind from Life', Carroll's Alice has access to magic realms that are also, magically, her own suggestively erotic, infinitely changing body. The loss of Wonderland is the loss of her magical childhood endowment: a little girl is infinite and an infinite allure, while a woman is confined because betrayed by sexuality and marriage, houses and walls. (1987, p. 99)

In 'The South West Wind from Life' Cameron used her out-of-focus technique to create an ethereal composition consisting of the floating head and shoulders of Ellen Terry hovering (completely out of proportion) over a natural landscape, thereby achieving an effect which though it might suggest Ariel in *The Tempest* does so surreally in a completely different style from that which her sister Kate was required to adopt in the role at the Princess's Theatre. For all the photograph's fluidity, Terry's eyes transfix the observer. Auerbach argues that

> when she modelled for Julia Cameron, Ellen Terry beautified the roles life demanded that she play: the eye of the camera was a grand epitome of the watching audience who from the beginning had given her her being. Off the stage, the passage from girl to woman was demanding incomprehensible humiliation, but when Ellen Terry illustrated Julia Cameron's visions, she understood her role at last. (p. 96)

Interestingly Auerbach detects the same process of acting to the camera with Carroll specifically in his photographs of children:

> Carroll's photographs of children differ from grand pre-Raphaelite female icons in that the latter tend to be marmoreal still-lives, while the former are remarkable for their mobility, their promise of perpetual activity and change. To elicit the essence of his sitters Carroll seems to have encouraged them to act, thus releasing the metamorphic potential he saw coiled within little girls: the hallmark of his photographs is his use of costumes, props, and the imaginative intensity of an improvised scene caught at midpoint. Carroll's love for the theatre was one of the sirens that lured him from the seemingly inevitable but 'unwelcome bed' of full ordination. His passionate affection for the young Ellen Terry, which seems to have been a more profound devotion than George Bernard Shaw's would be in the actress's middle age, his intensifying obsession with child actresses in general in his later years, his infusion of theatricality into his photographs of nonactresses – all suggest

Photography 133

that the mobile self-definition of acting crystallized the potential power he found in the little girl. His photographic allegiance to the performing self suggested a commitment to the metamorphic mystery of personality which few artists then as now, are brave enough to pledge. (1985, pp. 156-7)

Taking our cue from Nina Auerbach, it should not really come as a surprise that the theatrical element is most prominent in Carroll's photographs of young girls, since it was through his discovery of his own ability to entertain them that he struck up such a strong rapport with his audiences at Croft. Thereafter at endless home entertainments the roles tended to be reversed with Carroll as the audience. The camera served to make the relationship more reciprocal, with Carroll combining the role of stage-manager (producer) and audience. In fact Carroll's photographs of children in theatrical costume are predominantly of the daughters of Oxford friends rather than child actresses who belonged to a somewhat later period in his life. This is largely explained by the creation of suitable facilities for photographing in Christ Church following his occupation of what had been Lord Bute's rooms. There was, as Roger Taylor points out, a considerable delay in completing the alterations:

Dodgson moved into the rooms on 30 October 1868, and for the next few years pursued the possibility of having an adjacent studio. It took the best part of four years for the college authorities to agree and for Dodgson to have the studio built, but by October 1871 it was finished. A small and windowless room, on the stairs and close to the studio, was converted into a darkroom where he could prepare and develop his collodion plates…For the next eight years this studio and darkroom lay at the center of Dodgson's photographic activities, and he rarely took his camera elsewhere. (Taylor and Wakeling, 2002, p. 93)

Although prior to 1871 Carroll had taken some costume portraits of children, of which Agnes Weld as Little Red Riding-Hood at Croft in August 1857 and Alice Liddell as The Beggar Maid the following year stand out as particularly fine examples, it was not until after the alterations to his new accommodation were completed that what Gernsheim calls 'this outburst of costume pictures' (1969, p. 20) occurred. The reason for this was not simply the studio and darkroom but the storage space for costumes and other accoutrements.

Whilst it is true that some costume photographs of favourite models such as Xie Kitchin and Julia Arnold (several in Chinese dress) were taken in Badcock's Yard and therefore pre-date the completion of his studio and darkroom, of more significance is the fact that by that time Carroll had accommodation with storage space and it would have been no

134 *Lewis Carroll and the Victorian Stage*

problem to carry what he needed from his new rooms across the road to 105 St. Aldates. Once Carroll had all the amenities of storage, studio and darkroom in one place his output of costume photographs increased rapidly, as Edward Wakeling's register reveals. The Kitchin family is well represented, especially Xie with 'almost fifty portraits' including the 'Chinese Tea-Merchant' (on and off duty), Viola (*Twelfth Night*), in 'St George and the Dragon' with her three brothers, 'Dane' and the young musician in 'Most Musical, Most Melancholy'. As Roger Taylor observes, in 'every portrait of Xie it is her gaze that holds our attention' (Taylor and Wakeling, 2002, p. 97).

Of Carroll's favourite models the Hatch and the Arnold sisters were also involved in home theatricals, the former having a special prologue written for them by Carroll in February 1873 and the latter performing *The Mad Tea-Party* before him on 7 December 1874. So although the girls were not professional actresses they did have experience of performing, which they could bring to their poses before the camera. Ethel M. Arnold described Carroll's rooms as 'an El Dorado of delights':

> The large sitting room was lined with well-filled bookshelves under which ran a row of cupboards all round the four walls. Oh, those cupboards! What wondrous treasures they contained for the delectation of youth! Mechanical bears, dancing dolls, toys and puzzles of every description…all sorts of fancy dress (of which he kept an almost inexhaustible stock in the great cupboard). (*Atlantic Monthly* January 1929)

A similar picture is painted by Beatrice Hatch: 'He kept various costumes and "properties" with which to dress us up, and, of course that added to the fun. What child would not thoroughly enjoy personating a Japanese, or a beggar-child, or a gipsy, or an Indian?' (*Strand Magazine* June 1898) Beatrice herself wrote from experience, having been photographed by Carroll in French ('Vive la France') and Japanese ('Apis Japanensis') costume and her sister Ethel in – apparently – Dutch ('The Beast is Near') and Turkish. Evelyn Hatch (1933) was the subject of one of Carroll's surviving nude studies. Inevitably these have attracted a great deal of attention and controversy, with James Kincaid writing of Carroll living 'erotically by way of his camera' (1992, p. 303). Roger Taylor has delivered a less censorious verdict:

> This, then, is the sum of Dodgson's nude photography: an activity limited to eight sessions spread over thirteen years involving the children of six families (excluding Ada Smith, whose profession as a life model places her in a somewhat different category). It is not the record of a habitual voyeur, pornographer, or paedophile, but the response of an overtly sentimental

Photography 135

bachelor to the innocent beauty and grace of childhood. Whether this type of photography was Dodgson's way of satisfying or sublimating his sexual desires can never be known and will always remain fruitless speculation. Certainly the fear that this might be the case never troubled the families involved, and we can be certain that any whiff of impropriety would have been keenly scented. (Taylor and Wakeling, 2002, p. 107)

Carroll's characterisation of children in his article 'Stage Children' as 'innocence and sweet trustfulness and ignorance of the world' (*St James's Gazette* 2 September 1889) applies to his photographs as well as it does to child actors. And yet as Taylor observes (p. 103), actresses had long been associated with immoral behaviour and there were those who readily made a connection between them and the subjects of certain photographs. In its issue of 1 January 1869 the *Journal of British Photography* reprinted a leading article from the *Daily News* which drew attention to – amongst other things – 'the face of a pensive and good-looking girl' which featured 'constantly amongst theatrical *cartes*, and underneath it was a name fanciful and romantic enough for the stage': 'It was the portrait of a West-end courtesan, and its sale was organised and promoted by a woman who lends and sells clothes to prostitutes, and by the keeper of a casino.' In fact, as we have noted, Carroll did not photograph his child actress friends, but had he done so he would undoubtedly have been scrupulous in avoiding any such taint.

When in 1888, eight years after he had stopped photographing, the fourteen-year old Isa Bowman, probably his favourite child actress, visited Carroll in Oxford, he wrote his account 'Isa's Visit to Oxford', describing them going back to Christ Church and looking

at a lot of dresses, which the A. A. M. kept in a cupboard, to dress up children in, when they come to be photographed. Some of the dresses had been used in Pantomimes at Drury Lane: some were rags, to dress up beggar-children in: some had been very magnificent once, but were getting old and shabby. (Bowman, 1899, p. 52)

The subtext seems to be that Carroll himself (the 'Aged Aged Man') was also getting old and shabby, though he was only fifty-six and had another decade of life ahead of him. When he died there were several costumes still stored in his rooms at Christ Church, some of which were acquired by the Art and Antique Agency, 41 High Street, Oxford, which advertised them in its catalogue:

FANCY DRESS,
Used by LEWIS CARROLL's Child Friends.

136 *Lewis Carroll and the Victorian Stage*

(See *Strand Magazine*, April, 1898, in which these identical dresses are engraved.)

Fairy Prince Suit. – Green satin tunic heavily spangled and silver laced, with cap and sabretasche to match: green velvet breeches, golden laced; pink silk tights: £2 5s

Turkish Maiden Suit – Silk gauze tunic, gold trimming with green jewel ornament, lined; trousers green silk with gauze net over gilt spangled; long wide Indian gauze scarf; head dress to match, with imitation pearl drops and green beads; and scarlet spenser, gold lace trimming: £2

Engraved in *Strand Magazine*, April 1898, page 423.

Georgian Court Dress – Slate-green velveteen, with silver braid and buttons, lace at wrist; buff cloth breeches, velvet bands, lace at knees; red sword sash with gold braid, and green velvet scabbard: 30s...

Chinese Mandarin's Robe – Thick blue cotton with black and white pattern, 12s 6d

Similar to engraving on page 419 of the *Strand Magazine*...

Fairy Prince Suit – Dark crimson silk velvet; tunic with ermine round skirt, front, collar, sleeves: with sabretasche or gipsire to match; breeches with gold lace, cap with ermine; long pink silk stockings £2 10s

Red Fez – Lined, a trifle moth eaten, 2s 6d

Basket of Flowers, two muslin caps, blue serge bodice, red and white cotton skirt (some being part of the Dolly Varden costume, *Strand Magazine*, page 421): 6s

WE SEND ON APPROVAL IN SPECIAL CASES ONLY. (Stern, 1997, p. 92)

'The Turkish Maiden Suit' was that worn by Ethel Hatch in various photographs taken on 16 June 1877; 'Chinese Mandarin's Robes' were those worn by Xie Kitchin as the 'Tea-Merchant' (on and off duty) taken on 14 July 1873 and 'Basket of Flowers' as attributed (Wakeling register).

The theatre is of course renowned as the most evanescent art and even its trappings, though they may survive their wearer, become 'a trifle moth eaten' and decay. Barthes linked the theatre, photography and death, which in a sense Virginia Woolf had done several decades before him in her essay on Ellen Terry in *The Moment and other essays*:

> It is the fate of actors to leave only a picture behind them. Every night when the curtain goes down the beautiful coloured canvas is rubbed out. What remains is at best only a wavering, insubstantial phantom – a verbal life on the lips of the living. (1947, p. 165)

Human life, like the theatrical performance, expires, dies and disappears, but photographs attest that what we see 'actually existed'.

Notes

1 Typescript of talk given to the Leamington Literary Society by Miss Violet Dodgson on 17 October 1949. DFC (Dodgson Family Collection)/C/1/1-15, The Surrey History Centre, Woking.

2 Richard Foulkes, The Laroche Photographs of Charles Kean's Shakespeare Revivals, *Theatrephile*, vol. II, no. 8, pp. 29-33. This issue contains other articles relating to the Princess's Theatre, the Queen's Bazaar and Mr Mathews's Gallery of Theatrical Portraits.

3 The Royal Photographic Collection (PP2/25/8128) in the Royal Archives at Windsor Castle.

9 Carroll at the Theatre

> 'He was a splendid theatre-goer.'
> Ellen Terry, *The Story of My Life*

Carroll first attended a full-scale professional performance at the Princess's Theatre on 22 June 1855 when he saw Shakespeare's *Henry VIII* under the management of Charles Kean. His last visit to a theatre was to see J. M. Barrie's *The Little Minister* at the Haymarket Theatre on Saturday 20 November 1897. He enjoyed them both immensely. At the end of his diary entry about *Henry VIII* Carroll wrote: 'I never enjoyed anything so much in my life before' and he concluded his entry for *The Little Minister*, which he described as 'a beautiful play, beautifully acted', as follows: '*The Little Minister* is a play I should like to see again and again.' Sadly this was not to be as he fell ill during his Christmas visit to Guildford and died there on 14 January 1898. The striking thing about these two 'bookends' to Carroll's playgoing was how widely separated they were (by forty-two years) and that his enthusiasm for the theatre remained undimmed to the end. According to Evelyn Hatch: 'Going to the theatre was one of Mr Dodgson's favourite recreations, and with his usual precision he kept a "play-record" which showed how often young friends were taken to share his pleasure.' (Cohen ed., 1989, p. 121) Given his methodical records of his correspondence and photographs it is not surprising that Carroll should keep a similar log of his theatregoing. However it has not survived and the evidence has to be collected and collated from elsewhere: first and foremost in his diaries and then in his letters. Hugues Lebailly, who has undertaken this task meticulously, has calculated that Carroll attended the theatre on 479 occasions and saw 686 pieces (double and triple bills being common in the early years).[1]

Comparable records of individual theatregoing are rare indeed. At the beginning Carroll was contemporary with Henry Crabb Robinson, who was born in 1775, and at the end with Kate Terry Gielgud, who died in 1958. Along the way Carroll's chronicle intersects with Henry Morley, Theodor Fontane, G. H. Lewes, Charles Eyre Pascoe, Clement Scott, Henry James, Joseph Knight, George Bernard Shaw and William Archer. These identified authors will be preferred to the anonymous columns of the press as a point of reference for Carroll's theatrical judgement. The examination of what Carroll wrote about the theatre in those forty-two years provides a double insight, firstly into what was happening on the stage through the eyes of a man whose accomplishments encompassed mathematics, photography and authorship, and secondly into the mind and personality of that extraordinary and enigmatic individual.

As preceding chapters have revealed, Carroll had an innate disposition towards the dramatic from an early age, but he had to confront ingrained opposition from his father and search his conscience deeply before he ventured inside a playhouse. Thereafter Carroll adopted a relativist position, as his letter (already referred to in Chapter 1) of 12 May 1892 to A. R. H. Wright indicates. There he wrote 'all Christians agree...that we ought to abstain from *evil*, and therefore from all things which are *essentially* evil', a category into which the Revd Charles Dodgson and many another Victorian clerics would place the theatre. Carroll then listed five activities from which certain Christians advocated 'total abstinence', though in his view they were (only) *'capable* of being put to evil uses': wine, reading fiction, attending theatres, the attendance at social entertainments and mixing with human society in any form. Specifically on the subject of the theatre Carroll wrote:

> And so *I* say as to theatres, to which I often take my young friends, 'I take them to *good* theatres, and *good* plays: and I carefully avoid the *bad* ones.' In this, as in all things, I seek to live in the spirit of our dear Saviour's prayer for his disciples: 'I pray not that thou shouldest take them out of the world, but that thou shouldst keep them from the evil.'

The period of Carroll's playgoing was one of exceptional change, seeing a huge expansion in theatrical activity of every type to cater for the diverse tastes of the ever-increasing urban population of London and other cities. Patterns of playgoing were based on what social class people belonged to, where they lived, what transport was available and (particularly significant in Carroll's case) who might make up the party.

Carroll's theatregoing was predominantly (311 times) in London. As we have already noted, there were particular reasons why he saw so little in Oxford and Guildford was without a theatre. He attended the Theatre Royal in Brighton where he had connections, but, London apart, Eastbourne, where he holidayed annually for twenty-one years from 1877, provided him with the most opportunities – no less than sixty-three. Following the abolition of the Drury Lane and Covent Garden monopoly in 1843 there was an increase in theatre building, which reached its zenith towards the end of the century, led by the prolific architect C. J. Phipps. Whereas in the provinces a handful or less of theatres catered for most tastes in that town or city, in London theatres developed a particular style for a particular clientele, usually determined by the manager/actor-

140 *Lewis Carroll and the Victorian Stage*

manager in charge. In this context the theatres that Carroll never attended or stopped attending take on a significance alongside that of the theatres he did patronise. Similarly, even at favourite theatres there were plays he conspicuously did not attend. Carroll was a fair judge of acting and other theatre arts, but his crucial criterion as to whether a play was '*good*' or '*bad*' tended to be its moral content rather than its artistic merit. He never went to a play by Ibsen, Shaw or Wilde. His decision on whether or not to see a play relied more on word of mouth than his selective reading of reviews, as he wrote to Katherine Savile Clarke on 5 November 1887:

> I take in *The Theatre*, so I have *their* notice of *Shadows of a Great City*; and I have a certain amount of reliance that a play is fairly unobjectionable if they say nothing to the contrary; but as to *newspaper* notices, please don't trouble yourself: I haven't the smallest confidence in them. However, what I was hoping to get from *you* was some private opinion: one such opinion is worth all printed notices put together.

Usually Carroll's various antenna worked, though in the case of H. A. Jones's *The Dancing Girl* it was his careful reading of the review in the *Theatre*, rather than his friends, that saved him from a disagreeable evening, as he explained to Winifred Stevens in a letter of 27 November 1891:

> Thank you very much for your letter; but I'm sorry to say I must give up the plan of going to see *The Dancing Girl*. I had only heard it praised by friends, and had never acquainted myself with the plot. Now, that I have read, in the *Theatre*, a candidly and carefully written notice of the play, I have come to the conclusion that it is not a play I should care to witness, or to take any of my girl friends to.

Carroll acknowledged that 'a play would be ridiculous which represented human beings as sinless', conceded that 'it is splendidly acted' and protested that if the Stevens chose to see it he would not 'think the worse of you, in the least degree', but he had formed his 'own views in the matter' and they were clear enough. His views on Pinero's *The Second Mrs Tanqueray* were utterly unequivocal, as he made clear in his letter of 13 April 1894 to Mrs Greet, to whom he had already expressed his objections to *The Little Squire* (of which she was the co-author with Horace Sedger):

> As you name *The Second Mrs. Tanqueray*, I will add that I have not seen it, and do not mean to. The reviews are enough to settle that point. Friends have

Carroll at the Theatre 141

urged me to go: but I answer 'No. I consider it is a play that ought not to be acted.' And what ought not to be acted I feel that one ought not to witness.

Towards the end of his life – in the 'Naughty Nineties'– Carroll must have felt that he was traversing a theatrical minefield. Even his loyalty to seeing his friends on stage could be ill rewarded, as in the case of going to see Isa Bowman in *The Little Squire* at the Lyric Theatre in April 1894. Not content with fulminating in his diary, Carroll dispatched a letter of protest (7 April 1894) to the co-author Mrs W. Greet: 'I can assure you, it gave *great* pain to hear such flippant talk, about baptism and the soul, put into the minds of those two dear children.'

Happily at the outset of his theatregoing, when in any case he was younger and less censorious, there was little on the stage to which Carroll could take exception. How best to chart that progress from Charles Kean's Princess's Theatre in 1855 to the Haymarket in 1897? Alternative approaches include chronologically by year, by plays/authors, by actors or by theatres. I have elected in favour of theatres, since a particular theatre often embodies the taste of a particular time in terms of play, actors and style of production and the fluctuating fortunes of theatres are generally a good guide to fashion and favour.

The Princess's Theatre, Oxford Street
Charles Kean

As already noted, the (Royal) Princess's Theatre opened on the Oxford Street site of what had previously been the Royal Bazaar, the Queen's Bazaar and the Court Theatre on 28 September 1850 under the management of Charles Kean, the Eton-educated son of Edmund, and comedian Robert Keeley (Cole, 1859). The extended opening season encompassed the period of the Great Exhibition, the early months of which were disastrous for theatre business. Trade improved in the later months and in the longer term the Exhibition seems to have stimulated the market for the painstaking historical revivals of Shakespeare's plays (see Schoch, 1998) amongst the better-off and better-educated who had long since regarded the stage as a fount of immorality. In 1852 Keeley withdrew from the management, leaving Kean to pursue his archaeological bent in tandem with his formidable wife Ellen (formerly Tree). His appointment (in 1848) as director of the Royal Theatricals at Windsor Castle had given Kean considerable status. The moving force behind this initiative, which was intended to elevate stage as well as entertain the royal family, was Prince Albert, who had grown up in

142   *Lewis Carroll and the Victorian Stage*

Germany where court theatres were accepted as a matter of course. Kean organised a regular sequence of performances at Windsor, but Queen Victoria and her family also continued to patronise London theatres, the Princess's being a particular favourite (Rowell, 1978).

Kean may have regarded *The Merry Wives of Windsor* as an apt title for his first Shakespeare revival at the Princess's in 1851, though the royal family did not attend a performance there or command one at Windsor. Kean really got into his stride with *King John* and *Macbeth* in 1852 and Byron's *Sardanapalus* in the same year. As well as Shakespeare the Princess's specialised in romantic, 'gentlemanly' melodramas, most of them by Dion Boucicault.

Carroll was truly representative of the clientele that Kean wanted to attract: highly respectable, sober and righteous. The fact that, though he was already twenty-two and fascinated by the theatre when Kean began his management, it was five years before Carroll ventured inside the Princess's must be indicative of his indecisiveness, his self-control, his deference to his father, or all three. Two other men from similar backgrounds who regularly attended the Princess's and committed their impressions to paper were Henry Crabb Robinson and Henry Morley. After careers in the law and journalism, Crabb Robinson was one of the founders of University College, London, and of the Athenaeum (gentlemen's club) and he assiduously cultivated literary (Wordsworth, Coleridge, Hazlitt) and theatrical (Charles Young, Edmund Kean) contacts. When he attended the Princess's in the 1850s Crabb Robinson could compare Charles Kean with his father Edmund and Mrs Kean with Mrs Siddons, whom the young Carroll invoked in his prologue to *La Guida di Bragia*. Like Carroll, Crabb Robinson recorded his theatrical impressions in his diary, whereas Henry Morley, Professor of English Literature and editor of 'Morley's Universal Library', wrote for publication in the *Examiner*. Carroll knew the Morleys; he corresponded (28 June 1875) with and photographed the youngest daughter Edith. A committed educationalist, Morley regarded the theatre as a source of intellectual improvement. In contrast, all the available evidence of Carroll's interest in the theatre to date, albeit limited to home entertainments, is that he regarded it as fun. There is a very telling passage in his diary entry for that first theatre visit on 22 June 1855: 'This is the true end and object of acting – to raise the mind above itself, and out of its petty everyday cares.' Since Carroll went on to praise the scenery it seems reasonable to suppose that his remark applies to the whole theatrical experience, not just the acting. His use of the word 'mind' anticipates the title of a talk he gave in a Derbyshire vicarage in October 1884: 'Feeding the Mind'. Essentially what Carroll said is that, like the body, the mind

Carroll at the Theatre 143

needs 'the proper kind, amount, and variety of...mental food' (1907, p. 22). Carroll obviously regarded the (right kind of) theatre as a suitable mental food, the effect of which would be to release the mind from 'its petty everyday cares' in a process of recreation and refreshment. It was a release from everyday cares, not a means of taking them into a new context in which to deliberate on them further, let alone taking on board other cares or issues.

The passage quoted occurs in the middle of Carroll's ecstatic description of 'that exquisite vision of Queen Catharine [sic]' in which

> sunbeams broke in through the roof, and gradually revealed two angel forms, floating in front of the carved work on the ceiling : the column of sunbeams shone down upon the sleeping queen, and gradually down it floated a troop of angelic forms, transparent, and carrying palm branches in their hands: they waved these over the sleeping queen , with oh! such a sad and solemn grace.

Though nothing else he saw at the Princess's ever came up to this scene, Carroll consistently praised other scenic highlights, such as the wood scenes in *A Midsummer Night's Dream*, 'the visions' and the statue of Hermione in *The Winter's Tale*, the interpolated 'Historical Episode' of Richard II and Bolingbroke entering London in *Richard* II, the opening scene of the shipwreck and 'the concluding scene, where Ariel is left alone, hovering over the wide ocean, watching the retreating ship' in *The Tempest*, which he saw on 3 July 1857. As we have seen, Henry Morley had some reservations ('the shadow dance of fairies'), but generally he approved: 'I do not think the money ill spent upon stage-furniture, and certainly can only admire the exquisite scenery of the play [*A Midsummer Night's Dream*] now being presented at the Princess's' (1891, p. 133) and 'the splendours [of *Richard II*] are unimpeachable' (p. 141). Crabb Robinson found *The Winter's Tale* 'a treat to the eye' (Brown ed., 1966, pp. 201-2) and commended the scenery for *The Tempest* as 'fine...[a] great attraction' (p. 204) and for *A Midsummer Night's Dream* as 'beautiful' (p. 205). Eluned Brown's comment that Crabb Robinson 'came to feel that his age excelled in the theatre of spectacle and he was not ashamed to enjoy this' (p. 23) can be applied to Carroll and Morley too as a corrective to later (still continuing) disdain for that aspect of the Victorian theatre.

Even the German journalist and novelist Theodore Fontane, who whilst working for a press agency set up in London by the German government became an inveterate theatregoer, though he came from a different tradition, conceded:

11. Queen Katherine's Dream in *Henry VIII* at the Princess's Theatre

Carroll at the Theatre   145

Nevertheless, after a long period of resistance, I take Kean's side in the matter, and affirm that, even in the case of *un*historical plays, the principle is definitely that as well as striving to captivate by an appeal to the senses the theatre should *educate*...The Shakespeare he [Kean] offers is a *new Shakespeare*. Great and small must serve him: the archaelogist and the costumier; the British Museum and the pyrotechnist; heraldry, numismatics and the new laws of colour combinations – all are enlisted to overcome the apathy of the educated classes and to make Shakespeare popular again even in the higher circles of society. It has been a success. (Jackson ed., 1999, p. 32)

Though Fontane succeeded in bringing himself into sympathy with the British taste for historical scenery, he made little headway with that predilection closest to Carroll's heart: the child performer. Whereas on 22 June 1856 Carroll 'especially admired the acting of Little Mamillius' by 'Ellen Terry, a beautiful little creature, who played with remarkable ease' and thought Puck 'cleverly acted by the little Ellen Terry' on 16 December 1856, Fontane remained resistant to her charms. He acknowledged that after seeing her he 'could no longer even contemplate a Puck with a full bosom and plump arms', but nevertheless found her 'altogether intolerable: a precocious child brought up in the true English manner, old before her years' (Jackson ed., 1999, p. 46). Of Ellen Terry as Mamillius he was even more damning:

The presence of Little Mamillius is irksome, and he ruins the whole scene with his affectedness. Generally speaking, England is the land of spoiled children, and being brought up behind the scenes is the least likely way of putting a stop to all affectation. (pp. 51-2)

However Carroll's taste was shared by Queen Victoria herself as George Rowell has written:

Child performers always found a sympathetic response in the Queen. The Terry family were established favourites: an early Windsor performance, *King John,* was notable in this respect: 'The character of poor little "Arthur" was most touchingly and beautifully acted by Miss Kate Terry, a little girl of 9 years old. The scene between Arthur and Hubert was heartrending.'

The Victorian stage convention of casting actresses as small boys is no longer to the playgoer's taste, but the Queen delighted in it. Kate Terry's sister came to her notice in *A Midsummer Night's Dream* at the Princess's: 'Miss Ellen Terry (about 9 years old) played the part of "Robin" delightfully, and "Peaseblossom", "Mustard" [*sic*], etc., were represented by darling little children.' (1978, p. 71)

146   *Lewis Carroll and the Victorian Stage*

Though he does not appear to have objected to child performers as such, Crabb Robinson's estimation of Kate Terry as Ariel was strikingly at variance with Carroll's. Carroll described her on 3 July 1857 as 'the gem of the piece...exquisitely graceful and beautiful', especially when 'hovering' over the departing ship in the last scene, but to Crabb Robinson: 'The only great fault I can now recollect is that Ariel is too large and heavy – though a girl yet she is too bulky and coarse – yet she is well supported in the air – Mrs [Miss] Terry was Ariel.' (Brown ed., 1966, p. 204).

There were also divergent views about Mrs Kean. Ever eager to invoke Mrs Siddons, Carroll called 'Mrs. Kean a worthy successor to Mrs. Siddons as Queen Catherine' after seeing her for the first time on 22 June 1855. Fontane considered her as 'fine...in many respects, [though] her performance did not achieve its full effect', partly in his opinion 'because of the pomp with which it [the trial scene] was staged' (Jackson ed., 1999, p. 43). Crabb Robinson, though he did not make the direct comparison with Mrs Siddons that he was equipped to make, judged 'Mrs Kean [as Hermione] utterly powerless as an actress' (Brown ed., 1966, p. 202).

Carroll's enthusiastic patronage of the Princess's Theatre during the last four years of Charles Kean's management undoubtedly reflected Kean's successful appeal to 'the educated classes' whose tastes turned to lavish historical scenery and child performers. Theodor Fontane provides a useful contrast, suggesting that these tastes were particularly English. Amongst London theatres Fontane's preference was for Sadler's Wells in Islington, where since 1844 Samuel Phelps had drawn the local population to revivals of Shakespeare's plays that were well acted and without Kean's scenic excesses (see Allen, 1971). Fontane called Sadler's Wells 'the true Shakespeare stage' which furthermore was 'a people's theatre'. Discerning playgoers travelled to Islington from further afield: Fontane of course, Charles Dickens, Crabb Robinson and Morley. Crabb Robinson recorded visits to Massinger's *The Fatal Dowry* on 4 September 1845, *As You Like It* on 4 December 1847 and *Pericles* (albeit heavily bowdlerised) on 24 November 1854. Henry Morley was a regular at Sadler's Wells and reviewed the productions at length in the *Examiner*. Carroll went to Sadler's Wells only once, on 9 January 1874, to see *The Babes in the Wood* in which Katie Logan, Lizzie and Bert Coote were appearing, but he found it 'poor, as I expected, and rather vulgar. Katie has a poor part; the little Coote is hardly more than a clever baby.' In fact the 'little Coote' was the exception to Carroll's rule about healthy stage children: 'They are said to be killing the poor child with overwork, and she is suffering from some malady in the throat. She lies in bed all day, and almost lives on port-wine and oysters.' Phelps had long left Sadler's Wells by then and

Carroll at the Theatre

shortly afterwards 'it was to be turned into baths and washhouses' (Arundell, 1965, p. 164). The reasons why Carroll had not visited Sadler's Wells during its heyday under Phelps were its relative inaccessibility, its less than salubrious neighbourhood, and the predominance of Shakespeare without the compensating attractions of lavish scenery, the young Terrys and the lightweight afterpieces by John Maddison Morton, John Oxenford and J. R. Planché (see Davis and Emeljanow, 2001, Chapter 4). At least Carroll was in good company, for though Phelps's supporters tried to arrange a visit by Queen Victoria (Foulkes, 2002, p. 41), Dickens reported to Phelps on 25 February 1854: 'I am sorry to inform you that the difficulties in the way of the Queen's coming to Sadler's Wells are insurmountable. But a very just reference is made to you and the theatre in Colonel Phipps's letter' (Phelps and Forbes-Robertson, 1886, p. 390).

After Kean's departure the Princess's had a succession of – mostly brief – managements (Howard, 1970, p. 187). Carroll visited the theatre twice during George Vining's tenure, on both occasions to see a play by the prolific Irish-born playwright Dion Boucicault. On 20 August 1864 he went to *The Streets of London*, the title of which changed according to location: 'So *The Poor of Liverpool* became *The Poor of Leeds*, *The Poor of Manchester*, *The Streets of Islington* (when it played at Sadler's Wells Theatre) and *The Streets of London*, when it opened at the Princess's' (Fawkes, 1979, p. 148). Boucicault's drama incorporated powerful spectacle and, not surprisingly, what caught Carroll's attention were 'two wonderful scenes, Charing Cross on a winter's night, and a house on fire, a most real scene'. Drawing attention to the play's derivation from *Les Pauvres de Paris*, Morley was less convinced, finding 'its French origin uneffaced in an ingenious unreality of realism' (1891, p. 283). *Arrag-na-Pogue*, which Carroll saw on 8 April 1864, was 'that rarity, an original Boucicault play' (Fawkes, 1979, p. 155), further authenticated for Carroll by 'Mr. and Mrs. Boucicault' taking 'the chief parts' in 'a very effective drama'.

Wilson Barrett

Carroll's attendance at the Princess's during the 1870s was intermittent (*Goody Two Shoes* three times in 1873, W. G. Wills's *Jane Shore* on 25 May 1878 and *Uncle Tom's Cabin* with Carrie Coote on 9 October 1879), but following Wilson Barrett's assumption of the management in 1881 he became something of a regular. Born in Essex in 1846, Barrett, 'a member of a devout churchgoing family' (Thomas, 1984, p. 11), married Caroline

148   *Lewis Carroll and the Victorian Stage*

Heath who, having stood in for Mrs Kean at the Windsor Theatricals, eventually became official 'Reader to the Queen' (p. 18). At the Princess's Carroll saw Barrett in four of his greatest successes: *The Silver King* (four times), *Claudian* (three times) and *The Lights o'London* (once). Charles Lovett (2000) has dubbed *The Silver King* 'Lewis Carroll's favourite play', with its story of Will Denver mistakenly believing himself guilty of murder, emigrating, making a fortune, returning home to a poignant reunion with his family (children first) and the discovery of his innocence, but it has an even greater significance. Henry Arthur Jones, co-author with Henry Herman, solicited the interest of Matthew Arnold (D. Jones, 1930, pp. 61-2), who in due course reviewed the play in the *Pall Mall Gazette* where, having commented favourably on the audience ('a representative public, furnished from all classes, and showing that English society at large has now taken to the theatre'), he proclaimed that 'in general throughout the piece the diction and sentiments are natural, they have sobriety, they are literature' (Super, 1974, p. 95). For Carroll the attraction lay in the performances by Barrett, Mary Eastlake, Charles Coote and Phoebe Carlo, but the fact that Arnold rated the play as literature was the encomium that meant most to Jones. Carroll considered *Claudian* (by Herman and W. G. Wills) 'rather too tragic' and wrote (15 January 1884) to Barrett suggesting that 'a short sketch of the *plot* would be a most welcome addition to the playbill', thereby saving him 'the effort to make it out'. This and his enthusiastic description in his diary for 12 January 1884 of 'the downfall of the temple in the earthquake' as 'one of the best bits of stage business I ever saw' are indicative of Carroll's attitude towards the theatre as relaxation. At least when he did go (on 21 February 1885) to see Barrett in what was indisputably great literature, Carroll showed his shrewd judgement: 'His Hamlet is good, but uninteresting. Miss Eastlake as Ophelia is clever, but of course nothing like Miss Ellen Terry.'

Rather belatedly Carroll caught up with Barrett's early success *The Lights o'London* (London premiere 10.9.1881) on 5 June 1885 and a couple of months later saw him in *Hoodman Blind*, the melodrama he had written with H. A. Jones. On both occasions he praised the play and the acting, particularly Phoebe Carlo as the little boy, Kit, in the latter. Barrett continued to purvey his particular brand of righteous melodrama on British and overseas tours and in the West End. *The Sign of the Cross* (Mayer ed., 1994), the most sensational example of the genre, opened at the Lyric Theatre on 4 January 1896, but Carroll did not go to see it.

He did however return (on 28 November and 5 December) to the Princess's in 1896 for *Two Little Vagabonds* (by G. R. Sims and Arthur Shirley). He described it as

Carroll at the Theatre

149

a very sensational melodrama, capitally acted. 'Dick' and 'Wally' were played by Kate Tyndall and Sydney Fairbrother, whom I guess to be about 15 and 12. Both were excellent, and the latter remarkable for the perfect realism of her acting. There was some beautiful religious dialogue, between 'Wally' and a hospital nurse, – most reverently spoken, and reverently received by the audience.

Not for the first time, Carroll had drastically underestimated the ages of the performers, as Sydney Fairbrother knew only too well: 'we were both very happily married and each the proud mother of a delightful child – mine aged twelve months and Kate's about three years' (1939, p. 122). The belief that the two little vagabonds were actually being played by young performers was presumably integral to Carroll's response, but he was not alone, as G. B. Shaw noted:

> Albeit not used to the melting mood, the critics sobbed most pathetically over Two Little Vagabonds at the Princess's. This excessive appreciation of a drop of sentiment in a thirsty land is, perhaps, natural; but in my case Nature has not been so prodigal in her gift of tears as to justify me, a prudent man, in wasting many of them on Wally and Dick. (1954, vol. II, p. 206)

Nevertheless Shaw proclaimed himself 'anxious to shew my sense of the enterprise of the management at the Princess's, where popular drama at reasonable prices has been kept going with great energy throughout the year' (p. 208), and his fellow progressive critic William Archer recommended that 'tender souls...betake themselves [there] with a plentiful reserve of pocket handkerchiefs' (1897, p. 268). Thus although Carroll's tastes were – not surprisingly – fundamentally different from Shaw's and Archer's, it is clear that in holding them he represented a sizeable proportion of the playgoing public.

Carroll's patronage of the Princess's reflects its niche as a theatre. Charles Kean's Shakespeare revivals had appealed broadly to middle-class playgoers, whereas gradually through the 1880s and much more categorically in the 1890s there was a fragmentation into the respectably popular, the rather racy 'Society' plays, and the intellectual fare of the Independent Theatre and the Stage Society. Clearly the Princess's stood for the first as – staunchly – did Lewis Carroll.

150   *Lewis Carroll and the Victorian Stage*

The Olympic Theatre, Wych Street, The Strand
Frederick Robson

Though its origins went back to Philip Astley's Olympic Pavilion of 1806, famed for its feats of horsemanship, the Olympic Theatre as Carroll knew it opened on 26 December 1849, when the *Illustrated London News* (29 December 1849) described it as commencing its first season 'in gallant style' under the management of Walter Watts. But within the year Watts had hanged himself 'in Newgate prison [having] been sentenced to ten years' transportation for defrauding the Globe Insurance Company…to nearly £80,000' (Mander and Mitchenson, 1968, p. 275). Fortunately the Olympic Theatre was set on a firmer footing by subsequent managers: William Farren, Alfred Wigan and jointly Frederick Thomas Robson and W. S. Emden. Although Robson did not enter management until 1857 as an actor he had been the basis of the theatre's success since he first appeared there in *Catching an Heiress* in March 1853. His popularity grew with his performances in burleques of *Macbeth* and *The Merchant of Venice*, but the turning point was on 24 May 1853 when

> he played Jem Baggs in *The Wandering Minstrel*, a farce in which he sang 'Villikins and his Dinah'. He drew all fashionable London for the rest of the season and set the town singing the nonsense chorus of what has now almost become a 'Folk' song. (p. 276)

Carroll's familiarity with 'Villikins and his Dinah' has already been discussed in Chapter 4, but though he seems never actually to have been to *The Wandering Minstrel* he did see Robson in a number of his other roles. Popularly known as 'The Great Little Robson', he was in Barton Baker's words 'a great genius':

> who that saw him when in the full possession of his powers can ever forget the strange-looking little man with the small body and the big head, who played upon his audience as though they had been the keys of a piano, now convulsing them with laughter as he perpetrated some outrageous drollery, now hushing them into awe-struck silence by an electrical burst of passion or pathos, or holding them midway between terror and laughter as he performed some weirdly grotesque dance? (in Mander and Mitchenson, 1968, p. 276)

Carroll first saw Robson on 13 June 1856 in a rather weak farce *A Fascinating Individual* 'written for him by the Olympic actor H. Danvers' (Sands, 1979, p. 76), in which he was hardly seen at his best: 'Robson seems to me to rant in some parts, and in others to burlesque Kean: but he has the making of a great actor'. When he returned on 15 December to see

Robson in Francis Talfourd's *Jones the Avenger*, Carroll was much more impressed: 'Robson's acting was a perfect treat'. Henry Morley rated the play, 'a whimsical farce, adapted from the French', as 'not very good in itself', but it afforded Robson 'one or two fine opportunities of burlesquing tragic passion', in particular in 'a soliloquy that awakens laughter, by combining ludicrous ideas with the display of a passion as real...as Macbeth's' (1891, p. 137).

On 21 January 1857 Carroll was at the Olympic again to see

> a fairy extravaganza, *Young and Handsome*. Robson acted the part of 'Zephyr'. He certainly has the most versatile talent of any actor I know. This is an entirely new line, his acting was a marvellous combination of grace and lightness with rich comic humour. He appeared afterwards in a poor farce *Crinoline*, which gave little opportunity for good acting.

Although the author of the piece, J. R. Planché, attested that Robson 'left me nothing to desire' in his performance (1901, p. 351), Peter Thomson has judged that 'the challenge was beyond him' and by then he was succumbing to drink (2000, p. 147).

As Thomson points out, for 'many of his contemporaries' Robson's performance in the title role of Palgrave Simpson's *Daddy Hardacre* 'was his finest dramatic achievement', requiring him as it did 'to make contact with a darker self'. Adapted from *La fille d'avare*, the play 'reaches forward in English literature to George Eliot's *Silas Marner* (1861). Daddy Hardacre loves his daughter and his money – nothing else.' (p. 140) Crabb Robinson considered 'the play of conflicting passions – love of his gold and love of his daughter – was most excellent. The rage and despair were incomparable, when he found his hoard of gold gone' (Brown ed., 1966, p. 203). When he saw the play on 22 April 1857 Carroll thought 'some of it really grand tragic acting, almost awful, though now and then unintentionally recalling bits of his former burlesqued tragedy, which rather spoiled the effect'.

Though still falling short of rhapsodic, Carroll's appreciation of Robson was increasing, reflected perhaps by his attendance at the first night of *Masaniello* by Robert Brough on 2 July 1857:

> It was capitally acted by all, though Robson of course shone most, especially as the piece was clearly written for him...Robson had tremendous work in singing and dancing. One of his songs was a parody on the new Mrs. Barney Williams, 'Yankee Fixings'. He gave several admirable burlesques on 'bits' of Kean's acting, and towards the end, where he is driven mad by poison, he went through a marvellous tissue of raving, crying, laughing, scraps of plays, snatches of songs, etc.

12. Frederick Robson as Daddy Hardacre at the Olympic Theatre

Carroll at the Theatre

153

Carroll returned on 30 November 1857 and found that 'Robson was as wonderful as ever'.

As Richard Schoch has observed:

> for audience gathered at the Olympic Theatre in 1857, the theatrical impersonations piled one on top of the other – Shakespeare, Ristori, Kean, Planché, Talfourd, Brough, and even Robson himself – would have been instantly recognisable. To be sure, the pleasure of the scene lies in Robson's powers of mimicry *and* in the audience's sense of its own theatrical literacy, its ability to 'get' the jokes. (2003, p. 79)

Few members of the Olympic audience could have rejoiced in their own sense of 'theatrical literacy' more than Carroll, who even before he had attended a theatre was invoking Kemble, Liston and Siddons in his prologue to *La Guida di Bragia* and who at his very first play compared Mrs Kean with Mrs Siddons. Carroll was himself no mean exponent of parody, an art closely akin to burlesque.

With Charles Selby's *Boots at the Swan*, Henry Morley compared Robson with another contemporary actor, Robert Keeley, as he heightened 'the extravagance of a most laughable farce...to the utmost...there is not a long face to be seen in the house' (1891, p. 170). Though by no means 'a long face', Carroll, who saw this performance of Robson's twice, considered him 'too good an actor to be wasted on such things' (12 April 1858). Carroll appears to have seen Robson in John Oxenford's *The Porter's Knot* in December 1858, in which Sampson Burr, a porter, having amassed £2000 to enable his son to train as a doctor, discovers that the spendthrift boy is already in debt to that amount: 'This little tale abounds in opportunities of pathos, relieved and often deepened by humour.' (Marston, 1890, p. 368) Unfortunately Carroll's diary for this period has not survived and Robson does not feature in the extant diaries from 9 May 1862. He died in February 1864 aged only 43. In his versatility (mime, dance, song) and the range of emotions, which he could convincingly display within a short span, Robson belonged to that strain of comic genius in which the likes of Dan Leno and Max Wall might be included. His appeal extended not only to 'all fashionable London' or what Schoch calls 'the Brahmins [several Pre-Raphaelites, Dickens and Thackeray] who crowded the Olympic' (2002, p. 109), but also to theatre historians such as himself, Molly Sands and Peter Thomson, who have essayed that most difficult of tasks – conjuring up a long deceased performer – a task for which they did not avail themselves of Carroll's numerous observations and comments. Though these burlesques have

154   *Lewis Carroll and the Victorian Stage*

found an articulate advocate in Schoch the impression recurrently given by Carroll is the inadequacy of much of Robson's material, an awareness that may have been heightened by Carroll's own attempts to breathe life into slight pieces in his own solo performances. What comes across is the sense of an almost manic determination to triumph over such material, something which not even Robson could always achieve.

Tom Taylor

Concurrently with Robson's pre-eminence at the Olympic, some plays by Tom Taylor appeared in the repertoire. Carroll saw *Retribution* on 18 June 1856 and *A Sheep in Wolf's Clothing* on 22 April 1857, but typically he did not comment on them as such. Carroll used Taylor as an intermediary to establish contact with John Tenniel and the Terrys, a function that he was remarkably well equipped to undertake, being successively Professor of English Literature at University College, London, art critic for *The Times*, Secretary to the Board of Health, and editor of *Punch*. In addition he found time to write some seventy-five plays covering the whole spectrum of Victorian drama (Nicoll, 1946, vol. II, pp. 592-4), touching, in Winton Tolles's words, 'every existing field of dramatic activity' (1940, pp. 254-5). Tom Taylor's greatest success was *The Ticket of Leave Man*, first performed at the Olympic Theatre on 27 May 1863 with H. Neville as the ill-done-by 'Lancashire Lad' Robert Brierly and Horace Wigan as Hawkshaw, who 'set a pattern, together with the playwright, for the stage detective'. The only one of Taylor's plays still to receive an occasional revival, *The Ticket of Leave Man* is commended for its 'genuine social concern' (Banham ed., 1985, pp. 12-13). Knowing what we do of Carroll it is not likely that that was the attraction that took him to see it six times. On the first occasion, on 20 July 1863, when Henry Liddon evidently broke his rule not to enter a theatre, Carroll proclaimed it 'a very clever play. Beautifully acted particularly by Neville (the hero), and Atkins (a house-breaker)'. On his third visit on 2 October Carroll was in Taylor's box and when he went for the fourth time on 31 March 1864 he noted that it was the 265th performance of the play. In the end *The Ticket of Leave Man* ran for 406 performances, so in attending it six times and prevailing on Liddon to accompany him once Carroll was subscribing to one of the outstanding successes of the mid-Victorian stage.

As Winton Tolles says, 'the tremendous popularity of *The Ticket of Leave Man* and the favourable reception accorded *The Hidden Hand* and *Settling Day* re-established Taylor in the position...of house dramatist for the Olympic' (1940, p. 207). These two plays had the great advantage of Kate Terry in the cast playing opposite Henry Neville. Their stage partnership continued in *The Serf*, already considered in Chapter 6, which Carroll attended four times. In 1866 Kate Terry appeared in two older plays: Sheridan Knowles's *The Hunchback* and Bulwer Lytton's *Money*, both of which Carroll attended. The three other Terry sisters were also to be seen at the Olympic: Ellen (Mrs Watts) in *The Hunchback* on 20 June, providing with her sister 'about the best [acting] I have ever seen', Florence in *Nell, or the Old Curiosity Shop* (in Andrew Halliday's adaptation) and Marion [Polly] in Taylor's *Lady Clancarty* and John Oxenford's *The Two Orphans*.

In the Taylor play on 3 August 1874 Carroll thought 'Polly's acting was very nice, but it is not exactly a part that suits her, being too pert and forward for her refined and quiet style of acting'; in the Oxenford on 5 October 1878 'Marion was a delicious blind girl. Lizzie Coote had a "fast" part, which she played only too truthfully.' Lizzie Coote had previously appeared at the Olympic as 'a pretty...[if] perhaps a little too sentimental' Oliver on 9 July 1878 in Cyril Searle's *Nancy Sikes*, 'one of the most detestably realistic plays I ever saw'. In the same letter of 24 February 1880 to Tom Taylor Carroll confided: 'I'm afraid Lizzie will never rise to the higher grades of the profession. She has been too long in the burlesque and pantomime business to have much chance of ever being a refined actress.' But the Terry sisters were refined actresses and Carroll was appalled when any one of them was anything less.

During the score or so years in which Carroll patronised it the Olympic had passed through different phases: the heyday of burlesque with the *tour de force* performances of Robson, the plays of house dramatist Tom Taylor and the acting of the Terry sisters, principally Kate and Marion (Polly). Each was a high point for Victorian playgoers and Carroll supported all three.

The Adelphi Theatre, The Strand

Even in 1880 Henry James described the Adelphi as 'a fog-haunted house' in which 'on winter nights the murky atmosphere of the Strand is as thick within the theatre as outside it' (Wade ed., 1957, p. 151). Like so many London theatres the Adelphi went through several changes of name and successive alterations for many of which the architect playwright Samuel Beazley was responsible (Garlick, 2003). Carroll's first visit on 10 June 1856 was to a triple bill featuring the actor Edward Wright. He returned

156 *Lewis Carroll and the Victorian Stage*

on 13 December 1856 to see Boucicault's *Janet Pride*, a particular feature of which, as noted in Chapter 4, was

> the reproduction in the last act of the Central Criminal Court, with all the forms and furnishings of an Old Bailey trial, wonderfully accurate as it is, will be remembered among the dexterous feats of stage-appointment for which our theatres in these days are remarkable. (Morley, 1891, p. 93)

Furthermore the play was 'a fine vehicle...for [Ben] Webster [the manager] and [joint lessee] Madame Céleste' (Webster, 1969, p. 76) and with a drunken husband, forgery, a tottering wife and a dying infant, Carroll, though still very much a novice theatregoer, could confidently describe it after attending the performance on 13 December 1856 as 'a regular Adelphi drama'.

What is generally known as the second Adelphi Theatre was opened on 27 December 1858, still under the management of Benjamin Webster, but it was not until 16 July 1864 that Carroll went there, again to see *Janet Pride*. During the 1860s triple bills were still a regular feature at the Adelphi and Carroll saw pieces by H. J. Byron. John Maddison Morton, actor J. B. Buckstone and the theatre's lessee Ben Webster.

On 21 December 1865 Carroll availed himself of the opportunity to watch Joseph Jefferson in *Rip Van Winkle*, co-authored by the actor and Boucicault, and acclaimed it as 'one of the best pieces of acting I have seen for years'. The American actor recorded in his memoirs that he received 'a cordial welcome' in the play, which 'was entirely new to the English public, and its success secured for it a run of one hundred and seventy nights' (1949, p. 238). Though he did not remark upon them, the abundance of children (little Hendrick the innkeeper's son and Rip's own little daughter Meenie) no doubted added to Carroll's enjoyment. The 27 June 1870 found Carroll at a performance of *The Robust Invalid*, an adaptation of Molière's *Le Malade Imaginaire* by Charles Reade, who like Carroll combined an Oxford fellowship (at Magdalen College) with an intense interest in the theatre. The cast included George Vining, Florence Terry and Reade's beloved Laura Seymour, but it failed 'involv[ing] the author in a loss of four to five thousand pounds' (Coleman, 1903, p. 321).

Pantomimes

Benjamin Webster's thirty years as manager of the Adelphi ended in 1874 when he was succeeded by F. B. Chatterton, who in 1878 handed over to Agostino and Stefano Gatti. After Webster's departure Carroll's patronage

Carroll at the Theatre   157

of the Adelphi extended only to pantomime, beginning with *The Children in the Wood* by E. L. Blanchard on 13 January 1875. Although Blanchard unquestionably became Carroll's favourite author of pantomimes he actually described this one as 'poor', though when he had seen it previously at Drury Lane on 18 January 1873 he had rated it 'good, especially the dancing of the Vokes family'. In contrast Blanchard himself noted in his diary 'Adelphi pantomime, *Children in the Wood*, goes off well' (Scott and Howard eds, vol. II, p. 445).

Undeterred, Carroll returned to the Adelphi to see Blanchard's *Little Goody Two Shoes* (twice), *Little Red Riding Hood* (twice) and *Robin Hood and his Merry Little Men* (six times). A (if not *the*) reason for Carroll's enthusiasm was that these pantomimes were performed entirely by children. Thus his very full account of *Little Goody Two Shoes* on Saturday 13 January 1877:

> [I] took Evelyn [Dubourg] with me to the afternoon pantomime at the Adelphi, *Goody Two Shoes*, acted entirely by children. It was a really charming performance. The two Grattan children acted 'Goody' and 'Little Boy Blue': they seemed clever, but hardly worth the excessive praise they have received. Little Bertie Coote (about 10) was Clown, a wonderfully clever little fellow: and Carrie (about 8) was Columbine, a very pretty graceful little thing – in a few years time she will be just *the* child to act 'Alice', if it is ever dramatised. The Harlequin was a little girl named Gilchrist, one of the most beautiful children, in face and figure, that I have ever seen. I must get an opportunity of photographing her. Two twin sisters, Bella and Weevie Goddard, sang deliciously: but there was a more marvellous singer still, a child named ['Sinclair' crossed out] who acted 'Fairy Good-Nature', and whose voice, though not sweet, seemed to ring through the theatre. Little Bertie Coote, singing 'Hot Codlings', was curiously like the pictures of Grimaldi.

Edward Wakeling notes that 'a photograph of Connie Gilchrist attributed to Dodgson exists (Chicago Art Institute)' (Wakeling ed., vol. 7, p. 14, n. 8), but a little later she caught the eye of James McNeill Whistler (as she did of Frederick Leighton), who painted a portrait originally entitled 'A Girl in Gold', later changed to 'Connie Gilchrist – the Golden Girl', in which she is depicted 'in the short yellow tunic and high boots she wore in her "slipping-rope dance"' (Wyndham, 1951, p. 90; Whistler's portrait is reproduced opp. p. 80). Exhibited at the Grosvenor Gallery in 1879, the painting was bought by Henry Labouchere and eventually made its way to the Metropolitan Museum in New York. When it was painted Connie Gilchrist, the daughter of a civil engineer, had pursued her career with great determination to the Gaiety Theatre, where she attracted the

158   *Lewis Carroll and the Victorian Stage*

admiration of the seventh Earl of Orkney whom she married in 1892 and of Harry Furniss (1901, vol.I, p.66). Connie Gilchrist must stand as one of the foremost examples of Carroll's case in favour of the prospects of one sort and another offered by the stage to child actresses.

Just as he relied on the advice of friends in choosing which plays to see, Carroll encouraged them to go to *Little Goody Two Shoes*, writing to his publisher Alexander Macmillan on 4 February: 'Have you taken your young people (or your young "person" – for I suppose Olive still considers herself young) to see that most charming performance, the "Children's Pantomime" at the Adelphi?' (Cohen and Gandolfo eds, 1982, p. 134) On 11 February 1877 Carroll wrote to Gertrude Chataway, inviting her to attend *Little Goody Two Shoes* with him: 'It is all acted by children (there are nearly 100 in it) and two of them, the little Clown and Columbine, are friends of mine, and very nice children they are – and wonderfully clever.' In the event Evelyn and Olive Brooke, the daughters of the Revd Stopford Augustus Brooke, prolific author of books on literature and theology, accompanied Carroll. This was one of the occasions on which Carroll enlisted the assistance of Macmillans in securing his tickets. His letter of 2 March 1877 is typically detailed, even including a diagram: 'I want them dress-circle, front seats, about the place I have put a *. Two of them are for children under 12 (I mention in case children may be "half-price").' He added: 'We cannot arrive much before the thing begins – so, unless such seats are *numbered and reserved*, it would be better to get stalls (near middle of second or third row) but I'm afraid little children wouldn't see so well from the stalls.' (p. 135) Not unusually, Carroll's consideration for his young companions placed considerable demands on others.

Carroll saw *Little Red Riding Hood* on consecutive days in October 1877, when, presumably because it was outside the usual season for such entertainments, in the evening the pantomime shared the bill with Boucicault's *After Dark*. The Coote family was well represented in both: Lizzie Coote 'as "Area Jack", not a nice part for her, though she did it very cleverly' in the Boucicault and 'Carrie and Bertie Coote, as good as ever' and Connie Gilchrist 'that most delicious of Harlequins'. Having attended the evening performance on the 2 October, Carroll returned for the matinee of 'the Children's Pantomime' the next day, remarking that 'the Pantomime was a good deal longer than at night', though the point presumably was that it was a good deal *shorter at night* because of the double bill and the increased concern for the hours during which children were employed in theatres. As Tracy Davis has pointed out, matinees were partly a response to this (1986, p. 132). For Carroll there was the bonus of meeting Connie Gilchrist and her mother in the dressing-room afterwards.

Carroll at the Theatre   159

Carroll attended *Robin Hood and his Merry Little Men* six times during the 1877-8 season, taking a succession of child friends about whom he recorded more information than he did about the performances, suggesting that his priority may have been entertaining and enjoying the company of his guests rather than taking any special delight in the pantomime which on his first visit on 31 December 1877 he described as 'pretty, but not at all funny' with 'Connie Gilchrist, and Bertie and Carrie Coote' appearing 'as usual'. The *Illustrated London News* (29 December 1877) remarked that 'the pantomime of this year, like that of last, is performed by children...The performance is completely successful.'

During Benjamin Webster's lengthy management of the Adelphi Theatre the bill had been traditional in a somewhat dated way. The succeeding managements of Chatterton and Agostino and Stefano Gatti clearly tapped a huge well of public interest with their children's pantomimes, Carroll's enthusiasm for which was in no way singular, indeed, as Hugues Lebailly has suggested in the context 'of the universality of this fad for child prodigies', Carroll was often 'much more objective and balanced...than many' (1999, p. 29).

The Covent Garden Theatre, Bow Street, Westminster and
The Theatre Royal, Drury Lane, Catherine Street, Westminster

Having lost their patents, dating from 1660, in 1843 Covent Garden and Drury Lane struggled to find their niche in the new world of Victorian London's burgeoning theatre. Like many sightseers Carroll had gone 'to see the remains of Covent Garden Theatre' following the disastrous fire of 5 March 1856, but, although it reopened on 15 May 1858, Carroll did not enter the new theatre until 25 January 1865 and then for a pantomime, *Cinderella*, except to make one of his (very rare) opera visits (to *Norma*) on 2 April 1864. Even at *Cinderella* he had to endure 'a very dull English opera called *Constance*' by Frederick Clay and T. W. Robertson before he could enjoy that 'capital Pantomime' in which he judged that Clare Denvil, though only sixteen, had 'lost the beauty which, according to the photographs, she had as a child'. Carroll's intermittent visits to Covent Garden (one each in 1870 and 1878) concluded with *Jack and the Beanstalk* on 30 December 1878, 'which I chose because Lizzie Coote is acting "Quicksilver" in it...The Pantomime was gorgeous, but dull: Lizzie had but a poor part, specially as she could sing none of her songs, having a bad cold.' The pantomime was the work of Frank W. Green. several of whose other pieces Carroll had seen at the Theatre Royal, Brighton, during the 1870s. In Carroll's estimation Green was second only to

160 *Lewis Carroll and the Victorian Stage*

Blanchard, who also attended *Jack and the Beanstalk* at Covent Garden and described it as 'a brilliant spectacle, but the music-hall element very depressing' (Scott and Howard eds, 1891, vol. II, p. 483). Blanchard was particularly inclined to detect and disapprove of music-hall elements in pantomime, but his emphasis on the spectacle was borne out by Charles Eyre Pascoe in his *Dramatic Notes 1879*: 'Except, however, as a stage spectacle in which respect it merited warm praise, *Jack and the Beanstalk* called for no particular notice' (1883, pp. 1-2). Covent Garden and Drury Lane, which in their heyday had competed for the honours of the classical stage, now did so for supremacy in pantomime.

At the time of the Shakespeare tercentenary in 1864 Drury Lane still had pretensions as the 'National Theatre' with the veteran Samuel Phelps appearing as Falstaff in *Henry IV i*. Carroll, who had signally failed to see Phelps at Sadler's Wells, went twice (on 1 and 7 April) and though he considered that 'Phelps as Falstaff, and [Walter] Montgomery as Hotspur were about the best...the gem of the whole, to my mind was Lady Mortimer's Welsh song, most charmingly sung by Miss Edith Wynne'. At least Carroll, who had long prided himself on his knowledge of illustrious actors of the past, had seen Phelps and done so in one of his great roles. Phelps appeared as Posthumous in *Cymbeline* at Drury Lane on 28 October, when Carroll seized the opportunity to see Helen Faucit making a rare return to the stage as Imogen, one of her most renowned roles (Carlisle, 2000, pp. 211-12). Helen Faucit had retired in 1851 when she married Theodore Martin, later Prince Albert's biographer; the Martins lived at 31 Onslow Square, Carroll's Uncle Skeffington at 101. It seems possible that Carroll's diary entry for 28 June 1872 refers to her: 'I dined with Uncle Skeffington and was sorry to find Mrs. Martin ill.'

Though he had taken the opportunity provided by the tercentenary to see these two celebrated Shakespearian actors, Carroll can hardly be described as an enthusiast for the classical repertoire. On 7 July 1875 he did go to see the Italian tragedian Tomasso Salvini in *Hamlet* ('acted in Italian, which largely diminished the pleasure of hearing it'), but the lure of the pantomime was irresistible. He delighted in Blanchard's annual Drury Lane offerings: *Little King Pippin* (1866-7), *Faw, Fee, Fo, Fum; or, Jack the Giant Killer* (1867-8), the aforementioned *The Children in the Wood* (1872-3), *Aladdin, or the Wonderful Lamp* (1874-5) (Booth ed., 1976) and *Cinderella* (1878-9), which he saw twice. He wrote of *Little King Pippin* on 17 January 1866 as 'the most beautiful spectacle I ever saw in Pantomime. Percy Roselle's acting was quite the gem of the whole thing', though he learnt from Kate Terry, who accompanied him along with her sisters Marion and Florence, that 'he is 18 or 19' rather than 'about 8' as Carroll supposed. Not that the stage lacked genuine child

Carroll at the Theatre

161

performers for, as *The Times* review (27 December 1865) informs us, the Court of King Pippin was 'remarkable for one of those vast assemblages of juvenile performers, for which the Drury Lane pantomimes are famous. The little king...rules no less than 200 subjects' and in the ballet scene of *Harlequin Fortunatus* 'a hundred coryphées descend in a zig-zag line'. All these delights and transformation scenes too, but as always with Blanchard there was 'a moral allegory, his object on this occasion being to show that perfect happiness is by no means the necessary consequence of an ample fortune'.

Though it began at 'The Giant's Causeway by Moonlight' with 'The Monster Meeting of The Giants', *Faw, Fee, Fo, Fum; or, Jack the Giant Killer* also included 'The Cornish Drolls by Ninety Little Funny Fellows', the 'Grand Ballet by One Hundred Coryphées' (Blanchard, 1867, pp. 3-4), 'An Ice Scene in Russia' (Carroll's favourite) and 'Paris in Miniature, 1867...illustrated by 200 children' (p. 33). For all their visual effects, Blanchard's pantomimes were accomplished pieces of writing. As A. E. Wilson says, though 'Blanchard was not so addicted to the punning habit as were some of his rivals...on occasion he could turn out a pun with the best of them' as in the congress of giants: 'Og: I, that Giant Og propose that we eat up all things, / Go, the whole hog, in fact, with large and small things.' (nd, p. 67)

Edward Leman Blanchard, born in 1820 the son of actor William, was a gifted, hard-working, rather under-paid dramatist and journalist, who became more and more perturbed by the escalating intrusion of music hall into pantomimes. From 1869 to 1879 the Vokes family were increasingly prominent in the Drury Lane pantomimes; in *Aladdin* (on 6 January 1875) which Carroll thought 'dull as a whole, but worth seeing for the dancing of the Vokes family'. The Vokes family were the children of a theatrical costumier located at 19 Henrietta Street: Frederick (b. 1846), Jessie (b. 1851), Victoria (b. 1853) and Rosina (b. 1854). The Drury Lane 1878-9 pantomime *Cinderella*, which Carroll saw twice (6 and 20 January 1879) and rated 'good', seemed set to be another success for the proven formula with Blanchard furnishing 'the management with one of his usually clever and amusing stage-representations of fairy legend....[and] the principal characters...entrusted to members of the Vokes family', but it 'suddenly and unexpectedly closed' on 4 February 1879 (C. E. Pascoe, 1883, p. 5). Drury Lane pantomimes were hugely expensive with 'ordinary working expenses...never less than £1,000 per week' (Wagner, 1881, p. 32). Naturally the Vokes were particularly well paid and Frederick's refusal 'to consent to the reduction of his own and his sisters' salaries' was regarded as 'cruelty...thus allowing hundreds of poor *employés* to be thrown out of their expected work' (*Theatre* 1 March 1879). The problem was not so

162   *Lewis Carroll and the Victorian Stage*

much the pantomime itself as the 'exceptionally barren autumn' that preceded it, as a result of which the lessee F. B. Chatterton was '£32,000 in debt'. With Chatterton forced to close his pantomime (and give up his tenancy of Drury Lane) 'the field [was] clear to the rival pantomime at Covent Garden, then being run by the brothers A. and S. Gatti' (Wilson, 1934, p. 179). Thus in the pantomime rivalry between Drury Lane and Covent Garden those theatres were led by Chatterton and the Gattis, both of whom had made a success of child pantomimes at the Adelphi. Under Augustus Harris, who took over Drury Lane in 1879 aged 'only 27' (Macqueen-Pope, 1945, p. 284) the pantomimes became renowned for their lavish scenery and music-hall stars. Carroll never attended one.

Carroll certainly endorsed the popular enthusiasm for pantomimes, but with certain caveats. He was chary of the harlequinade, which he considered liable to be offensive to him (if not to the generality of the audience) and he left before it began on both of his visits to *Cinderella* at Drury Lane in 1879: ' Jan. 6. (M)...*Cinderella* was good: we left before the Harlequinade, which the papers condemn as very coarse'. His preference was for the decidedly moral offerings of Frank Green and E. L. Blanchard. He delighted in the spectacular scenery, including the transformation scenes and of course the masses of stage children, of whom according to Blanchard 'two or three thousand...[were] annually engaged in London for the Christmas entertainments'. Blanchard, like Carroll, was in no doubt of the importance to their families of this 'means of obtaining extra food and clothing at an inclement season of the year' (in Wagner, 1881, p. 34).

The Theatre Royal, Haymarket

The Little Theatre in the Hay-Market, as it was originally known, was built by John Potter, a carpenter, who 'hoped to obtain a licence in spite of the Patent Theatres but was unable to do so' (Mander and Mitchenson, 1963, p. 96). Nevertheless the theatre gradually achieved a level of legitimacy and was rebuilt to the designs of John Nash at a cost of £20,000 opening on 4 July 1821 with a revival of *The Rivals* by R. B. Sheridan. In 1853 John Baldwin Buckstone took over the management from Benjamin Webster. Buckstone himself was the author of the 'pantomime *The Butterfly's Ball and the Grasshopper's Feast, or Harlequin and the Genius of Spring*', which Carroll considered 'very good, and some of the scenery as gorgeous as the Princess's' when he saw

Carroll at the Theatre   163

it as part of a triple bill on 17 January 1856. He did not return until 1864, but became something of a regular for the next three years.

E. A. Sothern

On 16 May 1864, when no less than four pieces were performed, '*the piece of the evening*' was Tom Robertson's *David Garrick* 'in which Sothern acted the hero capitally, and Chippendale the old father quite as well, the heroine was a new actress from Manchester, Miss Nelly Moore'. Though, as Robertson acknowledged, his play was 'Adapted from the French of "Sullivan," which was founded on a German Dramatisation of a pretended Incident in Garrick's Life' (1889, vol. I, p. 147), it was to be staged in the same style ('practicable' doors, 'fire in fireplace, to burn' p. 149) as his so called 'Cup and Saucer' comedies which the Bancrofts had made the trademark of the Prince of Wales's Theatre. Sothern's trademark was the character of Lord Dundreary, 'a vile caricature of a vain nobleman, intensely ignorant, and extremely indolent', in Tom Taylor's *Our American Cousin*, which he had first played in 1858 at the Haymarket and which the *Athenaeum* (16 November 1861) described as 'certainly the *funniest* thing in the world'. Sothern's biographer T. Edgar Pemberton recalled that 'it was through a chance conversation with the adapter [Robertson]...that Sothern decided that *Garrick* should be the successor of *Dundreary...Garrick* became one of the most successful of his impersonations' (1890, p. 69). W. H. Chippendale was renowned for his performances in old comedies, his masterpiece being Sir Peter Teazle in Sheridan's *The School for Scandal*, in which Carroll saw him on 20 December 1864. Nellie Moore, the new actress from Manchester, had there become 'the first romance in...the life of Henry Irving' (Irving, 1951, p. 111) in whose pocket book her photograph pasted back-to-back with his was found after his death in October 1905. Carroll saw Sothern in two – what would now be described as 'spin-off'– plays *My Brother Sam* (by John Oxenford) in which he played Lord Dundreary's brother the Hon. Sam Slingsby and *Lord Dundreary Married and Done For* (by H. J. Byron), finding him 'very clever, but not equal to Dundreary' in the former (5 July 1865) and 'as good as ever' in the latter (27 June 1866). Sothern as Dundreary and related characters was the Haymarket's great attraction in the 1860s.

Carroll's return to the Haymarket in 1867 for the *Living Miniatures* has already been relayed in Chapters 4 and 7, but when he went to see Sothern in H. J. Byron's *The English Gentleman* on 20 July 1871 his

164   *Lewis Carroll and the Victorian Stage*

concern was for children in the audience rather than those on stage. He had offered to take the Cecil (Marquis of Salisbury's) children, but they had been unable to accept, which was just as well as Carroll resolved that 'in future I shall not take any children to a London theatre without ascertaining that the pieces acted are unobjectionable'.

W. S. Gilbert

During the 1870s the Haymarket became the showcase for a dramatist to some of whose lyrics Carroll did later take exception: W. S. Gilbert. Having dined with Alexander Macmillan at the Garrick Club, at which though never a member he was a not infrequent guest, Carroll saw *The Wicked World An Original Fairy Comedy* on 8 January 1873 and dismissed it summarily: 'I did not like it much.' The play starred Madge Kendal (as Selene a Fairy Queen), sister of dramatist T. W. Robertson, now married to William Kendal for whom she always insisted a suitable part was found. In this case Buckstone sent for her and told her 'that my husband was not suited for the part [of Sir Ethais] for which he had been cast and in that play it was an appalling part'. Appalling though the part was, the formidable Mrs Kendal insisted 'I do not play opposite anyone but my husband' (1933, pp. 168-9). Buckstone and Gilbert gave in. Dutton Cook found what he called the 'condition precedent' upon which the whole play depended 'perplexing', the long speeches tedious, certain 'observations upon the nature and results of earthly love...scarcely decorous', and the 'blank verse...unillumed by poetic thought', but he considered 'Miss Robertson', as he called her, 'well merited the applause her efforts obtained from the audience' (1883, pp. 171-3). Gilbert certainly agreed; he dedicated the play to her.

On 10 October 1876 Carroll saw Gilbert's *Dan'l Druce, Blacksmith*, which had opened the previous month. Another variant on the *Silas Marner* story, Carroll found 'much of the plot...absurdly improbable', but commended Hermann Vezin in the title role and Marion Terry 'as tender and graceful as possible' in the only female role in which Joseph Knight commended her 'quietude of manner' (1893, p. 144). In the audience one night was Marion Terry's eight-year-old niece Kate, who as the mother of John Gielgud ensured the continuation of the Terry dynasty for another distinguished generation. She was seeing her first play and over seventy years later recalled 'Dorothy's [Marion Terry's character] dove-grey dress, and her sweet face and gentle clear voice' (Terry Gielgud, 1953, p. 46). As an actress Marion Terry was gentle and genteel, qualities which

Carroll at the Theatre 165

Carroll admired, but when he saw her as Galatea, the role created by Madge Kendal, in the revival of *Pygmalion and Galatea* on 10 March 1877 he found her 'very sweet and charming, though perhaps a little wanting in *vis*', a quality which Lizzie Coote evidently had in abundance. With *Engaged* Marion Terry got the opportunity to create her own Gilbertian lead as Belinda Treherne and in doing so to develop what Jane Stedman has called

> a new principle of comic acting...that of playing comically without letting the audience see that the actor knows he is funny. As Belinda Marion Terry demonstrated an absolute command of this technique, uttering her lines with an irresistible seriousness which surprised reviewers who thought of her only as an *ingénue*. (1996, p. 151)

When he saw the play on 14 January 1878 Carroll detected what was going on: 'Marion Terry's mock heroics are delicious...She and Mr. Harold Kyrle seem to me to be the only two who carry out the author's idea, and let you see, through all their mock earnestness, that they are burlesquing the real thing.'

The Bancrofts

When Buckstone concluded his management of the Haymarket in 1878 his immediate successor was the American actor and manager John Sleeper Clarke, but his tenure was no more than an interregnum prior to the succession of Squire and Marie Bancroft in 1880. During the preceding fifteen years the Bancrofts were synonymous with the Prince of Wales's Theatre, which they had taken over in its former guise of the Queen's Theatre, Tottenham Court Street and transformed into one of the most elegant playhouses of its day. Though the realistic domestic comedies of T. W. Robertson were the mainstay of their repertoire the Bancrofts also included plays by Bulwer Lytton. H. J. Byron and W. S. Gilbert, all of which were treated in the same realistic style. Just what sort of clientele the Bancrofts' decorous auditorium and innovative staging attracted is still a subject for debate (see Davis and Emeljanow, 2001, pp. 145-7), but Carroll's presence vouchsafes its respectability. On his first visit to see Robertson's *Society* on 17 January 1866 Carroll took more note of the performances by Bancroft, Miss Wilton, as he still called Marie Bancroft, and John Hare than of Robertson's play or its scenery. Indeed it was their acting in the burlesque, H. J. Byron's *Little Don Giovanni* that pleased him most: 'All these, except Mr. Bancroft, had

166 *Lewis Carroll and the Victorian Stage*

good parts in the burlesque. Miss Wilton the hero, Mr. Clarke Leporello, Mr. Montgomery a policeman, and Mr. Hare a peasant girl.' In Robertson's *Caste* on 23 April 1867, though, he thought the third act when Polly (Miss Wilton) rehearses an operatic scene as a means of breaking the news to her sister 'that her husband supposed to be dead, has returned...[by] far the best bit', he seems to have delighted especially in the lower-class comedy of 'Hare, as Sam Gerridge, a gas-fitter, and Honey, as the drunken old father'. When he saw *Ours* on 19 December 1879 a dozen and more years had elapsed since Robertson's play had first been performed, but the revival had the inestimable advantage of Marion Terry as Blanche Haye: 'The whole play was a treat of uniformly good acting. Marion showed depths of pathos, beyond what I had thought her capable of.'

The Prince of Wales's had also afforded Carroll the opportunity to see Ellen Terry in Bulwer Lytton's *Money* of which he wrote after his first visit (of three) on 10 June 1875: 'It [*Money*] was one of the best pieces of acting I have seen for a long time. Mrs Bancroft as "Lady Franklin," and Mr. Honey as "Graves," were particularly good, but Mrs Watts as "Clara Douglas" was a perfect treat.' Dutton Cook commended Ellen Terry for the blend of 'grace and pathos' in 'the scenes with *Evelyn* in which she rejects his suit and relates the story of her father's sorrows...skilfully and powerfully' (1883, p. 285). When he returned on 12 July Carroll was disappointed that 'Mrs. Watts did not play', but his loyalty was rewarded on 22 July when Ellen Terry acted. Carroll did not go to see Ellen Terry in her outstanding success as Portia in the disappointingly short run (a mere thirty-six performances) of *The Merchant of Venice* from 17 April 1875, though as noted in Chapter 6 the actress had written to him offering a box. He saw her once more at the Prince of Wales's on 7 January 1876 in the Tom Taylor and Charles Reade play about the actress Peg Woffington, *Masks and Faces*, the ending of which Mrs Bancroft had had re-written so that the audience 'love Peg for her noble conduct, and weep with her in her suffering' (1889, p. 225). Without recourse to re-writing, Ellen Terry's performance as Mabel Vane 'move[d] the audience deeply, and secure[d] very hearty and well-deserved applause' (Cook, 1883, p. 298) and even-handedly Carroll wrote of the 'rare treat to see two such actresses as Mrs Bancroft and Ellen Terry in one piece'.

By the end of the decade Ellen Terry was joining forces with Henry Irving at the Lyceum and the Bancrofts were preparing to move to the Haymarket. Their main motive was to be able to accommodate 'the shoals' (Bancrofts, 1889, p. 284) of people who were turned away from the Prince of Wales's with its modest capacity of 600 and to accommodate them at the Haymarket, redesigned by C. J. Phipps to take 1159 seated. It was not only a matter of increased capacity. Bancroft identified 'the chief features in my rough outlines of the new theatre, made practical by Mr. Phipps' as creating 'the proscenium in the form of a large gold frame, and the abolition of the pit' (p. 294). Though the significance of the four-sided picture-frame proscenium has been noted and discussed by theatre historians, it was the abolition of the pit that prompted the strongest contemporary reaction: 'To take the events of that opening night in proper sequence. I must begin with the Pit Question, and the riot that occurred when the curtain rose' (p. 297), wrote Bancroft, but he had social and economic arguments on his side and the removal of the pit seats from the front of the stalls to the back prevailed.

Carroll visited the Haymarket under the Bancrofts only twice. On both occasions he saw Robertson's *School* (Marion Terry as Bella), but in hugely different circumstances. The first on 25 June 1880 was in high summer; the second on 18 January 1881 was on what the Bancrofts called 'Black Tuesday'. The latter occasion, on which Robertson's play was preceded by Saville Rowe's (aka Clement Scott) *The Vicarage,* provides a vivid illustration of the obstacles encountered by actors and audiences alike on an exceptionally severe winter night even in the heart of London. In a letter to a friend, Mrs Bancroft described the streets piled high with snow despite which 'every member of the company reached the theatre safely, several having come long distances'. When the curtain rose she could see 'the strangest picture...There were seven people in the stalls with topcoats, mufflers, fur cloaks, and large hoods...hardly anyone in the balcony' and elsewhere, including the occupants (if there were any) of the now distant pit, 'nothing but a row of noses'. The patrons in the stalls were so close that her 'gaze met the expression on their faces' and she 'could not restrain' her 'laughter any longer' whilst they like 'figures from Madame Tussaud's' made 'not a sound of applause or laughter throughout the evening'. Whilst the actors had naturally felt a professional obligation to get to the theatre, the audience 'must have loved the drama to come at all' (1889, pp. 312-13). Carroll had passed this ultimate test and furthermore had done so with two female companions, thereby being personally responsible for the presence of a significant proportion of those assembled:

We had a private conveyance, which Mrs. Drury hires occasionally: otherwise we might have had difficulty in getting a cab, in such deep snow. I took Minnie and Mrs. Thorold to the Haymarket, where *The Vicarage* and *School* were charmingly played to a nearly empty house (160 stalls having about 16 occupants). Marion Terry looking sweeter than ever. The new "Mr. Krux" is a Mr. Brookfield (an old Westminster boy, Paget tells me): so there

168   *Lewis Carroll and the Victorian Stage*

are at least three gentlemen in the piece, Mr. A. Cecil, Mr. Coulson (alias Conway), and this one. Probably Mr. Bancroft is one too.

Carroll's concern for the gentlemanly status of the cast clearly far exceeded any he may have had about the inclement climate.

Tree and after

Herbert Beerbohm Tree, the second son of Julius Beerbohm – a German merchant who settled in London – and his English wife, brought an aura of European mystery and panache to the London stage untainted by any trace of modesty (false or otherwise), as his entry in *The Green Room Book* reveals:

> he firmly established his reputation as an actor of the first rank; became lessee of the Comedy Theatre, 1887, opening with 'The Red Lamp'; in September, 1887, became manager of Haymarket Theatre, which he conducted with brilliant success for ten years (1906, p. 340).

Carroll managed to resist the attractions of Tree at the Haymarket until 30 April 1892 when he went 'to see Mr. Beerbohm Tree as "Hamlet". It was a real treat: Mrs. Tree was good as "Ophelia", and Mr. Kemble excellent as "Polonius". Mr. Tree emphasises the *love* of Hamlet for Ophelia.' When three years later Tree committed his thoughts on *Hamlet* to paper he did indeed have a good deal to say about the Prince of Denmark's relationship with 'the fair Ophelia', especially in the 'nunnery scene' which appeared to him to 'have all the clearness of a blue sky. It should be the endeavour of the actor (with the aid of such imaginative stage business) to make it so clear.' (1913, pp. 136-7) Even Tree's biographer Hesketh Pearson conceded: 'Where he failed completely was in purely romantic work, of which he gave the worst example in 1892 when he produced *Hamlet*.'(1956, p. 62) True to his word Tree did introduce 'stage business', though of a rather crass kind, to make his interpretation clear:

> Tree emphasized the sentimental lover-like aspect of Hamlet by returning quietly to kiss a tress of Ophelia's hair after the scene in which he rages at her, by reappearing alone with an armful of flowers for her grave after the quarrel with Laertes at her burial, and by dying to soft music as the chorus of angels sang him to rest and brought the curtain down. (p. 63)

Carroll at the Theatre

169

Maud Holt, whom Tree had married in 1884, was typical of the new generation of actresses, 'a thorough Greek scholar and musician '(*The Green Room Book*, 1906, p. 341) thanks to her education at The Queen's College in Harley Street (Foulkes, 1997, pp. 152-4). Though assessments of her acting ability were very variable, Maud Tree recalled that during the *Hamlet* production she was 'so intensely happy in the theatre' (Beerbohm, 1920, p. 74), unaware that out of it her husband was setting up a second home with May Pinney (Bingham, 1978, p. 51). As well as fathering two families offstage, Tree for some unaccountable reason also introduced numerous children on to the stage though even Maud confessed: 'I forget the object of so many children in Herbert's production of *Hamlet*, but there they undoubtedly were.' (p. 74) For Carroll children ('little eyases') in *Hamlet* must have been an element in what he described as 'a real treat'.

Carroll's visit to *Trilby* on 14 December 1895 was informed by his concern for two young women. It was an opportunity to see his protégée Dorothea Baird 'beautiful...intelligent and unaffected', though 'not yet an accomplished actress' (Archer, 1896, p. 335) in the title role and to try yet again to advance the career of Minna Quin whom Tree had agreed to see, which he did as Svengali 'a make-up in which I [Carroll] should not have in the least recognised him'. On 28 April 1897 Tree opened Her Majesty's Theatre (directly opposite his old one), which Shaw acclaimed as 'quite the handsomest theatre in London' (1954, vol. III, p. 117), but Carroll never went there.

Carroll did return to the Haymarket, for what we have already noted was his last theatre visit ever, on 20 November 1897 when he saw *The Little Minister*, which J. M. Barrie had rather belatedly (Hammerton, 1929, p. 191) adapted from his own novel and with which Cyril Maude opened his regime at the Haymarket, where it ran for 320 performances. Maude, who played the Revd Gavin Dishart ('The Little Minister'), believed that the play 'would not have drawn such large congregations for so great a number of nights had it not been for my wife's performance as "Babbie"' (1903, p. 203) and W. H. Leverton had no doubt that: 'She *was* "Lady Babbie,"...and, I think Sir James [Barrie] will agree' (1932, p. 77). William Archer did not: 'Miss Winifred Emery was a charming but scarcely ideal Babbie. Some of her effects were a little too obvious.' (1898, p. 331) and Shaw wrote of her 'play[ing] with her part like a child...amusing herself and the audience unboundedly' (1954, vol. III, p. 248). Carroll, who at one time might have demurred about a performance in which the actress evidently ignored his rule of disregarding the audience, proclaimed that: 'Mrs Maude was superb' and E. Gertrude Thomson, his companion at that matinee, confirmed that: 'He was

170   *Lewis Carroll and the Victorian Stage*

charmed with *The Little Minister*. Miss Winifred Emery, by her enchanting personation, won his warmest admiration.' (Cohen ed., 1989, p. 235)

It seems from descriptions of Tree's stage business as Hamlet and Winifred Emery's performance as Lady Babbie that a rather obvious style was to the fore, but perhaps Carroll, as he progressed through his sixties, found that more of a benefit (in terms of hearing and seeing) than an irritation and as a young performer himself he had after all relished audience approval. It was a reflection of the Haymarket's enduring status and appeal that Carroll's patronage extended over four decades.

The Savoy Theatre, The Strand

Though it was at the Haymarket Theatre that W. S. Gilbert's reputation as a playwright grew during the 1870s it was elsewhere that he embarked on the career as librettist, which will be forever associated with Arthur Sullivan and the Savoy. The first of these venues to be considered here was not even strictly speaking a theatre; it was the Gallery of Illustration at 14 Regent Street, Westminster, opened in 1856, which became the home of Mr and Mrs T. German Reed. In 1844 Thomas German Reed, then conductor of the Haymarket Theatre orchestra, married Priscilla Horton an actress with a beautiful contralto voice whose successes included Ariel in Macready's 1838 revival of *The Tempest*. In 1854 the couple undertook a tour of the provinces (Carroll saw them in Oxford in 1856) with an entertainment in which Reed played the piano and 'Mrs Reed sang amusing parodies of different vocalists. Mr George Grossmith was doing something similar.' (Williamson, 1895, p. 4) Following an encouraging season at the St Martin's Hall, Longacre, the Reeds set up at the Gallery of Illustration, which Carroll attended in the afternoon of 13 December 1856. The fact that Carroll attended an afternoon performance, long before matinees were introduced at regular theatres, is indicative of the distinctive character of the Gallery of Illustration. As Jane W. Stedman has written:

> The Reed performances were announced and conducted in completely non-theatrical terms. To the very last, they were 'illustrations', not 'plays'. Acts were called 'parts' and roles 'assumptions'. When the 1856 'gathering' assembled, it saw not a set, but an elegant drawing-room' (1967, p. 5)

albeit one with a capactity of 500. The German Reeds. 'an astute and talented couple', were in Macqueen-Pope's words 'cash[ing] in on the

Carroll at the Theatre 171

Victorian adoration of clean, wholesome entertainment without a vestige of vulgarity' (1951, p. 72). Carroll returned on 29 July 1862, by which time the Reeds had been 'strengthened by the addition of Mr John Parry, who had a marvellous mastery of the piano forte and a countenance capable of extraordinary facial contortions' (Williamson, 1895, p. 6). Carroll was back on 2 July 1864 for another 'afternoon entertainment – the Egyptian piece *The Pyramid, The Bard and his Birthday,* and Parry's *Mrs Roseleaf at the Sea-side* – the latter was far the best thing of the entertainment'.

Two years later on 23 June 1866 Carroll saw F. C. Burnand's *The Yachting Cruise* and John Parry's *The Wedding Breakfast,* describing the former as 'poor' and the latter as 'capital'. Not until 21 January 1873 did Carroll revisit the Reeds; he took three companions 'to the German Reeds. *Happy Arcadia* is well written and acted'. *Happy Arcadia* was the product of the partnership between W. S. Gilbert and the composer Frederic Clay in which they caught something of the *Bouffes Parisiens* (farcical, satirical, spectacular entertainments by composers such as Offenbach; regarded as indelicate, if not indecent, in England), but 'without, of course, the *Bouffes'* "coarseness"' (Stedman ed., 1967, p. 39). *Happy Arcadia* tells of four Arcadians who are thoroughly fed up with their supposedly idyllic existence and who during the course of the action exchange identities so that each performer essays two strikingly contrasting characters to great comic effect. Jane Stedman has identified many features of *Happy Arcadia* which reappear in later Gilbert and Sullivan operas (p. 43) and has made the general point that 'the Gallery of Illustration provided an ideal laboratory for his [Gilbert's] experiments by approximating more closely the future conditions of the Savoy' (p. 47).

There remained one further staging post *en route* to the Savoy Theatre: the Opera Comique, which opened on 29 October 1870 in the presence of the Prince of Wales (Mander and Mitchenson, 1968, p. 288). It was constructed back to back with the slightly earlier (1868) Globe Theatre and, like it, was 'jerry-built in the hope of big profits when the street [East Strand-Holywell Street] should be widened, and it was approached by long underground passages and stairs where, in the event of a fire, hundreds of persons would certainly have lost their lives...A theatre so recklessly planned would not now be permitted.'(Sherson, 1925, p. 253) Sherson explains the theatre's name in terms of the rage for *opéra bouffe,* but though many such pieces, suitably toned down, were very considerable successes: *Les Cloches de Corneville* 705 performances and *Madame Favart* 502, and even Carroll attended them, they were not performed at the Opera Comique. Gilbert and Sullivan's *The Sorcerer* first attracted him there on 14 January 1878, but he 'thought it poor, though

172   *Lewis Carroll and the Victorian Stage*

Mr. [George] Grossmith as Sorcerer was excellent'. Carroll's assessment was borne out by a modest run of 178 performances.

Carroll had not seen *H.M.S. Pinafore* during its hugely successful initial run of 571 performances from 25 May 1878, when C. E . Pascoe established its provenance as follows:

> It has the lightness, the brightness, the airy cleverness, in short all the good qualities of the French opera-bouffes – with none of the bad, – none of the blemishes which so often disfigure even the finest French humour. *H.M.S. Pinafore* has a purely English story, set in simple action and told in simple language. Its humour, its satire, its moral – all these are as clean, as honest, as healthy as the most rigid respectability could desire.' (1883, p. 49)

Not surprisingly Carroll was drawn to the so-called (because it was performed entirely by children) *Children's Pinafore*, which he saw on 14 January 1881, but it fell short of the standards his 'rigid respectability' desired. He found it 'pretty as a whole, though it grieved one to see the sweet bevy of little girls taught to say "He said damme."' Seven years later when he wrote his article 'The Stage and the Spirit of Reverence' the effect had not faded:

> I cannot find words to convey to the reader the pain I felt in seeing those dear children taught to utter such words to amuse ears grown callous to their ghastly meaning. Put the two ideas side by side – Hell (no matter whether *you* believe in it or not: millions do), and those pure young lips thus sporting with its horrors – and then find what *fun* in it you can! How Mr. Gilbert could have stooped to write, or Sir Arthur Sullivan could have prostituted his noble art to set to music, such vile trash, it passes my skill to understand. (*Theatre* 1 June 1888)

Gilbert experienced no such compunction, for not only did he put such words in the mouths of children he also put tickets in the hands of other children, in particular Kate Lewis (Kate Terry Gielgud) who went along to the matinee on 20 March 1880. The twelve-year-old's remarks on the performance 'acted by children – professional children –' show how much interest these young performers aroused in her as she refers to 'Harry and Emilie Grattan, son and daughter of H. Plunkett Grattan' who had previously appeared in *Uncle Tom's Cabin* at the Surrey and with Joseph Jefferson in *Rip Van Winkle* at the Princess's, which, as noted, Carroll had seen (Terry Gielgud, 1953, p. 53).

Frances Hodgson Burnett's *The Real Little Lord Fauntleroy* attracted Carroll to the Opera Comique twice on 10 January and 26 June 1889, though he had already seen it three times (18 June, 2 July and 11 July

1888) at Terry's Theatre. At Terry's on 18 June he delighted in Vera Beringer's performance as Lord Fauntleroy ('wonderful naturalness and spirit...one of the cleverest children I have seen on stage'), her sister Esme as Dick (both of them indebted to Mrs Kendal under whose 'superintendence' the play was produced), Alfred Bishop 'excellent as the old Earl, and Miss Winifred Emery charming and pathetic as Mrs. Erroll. Mr. Albert Chevalier also was very good as "Mr. Hobbs".' The *Illustrated London News* concurred : 'A better child's performance than that of Miss Vera Beringer has probably never been seen. It was not acting, but nature...this child is a born actress' (19 May 1888). For the daughter of the American-born authoress Mrs Oscar Beringer, accents were presumably not a problem, but at the Opera Comique on 10 January 1889 Carroll thought 'Vera is losing her spirit and naturalness a little'. He caught the play one last time on 26 June when Marion Terry had taken over as Mrs Erroll and was back at the Opera Comique on 11 July for the first performance of John Uniacke's *The Marquesa* with Violet Vanbrugh and Albert Chevalier as Lord Karne. Though also a music-hall artiste Chevalier was a reputable comic actor whose abilities Carroll recognised and respected.

The Savoy Theatre, 'built by Richard D'Oyly Carte with great consideration for the comfort of his patrons, was opened on 10 October 1881, with *Patience*, transferred from the Opera Comique where it had been running since April'. Another example of the work of the prolific theatre architect C. J. Phipps, the Savoy was of course renowned 'as the first theatre in the world to be lit throughout by electricity' (Ayre, 1972, pp. 411-12).

Though he pronounced it 'a little weak as a whole', Carroll saw *Patience* five times: 'It is entirely unobjectionable, which one is glad to say of one of Gilbert's plays, and the scenery and dresses are charming.' (31 December 1882) *Patience* therefore qualified as a suitable entertainment to which to take guests, but happily as he did so Carroll found himself enjoying it more: 'all the better on second hearing' (27 May 1882), 'as good as ever' (17 June and 12 August).

Carroll did not give *Iolanthe*, about which his verdict on 30 December 1882 was 'pretty, but uninteresting – very inferior to *Patience*', so much of an opportunity to grow on him, but more to his taste on 13 January 1885 was '*The Pirates of Penzance* acted by children...It was a very charming performance, and some of them have lovely voices.' William Beatty-Kingston reviewing the production in the *Theatre* (2 February 1885) took the opportunity not only to praise 'the half hundred children whose singing at the Savoy has been the wonder and admiration of

174   *Lewis Carroll and the Victorian Stage*

London during the past month', but also to launch into a patriotic eulogy of English musicality:

> These miniature mummers are living and indefeasible proofs of the disputed musicality of the English nation; for they are by no means 'infant wonders', but average children judiciously selected from some hundreds of youthful candidates for employment, belonging in part to the mysterious little world that is peopled by hangers-on to the dramatic profession, and in part to the work-a-day lower middle classes of society. That such children as these, after a few weeks' careful training...should perform so difficult a work as 'The Pirates of Penzance'...goes far to prove at least that what is conventionally called 'a musical ear' is a British national characteristic.

Whether or not he would have adopted or approved of such a chauvinist style, Carroll would not have dissented from Beatty-Kingston's description of and praise for these young performers. As with *Patience*, *The Mikado* stood Carroll in good stead as a piece to which he could take guests, which he did four times. In contrast he saw *The Yeomen of the Guard* ('not equal to *Patience*', 20 April 1889), *The Gondoliers* ('nothing to haunt the memory', 2 August 1890) and *Utopia (Limited)* ('not up to the standard of former Gilbert plays', 6 January 1894) only once each, although he had written to Enid Moberley Bell (on 10 October 1893) of *Utopia (Limited)* that 'if it turns out good (the *Standard* praises it tremendously) I shall be going a second time: and then, you know, I *might* take Iris: who knows?' Clearly it did not live up to expectations and nothing else by Gilbert and Sullivan ever matched *Patience*, an early indication of Arthur Jacobs's judgement that: '*Patience* itself would prove durable even when the artistic target of its satire had receded from public view.' (1986, p. 153)

The Savoy Theatre was the venue for a special theatrical occasion that Carroll attended on 21 June 1882: 'Florence Terry's last appearance', which has already been referred to in Chapter 6.

The Court Theatre, Lower George Street, Chelsea

In 1870 the former Ranelagh Chapel was converted into the New Chelsea Theatre; in 1871 after a 'more drastic reconstruction' by the architect Walter Emden it reopened as the Court Theatre under the management of Marie Litton (Mander and Mitchenson, 1963, p. 153). In 1875 John Hare, having enjoyed a successful period with the Bancrofts at the Prince of Wales's, invited William Kendal to become 'a silent partner for the

Carroll at the Theatre

remainder of the lease of the Court Theatre'. Kendal and Hare belonged to the new breed of financially astute actor-managers who made considerable fortunes (Davis, 2000, p. 165) and, as Madge Kendal relates, their venture at the Court was on a clearly defined financial footing (1933, p. 110). Carroll first visited the Court in 1877, the year in which Henry James wrote that 'a stranger in London' who 'asks where the best acting is to be seen...receives one of two answers. He is told either at the Prince of Wales's theatre or at the Court' (Wade ed., 1957, p. 107). James commended the ensemble at the Prince of Wales's and described Madge Kendal, who was then in the company, as 'the most agreeable actress on the London stage' (p. 108). Readers who knew the Court may well have picked up James's subtext for, having praised John Hare for his 'quiet natural' performance as Marmaduke Vavasour in the revival of *New Men and Old Acres* by A. W. Dubourg and Tom Taylor, he went on to deliver his verdict on Ellen Terry who appeared as Lilian Vavasour 'a part specially written for her', though actually first performed by Mrs Kendal at the Haymarket in 1869 (Manvell, 1968, p. 97). James began by acknowledging that Ellen Terry was 'picturesque...like a preRaphaelite drawing in a magazine...intelligent and vivacious...singularly delicate and lady-like', but 'the favour' which she enjoyed struck him, 'like that under which Mr. Henry Irving has expanded', as 'a sort of measure of the English critical sense in things theatrical':

> Miss Terry has all the pleasing qualities I have enumerated, but she has, with them, the defect that she is simply *not* an actress. One sees it sufficiently in her face – the face of a clever young Englishwoman, with a hundred merits, but not a dramatic artist. These things are indefinable; I can only give my impression. (Wade ed., 1957, p. 110)

Michael R. Booth in his perceptive study of Ellen Terry's acting takes the view that her 'sheer pictorial strength and pictorial beauty...could sometimes...be used, consciously or not, as a substitute for strength of character' (1988, p. 83), but for Carroll, as for so many admirers, it was the real Ellen Terry that they wanted as much as an impersonation of a character. Thus he wrote (16 January 1877) of her in *New Men and Old Acres*:

> Ellen Terry was wonderful, and I should think unsurpassable in all but the lighter parts. The gush of animal spirits of a light-hearted girl is beyond her now, poor thing! She can give a very clever imitation of it, but that is all.

176 *Lewis Carroll and the Victorian Stage*

Carroll was repining, as of course he did with many child friends, the lost 'gush of animal spirits of a light-hearted girl' for which he found such powers of 'clever imitation' (acting) a poor substitute. Carroll and James were the opposite sides of a coin: the former hankering for the real (youthful) Ellen Terry and the latter finding her own personality intrusive and no substitute for genuine acting.

When Carroll went to see Ellen Terry in the title role in *Olivia*, W. G. Wills's dramatisation of Oliver Goldsmith's *The Vicar of Wakefield* on 22 April 1878, it is apparent that Ellen Terry gave a performance that transcended his craving for personality and her tendency to rely upon it: 'the gem of the piece is "Olivia" herself, acted by Mrs. C. Kelly (Ellen Terry) with a sweetness and pathos that moved some of the audience (nearly including myself) to tears.' The fact that he refers not to Ellen Terry but to the character of Olivia as 'the gem of the piece' is of course significant and he goes on to describe the effect of Terry's vocal delivery: 'her exclamation "Pet!" was tenderness itself'. Though Henry James persisted in calling Ellen Terry 'amateurish' (Wade ed., 1957, p. 112), Joseph Knight wrote that her performance 'in one point at least, when she repelled the further advances of the man who has wronged her...touched greatness' (1893, p. 218) and Dutton Cook reckoned that:

> Only an artist of distinct genius could have ventured upon the impulsive abrupt movement by means of which she thrusts from her the villain who has betrayed her, and denotes the intensity of her scorn of him, the completeness of her change from loving to loathing. (1883, p. 361)

By then Ellen Terry had personal experiences of being rejected by men, but transmuting such experience into a stage performance to be repeated in this case for 138 performances is of course the actor's art.

Unlike Henry James, who favoured Madge Kendal at Ellen Terry's expense, Carroll was appreciative of both actresses. On 24 June 1879 he wrote: 'we saw Mrs. Kendal act superbly in *The Ladies' Battle*', an adaptation by her brother Tom Robertson of *La Bataille des Dames* by M. M. Scribe and Legouvé. Appropriately, given the piece's French origins, Madge Kendal's performance was so admired by the actor Coquelin that he was responsible for a piece of business ('discovering the first silver thread amongst the gold') being incorporated into the production at the Comédie Française (Kendal, 1933, p. 130). The bill included *Cousin Dick* by Val Prinsep, but, although she did not appear in his play, Mrs Kendal did sit for him to paint her portrait.

It was at the Court Theatre that the great Polish actress Helena Modjeska made her London debut in 1879, the year in which the Comédie

Française with Sarah Bernhardt played its historic season at the Gaiety Theatre (Foulkes, 2002a), but Carroll was rarely drawn to the numerous visiting actors (European and American) who increasingly in the ensuing decade regarded success in London (especially in Shakespeare) as the ultimate imprimatur (Foulkes 2002, pp. 108-23).

Carroll was happier with reassuringly familiar fare such as Tom Taylor's *To Parents and Guardians* and Marion Terry in *My Little Girl* by Dion Boucicault – the younger – who was to marry Irene Vanbrugh, and *Comrades*, the first play (in conjunction with B. C. Stephenson) by Brandon Thomas, the author of *Charley's Aunt*. On 26 May 1883 Carroll saw Marion Terry in *The Danischeffs*, adapted from the French by Lord Newry, erstwhile Christ Church undergraduate, in which she 'has much agony and screaming to do'. He saw her next on 16 May 1885 in *The Magistrate*, the first of A. W. Pinero's celebrated Court farces (to be followed by *The Schoolmistress* and *Dandy Dick*) which Carroll found 'a very funny piece' in which she 'has not much of a part' though the *Theatre* thought she 'made much of the small part of Charlotte Verinder' (1 April 1885). Funny though *The Magistrate* had been, Carroll did not return to the Court for Pinero's other plays, though he did see *Sweet Lavender* at Terry's on 10 August 1889. He did however attend the triple bill of *The New Sub* by Seymour Hicks, *Rosencrantz and Guildenstern* by W. S. Gilbert and *A Pantomime Rehearsal* by Cecil Clay four times during the summer of 1892. Described by H. G. Hibbert as 'the most popular one-act play of modern times', *A Pantomime Rehearsal* was created at Sir Percy Shelley's house in Boscombe where he had 'a perfectly equipped theatre'. Cecil Clay, a stalwart of the German Reed entertainments, was one of the guests, as were his wife Rosina (Vokes), her sister Victoria and (Alfred) German Reed 'to whom the Vokes girls hummed some of the songs of their entertainment, from which inspiration he vamped at the piano' (1920, p. 102). *A Pantomime Rehearsal* opened on 6 June 1891 at Terry's Theatre where it ran for 439 performances with a variety of other pieces; similarly at the Court it was, in the words of Ellaline Terriss, 'the backbone' (1928, p. 43) of a triple bill of which Carroll wrote on 2 July 1892 'in the last [*A Pantomime Rehearsal*], the songs and dances of Misses Ellaline Terriss and Decima Moore are fascinating'. On 16 January 1894 Carroll could appreciate Ellaline Terriss in '*Cinderella*, one of the prettiest and most refined pantomimes I ever saw' which was such a success at the Lyceum Theatre 'that it aroused interest in America, a country to which pantomime is not native and which does not understand it at all' (Terriss, 1955, p. 105). *Cinderella* transferred from the Lyceum to the Abbey Theatre, New York, with Ellaline Terriss in the title role.

178 *Lewis Carroll and the Victorian Stage*

There remained one further visit to the Court for Carroll, on 30 October 1897 when he took Beatrice Hatch and Margaret Mayhew to *The Children of the King* in which, as already noted in Chapter 7, Minna Quin was appearing as 'a super'. William Archer described Ernest Rosmer's play (translated by Carl Armbruster and 'revised' by John Davidson) with music by Humperdinck, as 'nursery romanticism', which with Cissie Loftus (a notable Peter Pan) 'graceful, unaffected, childlike' as the Goose-Girl and 'Miss Lina Verdi...delightful as the Broombinder's daughter' (1898, p. 288), was just what Carroll liked to make what he rated: 'A very pleasant day.'

The Lyceum Theatre, Wellington Street, The Strand

Writing of Samuel Beazley's designs for the 1834 Lyceum Theatre, Görel Garlick draws attention to its 'giant projecting portico of six fluted Corinthian columns of Portland stone' and the 'dome topped by a pilaster-glad lantern' which 'originally formed a handsome and striking climax to the theatre's exterior, the whole composition proclaiming the Lyceum's status as a theatre of national importance' (2003, p. 106). It took nearly four decades for the Lyceum to fully achieve that national importance and when Carroll first entered it in 1863 the Lyceum was in the hands of Charles Fechter, who, though (almost certainly) born in England (of a German father and French mother), was educated in France and spoke French as his first language. In G. H. Lewes's opinion Fechter pronounced 'English very well for Frenchman, but it is certain that his accent greatly interferes with due effect of the speeches.' (1875, p. 120) Carroll evidently experienced hearing problems when he saw Fechter and Kate Terry in *The Duke's Motto* on 27 March 1863, but he attributed that to having bad seats, presumably ones that made the deafness in his right ear more, rather than less, of a handicap. Nevertheless he pronounced the acting good, which he raised to 'very good' when he saw Fechter as Hamlet with Miss Terry 'a perfect treat' as Ophelia on 22 June 1864. That year was the tercentenary of Shakespeare's birth, in celebration of which a programme of events was planned under the leadership of Edward Flower in Stratford-upon-Avon in which Fechter had agreed to participate until as he put it: 'I find the general public turning against me' (Foulkes, 1984, p. 15) and he withdrew. Foreign actors performing in Shakespeare's plays as part of a national celebration of his birth was too much for some, not least certain English actors who felt their place had been usurped. Fechter had many admirers of whom G. H. Lewes, the author of the following description, was pre-eminent: 'Fechter is lymphatic, delicate, handsome.

Carroll at the Theatre 179

And with his long flaxen curls, quivering sensitive nostrils, fine eye, and sympathetic voice, perfectly represents the graceful prince.' (1875, p. 119)

In 1871 Hezekiah Bateman, the American manager married to Sam Cowell's half-sister Sydney, took the Lyceum with a view to furthering the stage careers of his four daughters, the eldest of whom was Kate, who had already achieved a measure of success in *Leah the Foresaken*, which Carroll saw on 5 July 1872. Henry Irving, whom Bateman had engaged as leading man, played Charles I ('too upright and honourable to succeed in Machiavelian arts', Wills 1898, p. 102) to Kate Bateman's Queen Henrietta Maria in W. G. Wills's *Charles I* which Carroll saw on 10 January and 16 April 1873. Carroll's first really positive endorsement of Irving came on 16 February 1874 when, having 'met for the first time', as fellow dinner guests, the Kendals, Carroll went to see Bulwer Lytton's '*Richelieu*, very finely acted by Irving'. But Carroll can hardly be regarded as an Irving enthusiast during the Bateman years at the Lyceum; he missed *The Bells* in which Irving's performance as Mathias had been a personal turning point on 25 November 1871 and he saw none of Irving's Shakespearian creations: Hamlet, Macbeth, Othello and Richard III. This changed dramatically when Irving inaugurated his own management at the end of 1878 with *Hamlet*, which Carroll promptly attended twice (7 and 20 January 1879), but his comments indicate what – or rather who – the real attraction was: 'to *Hamlet* at the Lyceum. Irving rather spoiled Hamlet for me by his extraordinary English. Ellen Terry as Ophelia was simply perfect. The play is superbly "mounted".' Carroll was by no means alone in criticising Irving's diction. It had been a target of three young Edinburgh men, Robert Lowe, George Halkett and William Archer in their pamphlet *The Fashionable Tragedian* in which Irving's pronunciation of 'blood' as 'ber-a-lud' was one of the examples cited (1877, p. 8). In Irving's defence Edward Gordon Craig later described this as 'a tendency…to enrich the sounds of words' (1930, p. 63).

Carroll made the first of his six visits to *The Merchant of Venice* on 10 January 1880 and the first of six visits to *Much Ado About Nothing* on 11 November 1882. As we have seen in Chapter 6 he made comments to Ellen Terry about both of them. Indeed his observations about the Lyceum in both his diaries and correspondence were nearly always about and/or directed to Ellen Terry. On 28 June 1879 in *Charles I* she 'made a charming Henrietta Maria'; in Tennyson's *The Cup* on 17 January 1881 as Camma she was 'the perfection of grace' and in its companion piece Mrs Cowley's *The Belle's Stratagem* she had 'two delicious scenes', but 'many of the other parts were poorly filled, as is the way at the Lyceum' (18 April 1881). Clement Scott concurred with Carroll about Terry's performances: 'Words fail me to express the singular charm and spell of

180   *Lewis Carroll and the Victorian Stage*

the Letitia Hardy [in *The Belle's Stratagem*] of Miss Ellen Terry. She is as
Georgian in her comedy graces as before she was Pagan in her rites as the
priestess Camma.' (Pascoe, 1883, pp. 22-3). Though the Lyceum
repertoire was not principally devised for Ellen Terry's advantage here
was a double bill that enabled her to show her strengths and versatility.

Twelfth Night served neither Irving (Malvolio) nor Terry (Viola)
particularly well. On 1 June 1884 Carroll considered Marion to be 'a
charming substitute for her sister' who was ill, but he did not return for
Ellen's Viola though he saw her reprise in *Olivia* twice. He thought that
Irving's comic performance made the end of C. Selby's old melodrama
Robert Macaire 'merely an extravagant farce' on 3 July 1888, but he
found no deficiencies in *Macbeth*: 'Miss Ellen Terry was *far* better than I
had thought possible. Irving was good. Alexander, as "Macduff" was
excellent. The scenery superb. Altogether it was a treat', he wrote on 11
May 1889. Carroll also approved of Irving's Wolsey ('some fine bits of
acting', 14 May 1892) and his King Lear ('excellent, nearly as good as in
"Shylock"', 3 December 1892) and (without being specific) Ellen Terry as
Queen Katherine and Cordelia. Overall then, though it was Ellen Terry
who attracted him to the Lyceum, Carroll became quite an admirer of
Irving too, even in roles such as Macbeth and King Lear in which he was
not without his detractors.

Carroll does not feature in Alfred Bryan's 'Distinguished Gathering'
showing the auditorium of the Lyceum occupied by some ninety
distinguished men (mainly) and women (Wilson, 1952, opp. p. 68), but
many were known to him (the Marquis of Salisbury, Val Prinsep, Lord
Newry, Tom Taylor, W. S. Gilbert, Arthur Sullivan, Anthony Trollope).
The fact that under Henry Irving the Lyceum realised what Görel Garlick
has called its 'status as a theatre of national importance', indeed a
National Theatre in all but name, was very much the achievement of
Henry Irving. However that achievement relied on the support of loyal
playgoers, of which Carroll was both a typical and unique example.
Happily Carroll lived long enough for Irving's knighthood in 1895, but he
died at the beginning of what A. E. Wilson called the 'Year of Disaster'
(1898): the calamitous fire at the scenery depot in February, which led to
Irving ceding control to the Lyceum Ltd., then Ellen Terry's departure and
eventually his own deposition as 'Lord of the Lyceum'.

Carroll at the Theatre   181

Along the Strand

If the Lyceum was the closest London got to the Comédie Française it was ironic that that company's celebrated London season in 1879 should have been at the Gaiety Theatre, 354 Strand, where under John Hollingshead, manager from 1868 to 1886, the 'main attraction was Burlesque; a form of topical "musical", blending Operetta, Music Hall and what we now know as Revue then called extravaganza' (Mander and Mitchenson, 1968, p. 105). Carroll attended the Gaiety only twice. The first time was a matinee on Saturday 13 January 1872. Hollingshead had introduced regular matinees in 1871 (prior to that they were limited to pantomimes and special occasions); matinees suited Carroll very well, not only for his own convenience as he grew older, but also to entertain young friends whom he could return to their families at an acceptable hour. Ellen Terry tried to persuade him of the disadvantages of matinees, but to no avail. The matinee Carroll attended on 13 January consisted of *Cox and Box* (Burnand and Sullivan), *Our Clerks* (Tom Taylor) and *The Spitalfields Weaver* (T. H. Bayly), but the real attractions were J. L. Toole and Nellie Farren who 'were irresistibly comic as the two clerks' in Taylor's play. In *The Spitalfields Weaver* 'Toole introduced his marvellous imitations of Phelps, Fechter, Webster, Compton and Buckstone, all in the same speech from *Hamlet*.' Carroll's other visit to the Gaiety was on 2 October 1878 when he saw H. J. Byron's burlesque (of Goethe) *Little Doctor Faustus* with Edward O'Connor Terry as Mephisto and Nellie Farren, described by Macqueen-Pope as 'that spirit of the gamin which always makes for adoration' (1949, p. 184) as Faust, both of whom Carroll rated as 'good'. Of Connie Gilchrist, whom he had admired so much at the Adelphi only two years earlier, as Siebel he wrote: 'she is losing her beauty, and can't act – but she did the old skipping-rope dance superbly'. The two years that Connie Gilchrist had aged had taken her from twelve to fourteen, a particularly significant passage of time for Carroll. Kate Vaughan fared even worse as Margaret, she 'was so offensive that I wrote to J. Hollingshead the manager'. If not for this then for some other reason Carroll never entered the Gaiety again.

Carroll found a more congenial venue at the Strand Theatre, 168-9 Strand, which he first attended on 18 July 1863 for a typical triple bill consisting of John Brougham's *While there's life there's hope*, H. J. Byron's *The Motto* and J. M. Morton's *My Wife's Second Floor*. In Byron's piece, 'a burlesque on the *Duke's Motto*', George Honey 'acted Fechter very well', which Carroll was well equipped to judge having seen Fechter himself in the role at the Lyceum on 27 March. The popularity of

182

Lewis Carroll and the Victorian Stage

burlesques of contemporary plays and performers indicates how familiar audiences were with them, if not at first hand then by repute. Carroll returned for similar fare at the Strand over the next three years, including on 13 July 1865 the burlesque opera *Windsor Castle* by Burnand and Montague Williams in which he judged 'the whole of the music...[as] original, a bold experiment' and *Kenilworth* by Andrew Halliday (24 July 1866). The opportunity to see Marion Terry in H. J. Byron's comedy *Weak Woman* took Carroll to the Strand on 11 June 1875, but he dismissed the play as 'rather weak'.

In 1879 Carroll was back no less than four times to see Offenbach's comic opera *Madame Favart* in an English version by H. B. Farnie. He particularly enjoyed Miss Florence St. John's performance in the title role of Madame Favart and was disappointed when she did not appear on 4 October, but she and Violet Cameron (Suzanne) were both performing when he returned on 20 December. Florence St. John, who had both married (for the first time) and made her stage debut at the age of fourteen, had been 'discovered' when playing in Liverpool by H. B. Farnie

> who engaged her to play Germaine in 'Les Cloches de Corneville' on tour, and afterwards at the Globe, where she appeared with great success; this was followed by 'Madame Favart', at the Strand in 1879, another enormous success; and 'Olivette', which firmly established her as a public favourite. (*The Green Room Book*, 1906, p. 300)

Carroll took a succession of guests to share the acting talent and other attractions of the twenty-four-year-old Miss St. John: Vere Bayne on 25 July, Mrs Vere Bayne on 13 September, Alice, Agnes and Evie Hull on 4 October and Jessie and Amyot Hull on 20 December, indicating that Farnie's *Madame Favart* contained nothing that could offend the delicate susceptibilities of English gentility. C. E. Pascoe correctly predicted that '*Madame Favart* seems likely to enjoy the patronage of supporters of opera-bouffe for some time to come' (1883, p. 53), as indeed it did to the tune of 502 performances, but furthermore Farnie had made a huge success with a piece that 'was at the outset a failure there [Paris], but coined money here' (Hibbert, 1920, p. 35). On 12 October 1880 Carroll was rather less enthusiastic about Farnie's *Olivette* in which Miss St. John had 'not so good a part as in *Madame Favart*, nor is the music (by Audran) so good as Offenbach – but it is fairly good'. However the prolific and shrewd Farnie had earned his reputation as 'the autocrat of comic opera' (Hibbert, 1920, p. 35) and *Olivette*, 'a farcical opera put on the stage in the most liberal manner' (Pascoe, 1883, p. 45), became a resounding success with 466 performances. This was modest when compared with H. J. Byron's *Our Boys*, which had run for 1362 performances at the Vaudeville (from 16 January 1875). Carroll did not see it there (he never went to the Vaudeville), but the revival at the Strand ran for 263 performances, two of which he attended and enjoyed.

13. Miss Florence St. John and Miss Emily Duncan in *Olivette* at the Strand Theatre

Another theatre that played host to some other Farnie offerings was the Globe, Newcastle Street, Strand, which stood back-to-back with the Opera Comique. Carroll had seen J. L. Toole as Hammond Coote, 'the Dickensian part [written] especially for him' (W. Trewin, 1980, p. 62), in James Albery's *Wig and Gown* there on 13 April 1874 and pronounced him 'very droll'. Farnie's *Blue Beard* was the Globe pantomime for 1874-5, 'and a very good one' Carroll noted on 9 January 1875, with Lydia Thomson as Selim and Lionel Brough in the title role. In 1881 Farnie was

184   *Lewis Carroll and the Victorian Stage*

back with *Les Cloches de Corneville*, with music by R. Planquette, which registered a run of 705 performances, of which Carroll attended that on 8 October 1881 and wrote: 'Mr. Shiel Barry made a wonderful miser. The music is delicious.' Carroll was to see *Les Cloches de Corneville* three more times in Eastbourne.

Carroll supported Wilson Barrett's brief tenure of the Globe by attending *The Golden Ladder* on 11 February 1888 and similar loyalty led him to see *Bootle's Baby* with Minnie Terry (daughter of Charles) on 2 July. His own interests took him there three times in January 1889 for the revival of Savile Clarke's dramatisation of the '*Alice*' books, which had originally been staged at the Prince of Wales (see Chapter 4), where his version of Thackeray's *The Rose and the Ring* was also staged in 1891.

Amongst the rapid turnover of managers at the Globe in the 1880s was the American Richard Mansfield, whose Richard III on 28 March 1889 Carroll pronounced '*splendid*' and the *Illustrated London News* (23 March 1889) 'the subtlest bit of acting, the highest example of his intelligence', but which later that year in his native American, where 'declamation and fustian' were still relished, attracted the cry of 'Give us more hump' (Wilstach, 1908, p. 188). The opportunities, which it offered to child actors enhanced the attraction of *Richard III* for Victorian playgoers. The *Illustrated London News* commended Bessie Hatton, who played the Prince of Wales, as 'a singularly clever and intelligent young actress, with an admirable elocutionary method', an opinion shared with Carroll who said she 'made a perfectly charming Prince of Wales: her enunciation is simply *delicious*'. About the other two child actors Isa and Nellie Bowman he was rather more guarded, describing the former as 'good as the little Duke of York' and the latter 'as sweetness itself' as Clarence's son. The Bowman sisters were already well known to Carroll and Isa was a particular friend of his, who in the year after his death published her book *The Story of Lewis Carroll*, which includes several photographs of herself as the Duke of York and a letter from Carroll addressed to 'My Lord Duke'. This letter is a wonderful repository of Carroll's precepts on acting. He took the lines: 'O then I see, you will part but with light gifts, / In weightier things you'll say a *beggar* nay' (Act III, Scene 1, line 118), pointing out that she was 'leaning on [emphasising] the word "beggar"', which was 'a mistake. *My* rule for knowing which word to lean on is the word that tells you something *new*, something that is *different* from what you expected.' Thus the words to be stressed are 'light' and 'heavy' (sic):

And the way to say the lines in the play is –
O, then I see you will *part* but with *light* gifts;

In weightier things you'll say a beggar nay.

Carroll also took her up on her (Irvingesque) pronunciation of 'thank' as 'thenk' in 'I *would*, that I might thank you as you call me' before proceeding to press home his other favourite theme:

> You are not as *natural*, when acting the Duke, as you were when you acted Alice. You seemed to me not to forget *yourself* enough. It was not so much a real *prince* talking to his elder brother and his uncle; it was *Isa Bowman* talking to people she didn't *much* care about, for an audience to listen to. I don't mean it was that all *through*, but *sometimes* you were *artificial*. Now don't be jealous of Miss Hatton, when I say she was *sweetly* natural. She looked and spoke just like a *real* Prince of Wales. And she didn't seem to know that there was any audience. If you are ever to be a good actress (as I hope you will), you must learn to *forget* 'Isa' altogether, and *be* the character you are playing. Try to think 'This is *really* the Prince of Wales, I'm his little brother, and I'm *very* glad to meet him, and I love him *very* much', and 'this is *really* my uncle: he's very kind, and lets me say saucy things to him', and *do* forget that there's anybody else listening! (Bowman, 1899, pp. 82-6; also in Cohen ed., 1979, vol. II, pp. 734-6)

Carroll's last visit to the Globe was on 4 January 1890 to see Frank Benson and his company perform on one of their rare forays into the capital in *A Midsummer Night's Dream*, a play not without application to aspiring actors. That, like his visit to the play at the Queen's Theatre on 10 October 1870, was not likely to be 'equal to the old rendering of it at the Princess's, with Ellen Terry as "Puck"'. Carroll had not seen the Princess's *King John*, but attended two consecutive performances at the Queen's on 2 and 3 July 1873.

The St. James's Theatre, King Street, Piccadilly

The 'Strange and Complete History' of the St. James's Theatre runs, as the sub-title of Barry Duncan's book (1964) indicates, from 1835 to 1957. Carroll visited three times in the 1860s when typical bills included pieces by Tom Taylor, John Maddison Morton and F. C. Burnand. The highlight was *The Adventures of a Love Letter* in which Charles James Mathews, the author of the piece, and his wife 'acted capitally'. There was also an early opportunity to see J. L. Toole, but he had 'little opportunity to show his comic powers' (26 January 1864). Carroll was not tempted to the St. James's during the 1870s, but on 20 July 1888, to his regret, he attended Pinero's *The Squire*, condemning it as 'the first distinctly objectionable

186   *Lewis Carroll and the Victorian Stage*

piece I have known Mrs. Kendal produce: and I can no longer take a young friend with confidence to her theatre, but I must always ask about the character of the play. I was so displeased with it that I came out after the second act.' *The Squire* was not even a new play, the Kendals had first staged it at the St. James's in 1881 when its similarities with Thomas Hardy's *Far from the Madding Crowd* had been noted by Austin Brereton, who wrote of being carried 'away from the busy world...into scenes of charming rural life' (Pascoe, 1883, p. 71). Carroll had seen a dramatisation of Hardy's novel performed by Charles Kelly's (aka Wardell) company at the Theatre Royal, Brighton on 2 September 1882 when he had described the plot as 'painful (there is a seduced girl who commits suicide) but not vicious' and 'the play good, and well acted'. As Hugues Lebailly says, with the Kendals at the St. James's Theatre Carroll felt that 'his trust in a manager's name' had been betrayed (2001, p. 25).

When George Alexander agreed terms with the Earl of Kilmorey (aka Lord Newry) for the St. James's in February 1891 he planned to create 'a theatre of high prestige and financial success upon the foundations of British authorship' (Mason, 1935, p. 7). The auditorium received the attention of Alexander's French wife Florence (Théleur) and he was no less attentive to the details of play selection and production. On 26 February 1891 *The Idler* by the Australian dramatist Charles Haddon Chambers opened with Marion Terry and Nutcombe Gould in the cast. Carroll saw it on 6 June 1891 and far from being disconcerted by this 'tale of a gold-mining fugitive from a drunken brawl murder, of blackmail, an averted duel, of pure love' (Duncan, 1964, p. 222) judged it 'an interesting play, well acted'. Carroll was even more taken with R. C. Carton's *Liberty Hall*, which he saw three times in March and April 1893. The critic of the *Illustrated London News* wrote:

> As you follow the story of 'Liberty Hall' it is difficult to believe that such a being as Ibsen ever existed, or that *any* school of playwrights has grown discontent with the fairies of the drama's childhood, and sought to replace them with beings whose motives and actions are supposed to resemble those of ordinary mortals. (10 December 1892)

That of course was just what appealed to Carroll, but he was not alone, *Liberty Hall* ran for 183 performances. John Russell Stephens quotes Carton as saying 'No dramatic author was ever more fortunate in his company – and *his* manager' (1992, p. 169) and though not all Alexander's authors might have expressed themselves as fulsomely he did maintain his commitment to 'British authorship' with plays by Oscar Wilde (*Lady Windermere's Fan* and *The Importance of Being Earnest*),

H. A. Jones (*The Masqueraders, The Triumph of the Philistines*), A. W. Pinero (*The Second Mrs Tanqueray*) to pluck out the best known from his list (Mason, 1935, pp. 235 et seq), but Carroll saw none of them. In most cases it was probably best for him that he did not do so, though it is difficult to suppose quite what put him off *The Importance of Being Earnest* except of course the reputation of the author, but that was not such an unusual reaction.

More Theatres

The theatrical map of London changed immensely during Carroll's time. New or reconstructed theatres sprang up in the 1880s and 1890 to cater not simply for increasing demand, but also for diversification of tastes: the Avenue (1882), the Comedy (1881), the Garrick (1889), the Lyric (1888), Toole's (re-opened 1882) and Daly's (1893) were all attended by Carroll.

Opened in March 1882 the Avenue (later the Playhouse) in Northumberland Avenue was rather cut off from other theatres. Carroll attended its opening pantomime, Joseph A. Cave's *Whittington and his Cat* three times, despite detecting on the first of them (1 January 1883) 'a piece of indecent fun in the harlequinade (about which I wrote to the Stage-manager)'. The Avenue struggled to find its identity and niche and Carroll visited it on only another three occasions. He went to the Comedy theatre in Panton Street just twice: to see Farnie's comic opera *Rip Van Winkle*, 'a very poor thing', on 30 April 1883, and Sydney Grundy's *Sowing the Wind* on 14 October 1893 with Cyril Maude, Winifred Emery and Brandon Thomas, with which he was well pleased, as was William Archer who rated 'the play...by far the best Mr Grundy has ever done' (1894, p. 232).

It was at the Garrick in Charing Cross Road that on 11 March 1893 Carroll saw B. C. Stephenson's and Clement Scott's *Diplomacy* (from Sardou's *Dora*) 'magnificently acted by Mr. Hare, the Bancrofts, Forbes-Robertson, Miss Olga Nethersole etc.' Such a venerable cast (Arthur Cecil too) was welcomed by William Archer: 'Mrs. Bancroft's voice and her crystalline laugh, both absolutely unimpaired...Mr. Arthur Cecil...has lost nothing in polish and humour', though 'Mr. Bancroft...seemed to me a trifle too deliberate' (1894, p. 55). To Kate Terry Gielgud 'Mr. Bancroft was fearfully slow – with a hesitation that rather suggested the absence of the prompter' and Arthur Cecil was 'not very audible' (1980, p. 4). In most audiences several generations of theatregoers overlap and inevitably have different responses to the same performance and performers. Thus of

188   *Lewis Carroll and the Victorian Stage*

Alabama by the American playwright Augustus Thomas, Archer wrote: 'it delighted me and the great majority of the Garrick audience, while it bored a minority, both in the gallery and the stalls'. With its unabashed sentimentality and 'bias towards the amiable' (1896, p. 268), not to mention Marion Terry in a small role, *Alabama* delighted Carroll so much that he saw it three times, remarking on the third (12 October 1895) that: '*Alabama* was as delightful as ever'. After his first visit on 8 November 1895 he described Barrie's *The Professor's Love Story* as 'a healthy and beautiful play, and splendidly acted' and on 30 November having 'suggested, in writing to Mr. Willard, how much we should like to come round and see him...between Acts II and III, he invited us to his room for a few minutes'. Carroll saw the play a third time on 7 March 1896. Though it comes as no surprise that Carroll should enjoy plays by the author of *Peter Pan*, he was far from alone in doing so, *The Professor's Love Story* having run successfully at the Comedy prior to the Garrick Theatre.

In 1891 Carroll went to the Lyric Theatre in Shaftesbury Avenue to see the comic opera *La Cigale* by F. C. Burnand with music by E. Audran, a reminder of Burnand's extraordinarily lengthy contribution to the Victorian stage, from his days at Cambridge University to his hugely popular *Ixion* and *Rumplestiltskin and the Maid* ('both capital burlesques') which Carroll saw in 23 and 24 June 1864 at the Royalty Theatre in Dean Street Soho, where on 5 October 1895 he saw Bourchier and Sutro's *The Chili Widow* which he dismissed as 'not very nice. As a literary production it is rubbish: and the acting is quite second rate'. Back to the Lyric, there on 18 June 1892 he saw the Gilbert and Cellier comic opera *The Mountebanks*, which he found rather dull and on 6 April 1894 Greet and Sledger's *The Little Squire*, which so incensed him that he protested to Mrs Greet as already recounted earlier in this chapter.

The location of Toole's Theatre in King William Street, Charing Cross, might, as Michael Reed has pointed out, have resulted in a nasty shock for a visitor who 'by mistake entered the door next to it, for he would have found himself in the mortuary of Charing Cross Hospital' (1992, p. 10). Carroll visited Toole's Theatre four times, apparently without undergoing such an unfortunate experience. He found J. L. Toole, who 'decided to call the house "Toole's Theatre"' (Hatton, 1889, vol. 2, p. 274) following its enlargement in 1882, 'very droll' in H. J. Byron's *The Upper Crust*, but 'not so well fitted' to Burnand's *Paw Claudian* in which he saw him on his first visit on 23 May 1884. 'Droll' was again the description for Toole in *The Butler*, a three-act comedy by Mr and Mrs Herman. Merivale in which he appeared with 'Violet Barnes [Vanbrugh]' as Lady Anne Babbicombe on 14 May 1887. The two appeared together

Carroll at the Theatre 189

again in *Dot*, a dramatisation of Dickens's *The Cricket on the Hearth* by her sister Irene's future husband Dion Boucicault, in which she 'was a pleasing May Fielding' and 'Toole was excellent as Caleb Plummer', on 14 January 1888. Carroll considered that J. M. Barrie's *Walker London*, which he saw on 23 April 1892, would 'have done well as a twenty-five minute farce, but was too thin for a three-act comedy'. Toole was supported by Irene Vanbrugh, in 'a stupid part as a learned Girton girl'.

Apart from Toole and Edward Terry, the only other manager to have the temerity (if not presumption) to name his theatre after himself was the American Augustus Daly. Carroll observed that 'the American theatre', as he called Daly's in Cranbourne Street off Leicester Square, was 'different from English ones: all that is not gilt is very dark: the effect is at once both tawdry and gloomy'. As to the performances in *Twelfth Night* on 24 February 1894, Ada Rehan was 'decidedly good, but not first-rate; and...too old for Viola', though altogether better than Violet Barnes who was 'ineffective' as Olivia. Carroll, who rarely attended performances by visiting (American or European) actors, had probably been drawn to *Twelfth Night* more by the presence of Violet Vanbrugh than Ada Rehan, but once there he judged their performances on merit. He had admired another American actress Mary Anderson in *Pygmalion and Galatea* at the Lyceum on 22 April 1885: 'very graceful and beautiful, [she] acts with real power'.

Brighton and Eastbourne

As already noted, Carroll was overwhelmingly a London playgoer. Whereas for previous generations spa towns (pre-eminently Bath of course) had been the main centres of entertainment for the leisured classes, in Carroll's day seaside resorts took over that function. Even on holiday the Victorians felt the obligation to take part in enjoyable and preferably worthwhile pursuits and, as Lowerson and Myerscough state, there was 'a crucial debate about how people should make use of their time' (1977, p. 3). The Prince Regent and his entourage had not concerned themselves greatly with this issue during their sojourns in Brighton and the town retained something of their indolence and indulgence. The Theatre Royal, which dated back to 1807, was substantially rebuilt in 1866 to the designs of C. J. Phipps, creating an auditorium 'shaped like a squeezed horseshoe, with three closely spaced, steeply raked balconies, supported by iron columns. The 1866 colour scheme was purple, cream and buff.' (Earl and Sell eds., 2000, p. 29) The venture had been financed

190   *Lewis Carroll and the Victorian Stage*

by a syndicate with Nye Chart as manager, but when he died aged only fifty-four in 1876 his wife took over and 'by the early eighteen-eighties the theatre was very prosperous indeed...on 5 December 1884, she [Mrs Chart] paid off the sum of £6,000 advanced to her husband under the mortgage by the syndicate which had helped him to buy the theatre in 1866' (Dale, 1980, p. 48).

Carroll first visited the Theatre Royal on 6 January 1874 and, as Stanley Goodman recalled, returned frequently thereafter:

> He paid equally regular visits in the Christmas holidays to Brighton, where he stayed with his old Christ Church friend, the Rev. Henry Barclay, at 11 Sussex Square and attended the pantomime at the Theatre Royal (where he also saw the stage version of *Alice* in 1887). (Cohen ed., 1989, pp. 172-3)

During the 1870s and early 1880s the Brighton pantomimes were by Frank W. Green, whom Carroll rated second only to E. L. Blanchard. A further attraction was Lizzie Coote, who for a time was a regular feature. On January 4 1878 Carroll took a party to '*Jack and the Beanstalk* which was extremely good as a whole. There was a pretty scene of children, the leading child being "Clara Elliston", a graceful and pretty child, a little like Xie Kitchin.' This (like several of Green's pantomimes) had been performed (in 1874) at the Surrey Theatre, a transpontine playhouse to which Carroll ventured only once, in January 1877 to see Lizzie Coote in its seasonal offering. Not even 'laureate Green' (Wilson, 1934, p. 155) could succeed every time and Carroll found his *Dick Whittington and his Cat* on 10 January 1882 'unusually dull', which cannot have been helped by its excessive length: 'the opening [i.e. excluding the harlequinade]...occupied four hours in its development', but for those who lasted the course: 'Mr. Sims is a supple harlequin, Miss King a capital columbine, Mr. English a good pantaloon; Miss Nelly Moore, harlequina' (*Stage* 30 December 1881). The Cootes were back for Green's *Little Red Riding Hood*, which Carroll saw on 9 January 1883, and his approval was endorsed by the *Stage* (29 December 1882): 'Miss Carrie Coote plays Riding Hood excellently. Miss Lizzie Coote is amusing as Boy Blue'. The published text of Green's pantomime commends his endeavour 'to provide a pretty and familiar nursery tale, told in a simple and entertaining style, combining wholesome fun, scenic display, tasteful dresses and effects' (Green, 1883). The opening chorus shows that Green was an accomplished wordsmith and rhymester:

Carroll at the Theatre

The Haunt of Maligna the Malignant.
'Come goblins grim, and lithe of limb,
Bestir within our cavern dim.
Come, demon brood, serve up thy food,
Put master in a merry mood.
The night hath sped, the bat hath fled,
The screech-owl hides his horned head,
The morn is breaking rosy red.' (p. 10)

Elsewhere Green shows his gifts for topicality (in the schoolroom scene: 'Miss Minerva Birch (school teacher): Answer all your questions, never say you can't / Then you'll increase my Government grant.' p. 20) and wit (when the Prince is about to marry the villain's daughter: 'Venema: "A handsome couple," people will remark. Tiptoppo: I shouldn't take her out till after dark.' p. 37).

Apart from pantomimes, Carroll saw *Alice in Wonderland* and spent the memorable day with Phoebe and Lizzie Carlo and Dorothy d'Alcourt, which he relayed in his letter to the *St. James's Gazette* (see Chapter 7). He caught up with plays that he had missed in London such as R. C. Carton's *Sunlight and Shadow* with Marion Terry and George Alexander, who transferred it (briefly) from the Avenue to the St James's as a preliminary to the inauguration of his management there. He also saw favourites again such as H. A. Jones's *The Silver King*, on 10 October 1891, which 'was really well done on the whole, though only by a tour company – Mr. H George being the hero, and evidently imitated Mr. Wilson Barrett – "Cissie" was nicely played by "Miss Polly Mallalieu"'. The family of comedian William Mallalieu was known to Carroll, who on 11 and 17 October 1891 wrote to Mary praising her sister Polly's performance.

Whereas in Brighton the Christmas pantomime was the primary attraction for Carroll, for him Eastbourne was only a summer resort, where from 1877 he took his annual holiday, staying with Mr and Mrs Dyer at 7 Lushington Road until in 1897 they moved to Bedford Well Road where he made what was to be his last visit (Jones and Gladstone, 1998, pp. 79-80). As David Cannadine writes in his authoritative account of its evolution, Eastbourne was 'almost entirely the creation of the House of Cavendish' (1980, p. 63) or more precisely the seventh Duke of Devonshire, who despite the fact that the family estate was heavily mortgaged continued to provide more and more capital for the development of the resort. The detailed planning was undertaken from 1859 onwards by Henry Currey and covered not only residential building, amenities (water and sewage), shops (none on the sea front), but also

192 *Lewis Carroll and the Victorian Stage*

recreational facilities, for the provision of which on a grand scale 'the Devonshire Parks and Baths Company' was set up in 1873 (p. 246). The Duke was 'obliged to dig further into his pockets', which he did with the conviction that, as he put it, Eastbourne needed 'a good assembly room, suitable for first class concerts, baths, etc.,...by which under proper management, the length of the present season would be increased, and also a great inducement held out to winter visitors' (p. 282). In fact the facilities catered for visitors all the year round with tennis courts, swimming bath, cricket pitch and eventually a theatre.

The annual *Devonshire Park Guide* provided full information for the 'class of visitors and residents whose demands for means of amusement and pastime were likely to be somewhat in advance of those provided at the majority of English watering-places' (p. 7). For their delectation there were 77 afternoon concerts, 78 evening concerts, 8 illuminated fetes and firework displays, 23 cricket matches, 9 days of lawn tennis tournaments, 3 smoking concerts and the companies booked for the Devonshire Park Theatre, which that year (1894) ranged from the 'Gaiety Girl' to the German Reeds and 'Charlie's Aunt' to 'Arms and the Man' (p. 26). As for the theatre itself:

> the upholstery and fittings were supplied by Maple, the tableau curtain [was] one of the most magnificent ever seen...the decorations of the walls and ceiling, by Schmidt, of Holloway, are chaste and elegant, ...and the Vestibule... is a gem of architectural design (*see illustration*) (p. 17)

Henry Currey, who, though his credits included St Thomas's Hospital, had never designed a theatre before, had done Eastbourne proud, as the first audience on 2 June 1884 must have realised, as must mere passers-by who could hardly fail to be struck by the two Italianate towers with pyramid roofs that flanked the façade, though they may not have appreciated that these were safety features comprising fireproof stairways and water tanks (Earl and Sell, 2000, p. 58).

As it happened another playhouse, this one by the hugely experienced theatre architect C. J. Phipps, had opened in Seaside Road, Eastbourne, in the previous year. Whereas the Devonshire Park Theatre had 'taken two years to build' (Thomas, 1997, p. 1), the Theatre Royal (later the Royal Hippodrome), also in the Italian style, went up in a matter of months:

> During January, 1883, a large dwelling house known as 'Aberdeen House', standing in its own grounds in Seaside Road, was being demolished to make room for this Theatre. The property was owned by a Mr. Simmons, who leased it to Mr. George Loveday, manager of Mr. J. L. Toole's world-famous

London Theatrical Company. The foundation stone was laid in April, and the building was scheduled to be built by July. It received its licence on July 16, and was called 'The Theatre Royal and Opera House'. Opening night was scheduled for 2nd August...[with] a special engagement for three nights only of the 'eminent Mr. J. L. Toole and his London company in an original comedy "A Fool and His Money".'[2]

Carroll began his regular holidays in Eastbourne in 1877, well before either the Theatre Royal or the Devonshire Park Theatre was even being planned, so they cannot be regarded as part of the resort's initial attraction for him. No doubt that was its refinement, the sense of superiority that led visitors such as himself to announce their arrival in the *Eastbourne Gazette* and *Eastbourne Chronicle*, and the aristocratic aura of the Devonshires, including the particular personal distinction of the seventh duke: 'First Smith's Prizeman at Trinity, Cambridge, where he took a First in Classics and Maths...Chancellor of London and then of Cambridge University, founder and benefactor of the Cavendish Laboratory'. Of him one contemporary observed: 'Had he not been a duke, he would have been a worthy professor of mathematics.' (Cannadine, 1980, p. 299)

During the years prior to the opening of the two purpose-built theatres Carroll attended performances in the Assembly Rooms, the Bijou Theatre, New Hall and Diplock's Assembly Rooms, but in 1884 he was able to see his favourite Gilbert and Sullivan piece *Patience* at the Devonshire Park and one of H. B. Farnie's most popular productions (705 performances at the Folly Theatre) *Les Cloches de Corneville* at the Theatre Royal with Shiel Barry as Gaspard, the miser giving what the *Eastbourne Gazette* described as 'a most remarkable impersonation. It is one of those pieces of powerful acting we are seldom permitted to see. He displayed surpassing powers of facial expression' (13 August 1884). Carroll saw *Les Cloches de Corneville* twice at the Theatre Royal in 1884 and once more at the Devonshire Park on 20 September 1887, when it was performed by Mr Warwick Gray's company of children.

In August 1886 the Theatre Royal played host to *The Mikado* with such success that 'many had to be denied admission', but Carroll favoured *La Fille de Madame Angot*, one of several English versions of C. Lecocq's comic opera, at the Devonshire Park, no doubt because it was performed by the aforementioned Mr Warwick Gray's company of children, which was only attracting 'fairly large audiences' (*Eastbourne Chronicle* 7 August 1886). Not even Carroll was all that impressed by the performers, but despite – or perhaps because of – this he called 'on Mr Warwick Gray...and saw the matron who looks after the boys (there are 20 boys and 20 girls) and spoke to some of the boys' and the next day (8

August) 'wrote to ask Mr. Gray to call (to talk about my idea of a Children's Theatre)' to which he referred in his letter to Savile Clarke at the end of the month. The next year Savile Clarke's adaptation of the 'Alice' books played at the Devonshire Park with Phoebe Carlo and Dorothy D'Alcourt: 'considering that the majority of the artistes were children, one cannot speak too highly of the performances' opined the *Eastbourne Chronicle* (20 August 1887) rather patronisingly. The rival *Eastbourne Gazette* was more impressed, particularly with Phoebe Carlo who 'plays as a child, although there is associated with her acting a piquant spirit that many older actresses strive in vain to obtain' (17 August 1887). Carroll must have hoped that Irene Vanbrugh, who was his guest at the time, was receptive to these finer points of acting.

14. Richard Corney Grain

Carroll at the Theatre   195

On 26 August 1889 Richard Corney Grain was part of the German Reed entertainment that attracted 'a large and fashionable audience' (*Eastbourne Gazette* 28 August 1889) to the Devonshire Park. Noted for his 'unwieldy form' and 'invariable propriety' (Hibbert, 1916, p. 153), Grain performed one of his most celebrated sketches *My Aunt's in Town*, of which David Williamson wrote: 'Can any one forget his funny description of a visit to the stores in company with his aunt, and his account of the deadly struggle over remnants? (1895, pp. 75-6) Not everything in Eastbourne was as irreproachable as the German Reeds. Carroll may have been thankful to the *Eastbourne Gazette* for warning him that *The Catspaw* at the Theatre Royal contained 'points about the "spy" brother, apart from his rascally plotting, which are objectionable' (14 August 1889). He ran no such risk in seeing *Bootle's Baby* by Hugh Moss featuring Maggie Bowman as Mignon at the Devonshire Park on 17 September, though he found her elocution indistinct. Other favourites at that theatre in the early 1890s included J. L. Toole and Irene Vanbrugh in Jerrold's *Paul Pry* (21 August 1891), Farnie's *Paul Jones* (12 and 15 October 1891), Pinero's *Sweet Lavender* (19 and 20 July 1892), the Benson company (17 and 20 August 1892) and *The Idler* which he saw three times also that August (22, 23 and 24). Carroll revisited *Liberty Hall*, which he had so enjoyed at the St. James's and which the *Eastbourne Gazette* (6 September 1893) endorsed as 'a refined and altogether delightful play'. Carroll and the newspaper would not have found themselves in step about the next week's offering: Wilde's *A Woman of No Importance* about which the *Eastbourne Gazette* (13 September 1893) sounded forth:

> It has not failed to please the jaded and fastidious taste of West End London...[where it] attracted an exceptionally large and fashionable audience...There is no need for prurient prudes of the species first pinned on cork by Mr. Charles Reade, to shake their heads at 'A Woman of No Importance'. There is no real harm in the play, which indeed enforces the teaching of the venerable couplet: –
> Know thou this task, enough the man to know,
> Virtue alone is happiness below!

Carroll probably did not regard himself as a 'prurient prude', but nevertheless stayed away. He had gone to see Albert Chevalier, albeit in a programme of coster songs rather than a play, when he gave a single 'Recital' at a considerably increased price of admission, on 22 July 1893. Carroll had evidently forgotten seeing Chevalier in *The Real Little Lord Fauntleroy*, though he had been 'decidedly good; but as a comic singer

196 *Lewis Carroll and the Victorian Stage*

(with considerable powers of pathos as well) he is quite first-rate' and he judged 'the songs...quite inoffensive, and very funny' and Chevalier's 'influence, on public taste...towards refinement and purity'. For once Carroll was ahead of the local press, the *Eastbourne Chronicle* (29 July 1893) pontificating that Chevalier's

> ditties represent a type of slang composition which might be expected to 'catch on' with the denizens of the gallery, but which, we think, acquires a false importance when it is feted and lauded by the cultured classes of the community.

The summer of 1894 brought the Martin-Harveys to Eastbourne in a triple bill, which Carroll saw on 31 August and Henry Irving and Ellen Terry to see his son (H. B.) in *A Bunch of Violets,* which attracted 'a crowded and fashionable audience' (*Eastbourne Gazette* 29 August 1894) of which Carroll was not part. He was though twice (4 and 8 September 1894) at *La Cigale*, a comic opera by Burnand and Audran at the Devonshire Park, and three times (5, 6 and 8 September 1894) at the melodrama *Our Eldorado*, written by and featuring F. A. Scudamore (see Redgrave, 1984, pp. 23-4) with a 'handsome child...[who] acted very prettily. In the bill she is "Marjorie Chetwynd", but we afterwards found her to be "Florence Ada White"'.

The repertoire of the Theatre Royal was not as refined as that at the Devonshire Park and Carroll sometimes found his sensibilities offended, as with Henry Pettitt's Adelphi melodrama *A Woman's Revenge* 'an unpleasant play, very poorly acted' (2 September 1895) and Clay M. Green's musical comedy *Hans the Boatman* ('poorly acted...coarse dialogue', 4 August 1896). As for Miss Go-Won-Go-Mohawk in *We-ton-No-Mah*, based on Fenimore Cooper's novel, on 28 September 1896, though 'a good audience applauded with exceeding demonstrativeness throughout this piece, and cheered their favourite characters almost every time they came upon the stage' (*Eastbourne Gazette* 30 September 1896), the hapless Carroll thought it 'so poor that I only saw two acts', a decision to which the behaviour of the audience may have contributed.

Such demonstrativeness would hardly have become the genteel ambiance of the Devonshire Park Theatre where on consecutive days (20 and 21 August 1896) Carroll was more at ease with the Edward Compton Comedy Company in *She Stoops to Conquer*: 'Mr Edward Compton was "Tony Lumpkin", and Miss Sidney Crowe was "Miss Hardcastle". It was decidedly good' and '*David Garrick*, which is about the best thing I have seen Mr. Compton do.' He was also well pleased with another familiar piece *Masks and Faces* (Taylor and Reade), on what was to be his last visit to the Devonshire Park Theatre on 31 August 1897; Ben Greet was 'a great deal better than I have seen him before [as Triplet] – "Peg Woffington" and "Mabel Vane" were both well acted; and the play as a whole was above average'. Happily Carroll also took pleasure in his final performances at the Theatre Royal: that most enduring of melodramas, Douglas Jerrold's *Black-Eyed Susan*, which he so enjoyed on 19 August that he returned the next day with his friend Winifred Schuster.

There were few, if any, other seaside resorts that could have provided Carroll with two attractive theatres catering for a range of tastes including his own. How best to characterise that taste? As with his choice of Eastbourne, Carroll's London playgoing formed what would now probably be called a 'profile' that was reasonably representative of his class, education and age, though for his gender his tastes were on the sentimental side. Having said that, one thing that an exploration of Carroll's theatregoing unquestionably demonstrates is that he shared his partiality for child performers with literally thousands of others and that he was not that unusual in regarding the theatre as a particularly appropriate pastime for his young friends. What he considered to be suitable for them often became the determining factor in his selection, but his own preferences were certainly not highbrow or intellectual. Throughout his life he delighted in comic acting and certainly developed a taste for sentiment. He enjoyed spectacular scenery, attractive costumes and spirited music. Most of Carroll's choices reflected the mainstream of theatrical taste at the time: Shakespeare at the Princess's Theatre, Robson at the Olympic and burlesques there and at other theatres, pantomimes, Ellen Terry (and her sisters) with and without Irving, the German Reeds and Corney Grain, Gilbert and Sullivan, H. B. Farnie and *opéra bouffe*, the plays of Tom Taylor and J. M. Barrie. On each occasion Carroll relished the whole experience of theatregoing (from the purchase or gift of the tickets to the visit backstage afterwards) as long as it remained untainted by indecorum of any kind. Above all, as the examples with which this chapter opened testify, for over forty years Carroll's enthusiasm for the theatre remained undiminished. In Ellen Terry's estimation Lewis Carroll was 'a splendid theatre-goer' (1908, p. 357).

Notes

[1]   Hugues Lebailly, 'Charles Lutwidge Dodgson et la Vie Artistique Victorienne', 1997, Volume Annexe: Fichiers, p. 52

[2]   The Royal Hippodrome souvenir programme September 1946 in the Eastbourne Public Library.

In Conclusion

In the quest to understand Lewis Carroll more fully through an exploration of his interest in the theatre, we have garnered what might be described as pieces in a jigsaw puzzle (not as far as I am aware a pastime he indulged in), which need to be assembled to create a composite picture.

The first piece is from Carroll's childhood and youth. There the image is vivid and clear. His innate sense of fun and capacity as a performer are reflected in his marionette theatre, charades, the magic lantern and his play-readings. His fascination with toy theatre needs to be seen in the context of the huge success of Signor Brigaldi and his puppets, who attracted large audiences to their performances and gave encouragement to amateurs at home. Carroll's single-handed performances of John Maddison Morton's *Away with Melancholy* and Henry Thornton Craven's *Done Brown* must have been rousing occasions ('more brandy') as he deployed half a dozen voices to create male and female characters. These plays were light, popular theatre, then much in vogue in London and the provinces. Indeed Carroll had seen them both on the professional stage. There was then little highbrow about the youthful Carroll's home entertainments. His choice of Henry Cockton's *The Life and Adventures of Valentine Vox The Ventriloquist* is revealing, as is his comment: 'Read *Valentine Vox* in the morning instead of working.' Carroll must have realised that he had a gift to entertain others, especially young children, and this was a means of expressing a vital part of himself as well as creating a relationship with them. There remains of course the, one is tempted to say brooding, presence of the Revd Charles Dodgson. His opposition to the professional theatre has long been well known, but reading his translation of Tertullian, in particular the virulent anti-theatrical sections, enforces the impression that his son encountered paternal disapproval. On the other hand Carroll did give his magic-lantern show at Croft School, where his father's acquiescence was presumably required.

The Revd Charles Dodgson's attitude towards the theatre can be seen as an undercurrent in his own education and that which he chose for his sons. Richmond School was evidently congenial to the young Lewis Carroll, who found in the Tate family kindred spirits and in Lucy Tate the prototype for many another young girl with whom he was to engage

In Conclusion 199

through his talent to amuse. Rugby School was by all accounts a bleak experience, but one wonders how Carroll coped with the ritual song. Shy though he undoubtedly was, might not this have been the occasion on which to tap that extrovert self which was to shine – indeed probably was already shining – in his entertainments at home. My attention to the Latin play at Westminster School may seem curious since Carroll did not attend the school, though he saw two performances there. However, the Latin play sheds light on two key characters in Carroll's life: his father and H. G. Liddell. I suggest that the Revd Charles Dodgson's choice of schools for his sons may have been influenced by his experience of the Latin play at Westminster, but that Liddell's prompt support for the play – which Samuel Wilberforce had effectively banned – is indicative of his and his wife's love of the theatre.

This antagonism between Liddell and Wilberforce over the Latin play seems likely to have spilt over into their new roles as Dean of Christ Church and Bishop of Oxford, with particular relevance to the expectation that Carroll should take priest's orders. Liddell and Wilberforce were both formidable figures in the academic and ecclesiastical establishment of the day. Liddell's action in restoring the Latin play must have been widely seen as a rebuff for Wilberforce. That success can hardly have heightened Liddell's inclination to defer to Wilberforce, particularly on a matter in which the theatre featured. It is generally accepted that Carroll's love of the theatre was one, if not the, reason for his reluctance to take priest's orders and if that was the case then it is scarcely surprising that Liddell should come to Carroll's rescue. Having said that, it has to be acknowledged that Carroll's behaviour in Oxford was highly circumspect as far the theatre was concerned. Early on he attended entertainments by Fanny Kemble and the German Reeds, though thereafter he generally avoided the professional theatre. Carroll clearly enjoyed some early undergraduate performances, but his interest appeared to wane and when OUDS blossomed under Jowett's encouragement Carroll was nowhere to be seen. By then Carroll had influential contacts in the theatrical profession, but, though he did not hesitate to use them in other ways, he did not deploy them in Oxford. There he seems to have been content to keep a very low profile.

The 'Alice' books gave Lewis Carroll a new identity. His relationship with the Liddell sisters mirrored previous and future relationships with other young girls in many of which the theatre in some form or other was central. This was not really the case with the Liddells, though their shared taste for popular music in the form of 'Villikins and his Dinah' has been noted and it is apparent that the 'Alice' books both owe a good deal to the contemporary theatre, as Tenniel's drawings do to the enthusiasm he shared with Carroll. The dramatisation of the 'Alice' books by Savile Clarke was something Carroll had long hoped for and when it happened he took a close interest in it. Carroll's letters to Savile Clarke are a wonderful repository of his views on the theatre. He comes across as a shrewd judge of acting, in particular the respective merits of Phoebe Carlo and Isa Bowman as Alice and the failings of the Red and White Queens. His insistence on clear pronunciation and correct emphasis addresses the essential basics of stage performance. His preoccupation with 'anything suggestive of coarseness' signals the growing preoccupation of later years, but his concern for and generosity towards Savile Clarke are irreproachable.

The exploration of home entertainments takes us away from the professional theatre, though their popularity from the 1850s onwards undoubtedly contributed to the surge in middle-class audiences and recruits to the stage. Indeed it is significant that having denied himself the delights of theatregoing for eighteen months following his father's death Carroll eased himself back into the habit after what amounted to almost a frenzy of home entertainments during Christmas-New Year 1869-70. This exuberant participation in charades, dumb-shows, *tableaux vivants* and such like was clearly not at all unusual for men of Carroll's age and background. The drawing of 'Una and the Lion' in the *Illustrated London News* of 28 December 1872 shows Uncle Jack in (fairly willing) thrall to his niece Susie, whose appearance is reminiscent of Tenniel's Alice. Uncle Jack's resemblance to Carroll's friend George MacDonald is reinforced by the accounts of his wholehearted participation in such antics by his son Greville and actor Johnston Forbes-Robertson.

Perhaps the family whose domestic hearth Carroll most wanted to share was the Terrys. He finally succeeded in meeting them all in 1864 and photographed them the following summer. He remained in contact, with Ellen in particular, for the rest of his life.

Carroll had admired Kate and Ellen Terry as actresses from his early theatregoing at the Princess's Theatre and followed their careers and those of their sisters Marion (Polly) and Florence. Loyal though he was to them, they were not above criticism. Sometimes this was deserved (an unsuitable role for instance); sometimes it was rather gratuitous (as with Ellen Terry in *Faust*). Carroll had no compunction in calling for favours, usually in the form of tickets, gifts for his companions and help for his protégées, but such behaviour was customary at the time. Ellen Terry's could not be so described with her marriage to G. F. Watts, her relationship with E. W. Godwin (two children) and her closeness to Henry Irving. As his letters reveal, Carroll, though he broke off direct contact for a period, was essentially sympathetic towards Ellen Terry and defended

In Conclusion 201

and justified her actions. His attitude cannot but be described as sympathetic and by the standards of the day even liberal and enlightened.

Carroll's apparent disregard for the wellbeing of children (as young as five) appearing at 11pm on the stage of the Princess's Theatre in the 1850s originally struck me as culpable. However it seems unfair to single him out from that audience (and others) to shoulder the blame for what at the time was hardly a contentious matter. The popularity of child performers continued throughout the Victorian period and was clearly shared by thousands of playgoers, so in this respect Carroll cannot be accounted exceptional. He was, though, in his interest in the working conditions of young actors and actresses and his common sense seems to have influenced the legislation passed in 1889. On that occasion he opposed the prescriptive intervention of vigilante groups, supporting instead the freedom of families to run their own lives within the safeguards laid down by the government. He undoubtedly regarded his encouragement of child performers as a means of helping them realise their talent and benefit their families financially. Though the tone of his attempts to further the stage aspirations of what he called 'real *ladies*' strikes us as irredeemably snobbish, he was often far more progressive than their own parents. With both minors and protégées Carroll showed himself to be sympathetic to the advancement of women whilst in no way countenancing any compromise of their personal safety or respectability.

The issue of respectability inevitably arises with Carroll's photographs of young girls without necessarily dwelling on the few (surviving) nude studies. The close links between the theatre and photography are evident from the work of Laroche – in particular – in the 1850s. With his twin enthusiasms for the theatre and photography it is not surprising that Carroll should want to take subjects in theatrical costumes as he was well equipped to do after his move into more spacious accommodation at Christ Church. Several of his models, though not professional actresses, had experience of home theatricals and with them Carroll seems to have established something of the actor-audience relationship that he had enjoyed in different guises from his entertainments at Croft onwards. Protective as he was of children and women working in the theatre, he would hardly have risked tainting his photographic subjects in any way.

Though his practice of taking young female companions to the theatre was a rather late development, his preoccupation with not exposing them to anything remotely objectionable should be registered now. His early theatregoing was less fraught. Charles Kean's Shakespeare revivals could be relied upon to enchant the eye and delight the ear without any risk of offence. Burlesques, though they were a rather racier form of entertainment, generally avoided excess and Carroll appreciated the genius of Frederick Robson at the Olympic and lesser talents in the same genre at other theatres. He was as gripped as anyone by wholesome melodrama from the prolific pen of Boucicault and other exponents. His enthusiasm for pantomime, especially when performed partly if not wholly by children, was tempered by alertness to any coarseness, especially in the harlequinade. Though the employment of children reached its height with pantomimes they were a feature in many plays and obviously were a significant attraction for audiences who sustained long runs. The comedies of W. S. Gilbert, his collaboration with Arthur Sullivan and the English strain of *opéra bouffe* account for a significant proportion of Carroll's playgoing. Though he did on occasion take exception to Gilbert's work, Carroll evidently had no difficulty with H. B. Farnie's numerous concoctions in which the charms of Florence St. John and her ilk were displayed. This, after all, was essentially theatre as fun, as Carroll's childhood entertainments had been, and as long as decorum was preserved he and the tens of thousands of other theatregoers who kept them running for months, years even, were happy. Carroll was loyal to the Terry sisters and became a regular at the Lyceum Theatre after Ellen joined Irving there. Marion Terry's choice of plays caused him some problems in the 1880s and 1890s, by which time he had become set in his ways and unreceptive to the wave of new drama not only by the advanced guard of Ibsen and Shaw but also by Pinero, Wilde and Jones. However, as both Shaw and Archer acknowledged, there was still a public for old-fashioned sentimental plays and Carroll was undoubtedly representative of it.

In summary then it is difficult to find anything exceptionable in Carroll's playgoing. Even his taste for child performers, far from being dubious, was clearly shared by many of his contemporaries. This serves to normalise Carroll as, it seems to me, has most of this exploration of him and the theatre of his day. What picture do we have now that the different pieces of the jigsaw are in place? Though essentially shy, in his youth he had a carefree, extrovert side to his personality, which found expression in home entertainments. These may well have attracted paternal disapproval, but Carroll persisted, presumably because of the sense of release that he experienced and his success in creating relationships with his young audiences. This connection between performance and companionship must have become bedded deep in his personality. It manifested itself in his continuing enthusiasm for amateur theatricals and other like pastimes, and not only attending plays but also taking children with him and befriending young performers. Carroll recognised that – to use his own words – 'a taste for *acting* is one of the strongest passions of human

In Conclusion 203

nature'. His awareness of the almost universal impulse amongst the young to act and/or watch others acting provided Carroll with the means by which he engaged with them, be it through his own entertainments, acting to camera, encouraging their careers or the shared experience of watching a play. Quite simply the theatre was the golden strand that wove joy into his life.

References

Adderley, J. G. 1888. *The Fight for Drama at Oxford*, Oxford.

Allen, Shirley. 1971. *Samuel Phelps and the Sadler's Wells Theatre*, Middletown, CT.

Altick, R. 1978. *The Shows of London*, Cambridge, Mass and London.

Alumni Oxiensis 1715-1886, 1888. Oxford and London.

Amor, Anne Clark. 1995. *Lewis Carroll Child of the North*, Luton and Croft.

Amor, Anne Clark ed. 1990. *Letters to Skeffington Dodgson from His Father*, London.

Archer, William. 1894. *The Theatrical World for 1893*, London.

1896. *The Theatrical World for 1895*, London.

1897. *The Theatrical World for 1896*, London.

1898. *The Theatrical World for 1897*, London.

Archer, William, Halkett, George and Lowe, Robert W. 1877. *The Fashionable Tragedian*, London.

Arnold, Ethel. 1929. Reminiscences of Lewis Carroll. In *Atlantic Monthly*, January to June, pp. 781-9.

Arundell, Dennis. 1965. *The Story of Sadler's Wells Theatre*, London.

Auerbach, Nina. 1985. *Romantic Imprisonment Women and other Glorified Outcasts*, New York.

1987. *Ellen Terry Player in Her Time*, London.

Ayre, Leslie. 1972. *The Gilbert and Sullivan Companion*, London.

Barker, G. F. and Stenning, Alan H. eds. 1928. *The Record of Old Westminsters*, 2 vols, London.

Baker, Michael. 1978. *The Rise of the Victorian Actor*, London.

Bakewell, Michael. 1997. *Lewis Carroll A Biography*, London.

Bancroft, Squire and Marie. 1889. *Mr and Mrs Bancroft On and Off the Stage*, London.

Banham, Martin ed. 1985. *Plays by Tom Taylor*, Cambridge.

Barish, Jonas. 1981. *The Anti-theatrical Prejudice*, Berkeley, Los Angeles and London.

Barnes, Kenneth. 1958. *Welcome Good Friends*, London.

Barthes, Roland. 1982. *Camera Lucida Reflections on Photography*, London.

Beaver, Patricia. 1974. *Victorian Parlour Games for Today*, London.

References

205

Beerbohm, Max. 1920. *Herbert Beerbohm Tree Some Memories of Him and His Art*, London.

Benson, Constance. 1926. *Mainly Players: Bensonian Memories*, London.

Bettany, F. G. 1926. *Stewart Headlam: A Biography*. London.

Bill, E. G. W. and Mason, J. F. A. 1970. *Christ Church and Reform 1850-1867*, Oxford.

Bingham, Madeleine. 1978. *'The Great Lover.' The Life and Art of Herbert Beerbhom Tree*, London.

Blake, Kathleen. 1974. *Play, Games and Sport The Literary Works of Lewis Carroll*, Ithaca and London.

Blanchard, E. L. 1867. *Faw, Fee, Fo, Fum; or, Jack the Giant-Killer*, London.
1872. *The Children in the Wood; or Harlequin Queen Mab and the World of Dreams*, London.

Booth, Michael R. 1981. *Spectacular Theatre 1850-1910*, London.
1988. Ellen Terry. In Stokes, John, Booth, Michael R., and Bassnett, Susan, *Bernhardt, Terry, Duse the actress in her time*, Cambridge.
Nd. *Prefaces to English Nineteenth-Century Theatre*, Manchester.

Booth, Michael R. ed. 1976. *English Plays of the Nineteenth Century Pantomimes, Extravaganzas and Burlesques*, Oxford.

Bowman, Anne. 1891. *Acting Charades and Proverbs Arranged for Representation in the Drawing-Room*, London.

Bowman, Isa. 1899. *The Story of Lewis Carroll Told for Young People by The Real Alice in Wonderland*, London.

Bowring, John ed. 1962. *The Works of Jeremy Bentham*, 11 vols, London and New York.

Bradley, H. C. 1900. *Rugby*, London.

Bratton, J. S. 1975. *The Victorian Popular Ballad*. London.

British Parliamentary Papers, Stage and Screen 1, 1968, Shannon.

Brown, Eluned ed. 1966. *The London Theatre 1811-1866 Selections from the diary of Henry Crabb Robinson*, London.

Bulwer Lytton, Edward. 1971. *England and the English*, 2 vols, Shannon.

Burnand, F. C. 1856. *Villikins and his Dinah*, in *Lacy's Amateur Theatre*, vol. 1–6, London.
1880. *Personal Reminiscences of the "A. D. C." Cambridge*, London.
1903. *Records and Reminiscences Personal and General*, London.

Calvert, Mrs Charles. 1911. *Sixty-Eight Years on the Stage*, London.

Carleton, John. 1965. *Westminster School*, London.

Carlisle, Carol J. 2000. *Helen Faucit Fire and Ice on the Victorian Stage*, London.

206   *Lewis Carroll and the Victorian Stage*

Cannadine, David. 1980. *Lords and Landowners: the Aristocracy and the Towns 1774-1967*, Leicester.

Carpenter, Humphrey. 1985. *O. U. D. S. A Centenary History of the Oxford University Dramatic Society*, Oxford and New York.

Carroll, Lewis. 1887. 'Alice' on the Stage. In *Theatre* 1 April, pp. 179-84.
1888. The Stage and the Spirit of Reverence. In *Theatre* 1 June, pp. 285-94.
1889. Stage Children. In *Theatre* 2 September, pp. 113-17.
1907. *Feeding the Mind*, London.
1931. *La Guida di Bragia*. In *Queen* 18 November, pp. 37-40 and 66.
1997. ed. Alexander Woollcott, *The Complete Illustrated Lewis Carroll*, Ware.

Cassell's Book of Sport and Pastimes, 1881, London.

Clark, Anne. 1979. *Lewis Carroll A Biography*, London.
1981. *The Real Alice*, London.

Cockton, Henry. 1840, *The Life and Adventures of Valentine Vox The Ventriloquist*, London and Birmingham.

Cohen, Morton N. 1982. The Actress and the Don: Ellen Terry and Lewis Carroll. In Guiliano, Edward ed. *Lewis Carroll A Celebration*, pp. 1-14, New York.
1995. *Lewis Carroll A Biography*, London.

Cohen, Morton N. ed. with the assistance of Roger Lancelyn Green, 1979. *The Letters of Lewis Carroll*, 2 vols, London.
1979a. *The Russian Journal – II A Record Kept by Henry Parry Liddon of a Tour Taken with C. L. Dodgson in the Summer of 1867*, New York.
1989. *Lewis Carroll Interviews and Recollections*, London.
1989a. *The Selected Letters of Lewis Carroll*, London.

Cohen, Morton N. and Gandolfo, Anita eds. 1982. *Lewis Carroll and the House of Macmillan*, Cambridge.

Cohen, Morton N. and Wakeling, Edward eds. 2003. *Lewis Carroll and His Illustrators Collaborators and Correspondence 1865-1898*, Basingstoke and Oxford.

Cole, J. W. 1859. *The Life and Theatrical Times of Charles Kean FSA*, 2 vols, London.

Coleman, John. 1903. *Charles Reade As I Knew Him*. London.

Collingwood, Stuart Dodgson. 1898. *The Life and Letters of Lewis Carroll*, London.
1898a. Before 'Alice'- The Boyhood of Lewis Carroll. In *Strand Magazine* vol. XVI, no. 91, pp. 616-27.
1899. *The Lewis Carroll Picture Book*, London and Glasgow.

References

Cook, Dutton. 1883. *Nights at the Play A View of the English Stage*. London.

Cook, Olive. 1963. *Movement in Dimensions*, London.

Coyne, J. Stirling. 1850. *Willikins and Hys Dinah*, London.

Craig, Edith and St. John, Christopher. 1933. *Ellen Terry's Memoirs*, London.

Craig, Edward Gordon. 1930. *Henry Irving*, London.

1957. *Index to the Story of My Days*, London.

Craven, H. Thornton. Nd. *Done Brown*, London.

Crutch, Denis, 1973. Lewis Carroll and the Marionette Theatre. In *Jabberwocky*, Spring, pp. 1-9.

Dale, Anthony. 1980. *The Theatre Royal Brighton*, London.

Davidson, Randall and Benham, William. 1892. *The Life of Archibald Tait*, 2 vols, London.

Davies, Ivor Ll. 1976. Archdeacon Dodgson. In *Jabberwocky*, vol. 5, no. 2, pp. 46-9.

Davis, Jim and Emeljanow, Victor. 2001. *Reflecting the Audience London Theatregoing 1840-1880*, Hatfield.

Davis, Tracy. 1986. The Employment of Children in the Theatre. In *New Theatre Quarterly*, vol. 2, no. 6, pp. 117-35.

1991. *Actresses as Working Women Their Social Identity in Victorian Culture*, London.

2000. *The Economics of the British Stage 1800-1914*, Cambridge.

Dent, Hugh R. 1938. *The House of Dent 1888-1938*, London.

De Sausmarez, Frederick B. 1932. Early Theatricals at Oxford. In *Nineteenth Century*, February, pp. 235-8.

Devonshire Park Guide, The. 1894, Eastbourne.

Dimond, Francis and Taylor, Roger. 1987. *Crown and Camera*, London.

Disher, Maurice Willson. 1955. *Victorian Song From Dive to Drawing Room*, London.

Dodgson, Charles ed. 1842. *Tertullian*, Oxford and London.

Donaldson, A. B. 1902. *Five Great Oxford Leaders*, London.

Duncan, Barry. 1964. *The St. James's Theatre Its Strange and Complete History 1835-1957*, London.

Earl, John and Sell, Michael eds. 2000. *The Theatres Trust Guide to British Theatres 1750-1950 A Gazetteer*, London.

Engen, Rodney. 1991. *Sir John Tenniel Alice's White Knight*, Aldershot.

Faber, Geoffrey. 1957. *Jowett - A Portrait with Background*, London.

Fairbrother, Sydney. 1939. *Through an Old Stage Door*, London.

208   *Lewis Carroll and the Victorian Stage*

Fawkes, Richard. 1979. *Dion Boucicault*, London.

Fisher, John ed. 1973. *The Magic of Lewis Carroll*, London.

Fitzgerald, Percy. 1870. *Principles of Comedy and Dramatic Effect*, London.

    1881. *The World behind the Scenes*, London.

    1890. *The Story of Bradshaw's Guide*, London.

    1893. *Henry Irving*, London.

Forbes-Robertson, Johnston. 1925. *A Player Under Three Reigns*, London.

Forshall, Frederic H. 1884. *Westminster School Past and Present*, London.

Foulkes, Richard. 1972. Henry Irving and Laurence Olivier as Shylock. In *Theatre Notebook*, vol. 28, no. 1, pp. 26-36.

    1984. *The Shakespeare Tercentenary of 1864*, London.

    1986. The Laroche Photographs of Charles Kean's Shakespeare Revivals. In *Theatrephile*, vol. 2, no. 8, pp. 29-33.

    1992. *The Calverts Actors of Some Importance*, London.

    1997. *Church and Stage in Victorian England*, Cambridge.

    2002. *Performing Shakespeare in the Age of Empire*, Cambridge.

    2002a. The French Play in London: The Comédie Française at the Gaiety Theatre 1879. In *Theatre Notebook*, vol. 56, no. 2, pp. 125-31.

Foulkes, Richard ed. 1992. *British Theatre in the 1890s Essays on drama and the stage*, Cambridge.

Francis, David. 1968. *The Origins of the Cinema*, Cardiff.

Freilgrath-Kroeker, Kate. 1880. *Alice and Other Fairy Plays for Children*, London.

Furniss, Harry.1901.*Confessions of a Caricaturist*, 2 vols, London.

Gandolpho, Anita. 1983. C. L. Dodgson's Russian Journey. In *Jabberwocky*, vol. 12, no. 4, pp. 91-6.

Garlick, Görel. 2003. *To Serve the Purpose of the Drama The Theatre Designs and Plays of Samuel Beazley 1786-1851*, London.

Gattegno, Jean. 1977. *Lewis Carroll Fragments of a Looking-Glass From Alice to Zero*, London.

Gernsheim, Helmut. 1968. *History of Photography*, London.

    1969. *Lewis Carroll Photographer*, New York.

    1975. *Julia Margaret Cameron Her Life and Photographic Work*, London.

Gielgud, Kate Terry. 1953. *An Autobiography*, London.

    1980. *A Victorian Playgoer*, London.

Gordon, Colin. 1982. *Beyond the Looking Glass*, London.

References 209

Green, Frank W. 1878. *Robinson Crusoe*, Liverpool.
   1883. *Little Red Riding Hood*, London.
Green, Roger Lancelyn ed. 1971. *The Diaries of Lewis Carroll*, 2 vols, Westport, CT.
Green Room Book, The. 1906. London.

Hammerton, J. A. 1929. *Barrie: The Story of a Genius*, London.
Hansard's Parliamentary Debates Session 1889 7th volume.
Hargreaves, Caryl. 1932. Alice's Recollections of Carrollian Days. In *Cornhill Magazine*, July, pp. 1-12.
Hatch, Beatrice. 1898. Lewis Carroll. In *Strand Magazine*, vol. XV, pp. 413-23.
Hatch Evelyn. 1933. *A Selection from the letters of Lewis Carroll to His Child-friends*, London.
Hatton, Joseph. 1889. *Reminiscences of J. L. Toole*, 2 vols, London.
Hibbert, H. G. 1916. *Fifty Years of A Londoner's Life*, London.
   1920. *A Playgoer's Memories*, London.
Hill, Brian. 1973. *Julia Margaret Cameron A Victorian Family Portrait*, London.
Howard, Diana. 1970. *London Theatres*, London.
Hudson, Derek. 1995. *Lewis Carroll*, London.
Hughes, Thomas. 1966. *Tom Brown's School Days*, London.
Hunt, James. 1854. *Stammering and Stuttering Their Nature and Treatment*, London.
   1859. *A Manual of the Philosophy of Voice and Speech Especially in relation to the English Language and the Art of Public Speaking*, London.

Irving, Laurence. 1951. *Henry Irving*, London.
   1967. *The Successors*, London.

Jackson, Russell ed. 1999. *Shakespeare in the London Theatre 1855-58 by Theodor Fontane*, London.
Jacobs, Arthur. 1986. *Arthur Sullivan A Victorian Musician*, Oxford.
Jefferson, Joseph. 1949. *"Rip Van Winkle" The Autobiography of Joseph Jefferson*, London.
Johnston, J. O. 1904. *The Life and Letters of Henry Parry Liddon*, London.
Jones, Doris Arthur. 1930. *The Life and Letters of Henry Arthur Jones*, London.
Jones, Jo Elwyn and Gladstone, Francis. 1995. *Red King's Dream or Lewis Carroll in Wonderland*, London.

1998. *The* Alice *Companion A Guide to Lewis Carroll's* Alice *Books*, Basingstoke and London.

Kendal, Madge. 1933. *Dame Madge Kendal by Herself*, London.
Kincaid, James. 1992. *The Erotic Child and Victorian Culture*, New York and London.
Knight, Joseph. 1893. *Theatrical Notes*, London.
Knight, William G. 1997. *A Major London 'Minor' The Surrey Theatre 1805-1865*, London.

Lavie, Germain. 1855. *The Westminster Play, Its Actors and Its Visitors*, London.
Leach, Karoline. 1999. *In the Shadow of the Dreamchild A New Understanding of Lewis Carroll*, London and Chester Springs.
Lebailly, Hugues. 1997. 'Charles Lutwidge Dodgson et la Vie Artistique Victorienne', Thèse de Doctorat, Université des Sciences Humaines de Strasbourg.
1999. C. L. Dodgson and the Victorian Cult of the Child. In *Carrollian*, no. 4, pp. 3-31.
2001. Charles Lutwidge Dodgson's Diaries: The Journal of a Victorian Playgoer (1855-1897). In *Carrollian*, no. 7, pp. 16-39.
Lennon, Florence Becker. 1947. *Lewis Carroll*, London.
Leverton, W. H. 1932. *Through the Box-office Window Memories of Fifty Years at the Haymarket Theatre*. London.
Lewes, G. H. 1875. *On Actors and the Art of Acting*, London.
Lloyd, Chris. 1991. The Theatre. In *Memories of Darlington, Northern Echo*, pp. 15-17.
Lobb, K. M. 1955. *The Drama in School and Church*, London.
Lovett, Charles. 1990. *Alice On Stage A History of the Early Theatrical Productions of Alice in Wonderland*, Westport CT and London.
2000. Lewis Carroll's Favourite Play. In *Carrollian*, no. 5, pp. 3-19.
Lowerson, John and Myerscough, John. 1977. *Time to Spare in Victorian England*, London.
Lusus Alteri Westmonasterienses Pars Secunda (1867), 3 vols, 1863-1906, London.

MacDonald, George. 1867. *Unspoken Sermons*, London.
1905. *Phantastes*, London.
MacDonald, Mrs George. 1870. *Chamber Dramas for Children*, London.
MacDonald, Greville. 1924. *George MacDonald and His Wife*, London.
1923. The Spirit of Play. In *Hibbert Journal*, vol. 21, pp. 353-66.
1932. *Reminiscences of a Specialist*, London.

References

Mackinnon, Alan. 1910. *The Oxford Amateurs. A Short History of the Theatricals at the University*, London.

Macqueen-Pope, W. 1945. *Theatre Royal Drury Lane*, London.

1949. *Gaiety Theatre of Enchantment*, London.

1951. *Ghosts and Greasepaint*. London.

Mander, Raymond and Mitchenson, Joe. 1963. *The Theatres of London*, London.

1968. *The Lost Theatres of London*, London.

Manvell, Roger. 1968. *Ellen Terry*, London.

Marston, Westland. 1890. *Some Recollections of Our Recent Actors*, London.

Martin-Harvey, John. 1933. *The Autobiography of Sir John Martin-Harvey*, London.

Mason, A. E. W. 1935, *Sir George Alexander and the St. James' Theatre*, London.

Maude, Cyril. 1903. *The Haymarket Theatre Some Records and Reminiscences*, London.

Maurice, F. D. 1853. *Theological Essays*, London.

Mavor, Carol. 1995. *Pleasures Taken Performances of Sexuality and Loss in Victorian Photographs*, Durham and London.

Mayer, David ed. 1994. *Playing out the Empire*, Oxford.

Meacham, Standish. 1970. *Lord Bishop The Life of Samuel Wilberforce*, Cambridge, Mass.

Melville, Joy. 2003. *Julia Margaret Cameron Pioneer Photographer*, Stroud.

Moore, Katharine. 1974. *Victorian Wives*, London.

Morley, Henry. 1891. *The Journal of a London Playgoer*, London.

Morley, Malcolm. 1966. *Margate and its Theatres*, London.

Morris, Frankie. 1983. Alice and King Chess. In *Jabberwocky*, vol. 12, no. 4, pp. 75-90.

Morton, John Maddison. 1850. *Away with Melancholy*, London.

Moses, Belle. 1910. *Lewis Carroll in Wonderland and At Home*, New York and London.

Nelson, Claudia. 1991. *Boys will be Girls The Feminine Ethic and British Children's Fiction 1857-1917*, New Brunswick and London.

Newark, Charles H. 1848. *Recollections of Rugby by an Old Rugbaean*, London.

Nicoll, Allardyce. 1946. *A History of Late Nineteenth Century Drama 1850-1900*, 2 vols, Cambridge.

Orens, J. R. 1978. *Lewis Carroll and the Dancing Priest*. In *Jabberwocky*, vol. 7, no. 2, pp. 31-5.

Pascoe, C. E. 1883. *Dramatic Notes A Chronicle of the London Stage 1879-1882*, London.

Pearson, Hesketh. 1956. *Beerbohm Tree His Life and Laughter*, London.

Pemberton, T. Edgar. 1890. *A Memoir of Edward Askew Sothern*, London.

1895. *John Hare Comedian 1865–1895 A Biography*, London.

1902. *Ellen Terry and her Sisters*, London.

Phelps, W. May and Forbes-Robertson, Johnston. 1886. *The Life and Life-work of Samuel Phelps*, London.

Planché, James Robinson. 1901. *Recollections and Reflections*. London.

Playfair, Nigel. 1930. *Hammersmith Hoy*, London.

Pollock, Frederick ed. 1876. *Macready's Reminiscences*, London.

Redgrave, Michael. 1984. *In My Mind's Eye*, London.

Reed, Michael. 1992. J. L. Toole's theatre of farce: ancient and modern. In Foulkes, Richard ed. *British Theatre in the 1890s Essays on drama and the stage*, Cambridge.

Rees, Terence. 1978. *Theatre Lighting in the Age of Gas*, London.

Richards, Jeffrey ed. 1994. *Henry Irving Theatre, Culture and Society*, Keele.

Robertson, T. W. 1889. *The Principal Dramatic Works of Thomas William Robertson with A Memoir by His Son*, 2 vols, London.

Robson, Catherine. 2001. *Men in Wonderland The Lost Girlhood of the Victorian Gentleman*, Princeton and Oxford.

Rosenfeld, Sybil. 1984. *The Georgian Theatre of Richmond Yorkshire*, London.

Rowell, George. 1978. *Queen Victoria Goes to the Theatre*, London.

Ruskin, John. 1885. *Ethics of the Dust Ten Lectures to Little Housewives on The Elements of Crystallisation*, New York.

1949. *Praeterita*, with an introduction by Kenneth Clark, London.

Sands, Molly. 1979. *Robson of the Olympic*, London.

Sargeaunt, John. 1898. *Annals of Westminster School*, London.

Sarzano, Frances. 1948. *Sir John Tenniel*, London.

Schoch, Richard W. 1998. *Shakespeare's Victorian Stage Performing History in the Theatre of Charles Kean*, Cambridge.

2002. *Not Shakespeare Bardolatry and Burlesque in the Nineteenth Century*, Cambridge.

2003. Shakespeare Mad. In Marshall, Gail and Poole, Adrian eds. *Victorian Shakespeare*, 2 vols, London, vol. 1, pp. 73-81.

References

Scott, Clement. 1870. *Drawing-Room Plays and Parlour Pantomimes Collected by Clement Scott*, London.

1899. *The Drama of Yesterday and Today*, 2 vols, London.

Scott, Clement and Howard, Cecil. 1891. *The Life and Reminiscences of E. L. Blanchard*, London.

Shaberman, R. B. 1976. Lewis Carroll and George MacDonald. In *Jabberwocky*, vol. 5, no. 3, pp. 67-88.

Shattuck, Charles ed. 1962. *William Charles Macready's King John*, Urbana, IL.

Shaw, G. B. 1954. *Our Theatres in the Nineties*, 3 vols, London.

Sherson, Erroll. 1925. *Lost Theatres of London*, London.

Simpson, J. B. Hope. 1967. *Rugby School Since Arnold*, London.

Simpson, Roger. 1994. *Sir John Tenniel Aspects of His Work*, London.

Speaight, George. 1946. *Juvenile Drama The History of the English Toy Theatre*, London.

1955. *The History of the English Puppet Theatre*, London.

Spielmann, M. H. 1895. *The History of Punch*. London.

St. John, Christopher. 1907. *Ellen Terry*, London.

Stedman, Jane W. 1996. *W. S. Gilbert A Classic Victorian and His Theatre*, Oxford.

Stedman, Jane W. ed. 1967. *Gilbert Before Sullivan*, Oxford.

Steen, Marguerite. 1962. *A Pride of Terrys*, London.

Stephens, John Russell. 1992. *The Profession of Playwright British Theatre 1800-1900*, Cambridge.

Stern, Jeffrey. 1997. *Lewis Carroll Bibliophile*, London.

Super, R. H. ed. 1974. *The Complete Works of Matthew Arnold*, vol. X, London.

Tanner, Lawrence. 1951. *Westminster School*, London.

Taylor, Roger and Wakeling, Edward. 2002. *Lewis Carroll Photographer*. Princeton.

Tennyson, Charles. 1959. They Taught the World to Play. In *Victorian Studies*. Vol. II, pp. 211-22.

Tennyson, Hallam. 1897. *Tennyson A Memoir by his Son*, 2 vols, London.

Terriss, Ellaline. 1928. *Ellaline Terriss By Herself and With Others*. London.

1955. *Just a Little Bit of String*, London.

Terry, Ellen. 1908. *The Story of My Life*, London.

1933. *Ellen Terry's Memoirs*. See Craig, Edith and St. John, Christopher.

Thackeray, Anne. 1996. *From an Island*, Newport, Isle of Wight.

214   *Lewis Carroll and the Victorian Stage*

Thomas, Donald. 1996. *Lewis Carroll A Portrait with Background.* London.

Thomas, Edward. 1997. *The Playhouse on the Park A History of the Devonshire Park Theatre*, Eastbourne.

Thomas, J. 1984. *The Art of the Actor-Manager Wilson Barrett and the Victorian Theatre*, Epping.

Thompson, Revd Henry C. 1899. *Henry George Liddell DD Dean of Christ Church, Oxford A Memoir*, London.

     1900. *Christ Church*, London.

Thomson, Peter. 2000. *On Actors and Acting*, Exeter.

Tolles, Winton. 1940. *Tom Taylor and the Victorian Drama*, New York.

Tree, Herbert Beerbohm. 1913. *Thoughts and After-Thoughts,* London.

Trench, Maria. 1900. *The Story of Dr Pusey's Life*, London.

Trewin, Wendy. 1980. *All on Stage Charles Wyndham and the Alberys,* London.

Truss, Lynne. 1997. *Tennyson's Gift*, London.

Tweedie, Mrs Alec. 1904. *Behind the Footlights*, London.

Vanbrugh, Irene. 1949. *To Tell My Story*, London.

Wade, Allan ed. 1957. *Henry James The Scenic Art*, New York.

Wagner, Leopold. 1881. *The Pantomimes and All About Them*, 1881.

Wakeling, Edward ed. 1993-2004. *Lewis Carroll's Diaries*, 8 vols, London.

Webster, Margaret. 1969. *The Same Only Different. Five Generations of a Great Theatrical Family*, London.

Wenham, Leslie P. 1958. *The History of Richmond School, Yorkshire*, Arbroath.

Wilberforce, Reginald. 1905. *Bishop Wilberforce*, Oxford and London.

Williamson, David. 1895. *The German Reeds and Corney Grain*, London.

Wills, F. 1898. *W. G. Wills Dramatist and Painter*, London.

Wilson, A. E. 1934. *Christmas Pantomimes*, London.

     1952. *The Lyceum*, London.

     Nd. *Pantomime Pageant*, London.

Wilstach, Paul. 1908. *Richard Mansfield The Man and the Actor*, London.

Wood, R. Derek. 1975. *The Colotype Patent Lawsuit of Talbot v. Laroche 1854*, Bromley.

Woolcott, Alexander ed. 1997. *The Complete Illustrated Lewis Carroll*, Ware.

Woolf, Virginia. 1947. *The Moment and other essays*, London.

Wroth, Warwick. 1907. *Cremorne and the Later London Gardens*, London.

Wyndham, Horace. 1951. *Chorus to Coronet*, London.

Ziegler, Georgianna. 2003. Alice Reads Shakespeare. Charles Dodgson and the Girl's Shakespeare Project. In Miller, Naomi J. ed. *Reimagining Shakespeare for Children and Young Adults,* London.

Journals

Atlantic Monthly
Carrollian
Cornhill Magazine
Eastbourne Chronicle
Eastbourne Gazette
Era
Gazette, The (Library of Congress)
Hibbert Journal
Illustrated London News
Jabberwocky
Journal of British Photography
New Theatre Quarterly
Punch
Queen
Rugbaean
Rugby Miscellany
Spectator
St James's Gazette
Stage
Strand Magazine
Theatre Notebook
Theatrephile
The Times
Victorian Studies

Index

Academy (Royal) of Dramatic Art, 117, 119
Adderley, J. G., 40-1
Albert, Prince Consort, 29-32, 38, 127, 141-2, 160
Alexander, George, 180, 186, 191
Anderson, Mary, 189
Arnold, Ethel, 43, 60, 97, 134
Arnold, Julia, 43, 60, 133, 134
Arnold, Lucy, 100, 102, 103
Arnold, Thomas, 24, 34, 43

Bancroft, Marie, 105, 165-8, 187
Bancroft, Squire, 105, 165-8, 187
Baird, Dorothea, 103, 121, 122, 169
Barnes, Kenneth, 118
Barnes, Revd Reginald, 67, 118, 119
Barrie, J. M., 3, 197
  Little Minister, The, 138, 169-70
  Professor's Love Story, The, 187-8
  Walker London, 188
Barrett, Wilson, 2, 120, 147-8, 183, 191
  Sign of the Cross, The, 148
Barry, Shiel, 183, 193
Bateman, Hezekiah, 178-9
Bayne, T. Vere, 28, 39
Benson, Frank, 42, 122, 185, 195
Bentham, Jeremy, 69-70
Beringer, Vera, 66, 67, 173

Blanchard, E. L., 13, 75, 160, 162
  Aladdin, or the Wonderful Lamp, 160, 161
  Children in the Wood, The, 55, 110, 157, 160
  Cinderella, 159, 160, 161, 162
  Faw, Fee, Fo, Fum; or, Jack, the Giant Killer, 56, 160, 161
  Little Goody Two Shoes, 157, 158
  Little King Pippin, 160-1
  Little Red Riding Hood, 157, 158
  Robin Hood and his Merry Men, 110, 157, 159
Boucicault, Dion, 202
  After Dark, 158
  Arrag-na-Pogue, 147
  Janet Pride, 55, 156
  Rip Van Winkle, 156, 172
  Streets of London, The, 147
  Trial of Effie Deans, The, 55
Boucicault, Dion (the younger)
  Dot, 188
  My Little Girl, 177
Bourchier, Arthur, 42, 44, 119
  Chili Widow, The, (with Alfred Sutro), 188
Bowman, Isa, 65, 66, 67, 103-4, 135, 184-5
Bowman, Maggie, 195
Bowman, Nellie, 184
Brigaldi, Signor, 9, 198
Brighton, 86, 112
  Theatre Royal, 110, 112, 139, 159, 185, 189-91

Index

217

Brough, Robert, 153
Masaniello, 151
Buckstone, J. B., 156, 162, 164
Bulwer Lytton, Edward George, 26, 69-70, 165
Money, 155, 166
Richelieu, 179
Bunsen, Chevalier, 27, 35
Burnand, F. C., 11, 58, 62, 185
Cox and Box, 58, 96, 181
La Cigale, 188, 196
Ixion, 188
Paw Claudian, 188
Rumplestiltskin and the Maid, 188
Villikins and his Dinah, 36, 41
Windsor Castle, 181
Yachting Cruise, The, 171
Burnett, F. C. Hodgson
Real Little Lord Fauntleroy, The, 98, 172-3, 195
Byron, H. J., 156, 165
English Gentleman, The, 164
La! Sonnambula, 40
Little Doctor Faustus, 181
Little Don Giovanni, 166
Lord Dundreary Married and Done For, 163
Maid and the Magpie, The, 39
Motto, The, 181
Our Boys, 182
Upper Crust, The, 188
Weak Women, 182
Yellow Dwarf, The, 56, 78

Calvert, Mrs Charles, 88, 120-1
Cambridge, 11, 21
ADC, 11
Cameron, Julia Margaret, 130-2
Cameron, Violet, 182
Carlo, Lizzie, 112, 191

Carlo, Phoebe, 62, 64, 65, 66, 67, 112, 148, 191, 193, 199
Carroll, Lewis
Alice's Adventures in Wonderland, 37, 44, 51, 53-4
'Alice' on the Stage, 53-4
Feeding the Mind, 142-3
Guildford Gazette Extraordinary, 76-7
La Guida di Bragia, 13-15, 44, 142, 153
marionette theatre, 1, 2, 3, 8-15, 198
Morning Clouds, 59
Priest's orders, 1, 32, 34-5, 46-7, 50, 199
Phantasmagoria, 51, 72
Russia, trip to, 1, 48-9
School of Dramatic Art, 117
'Shakespeare for Girls', 117
'Stage Children', 113-17, 135
'The Stage and the Spirit of Reverence', 100
stammer, 18
stories, 15, 51
Sylvie and Bruno, 81
Tory, 84, 117
Through the Looking-Glass and What Alice Found There, 53, 54, 56
Carton, R. C.
Liberty Hall, 98, 186, 195
Sunlight and Shadow, 191
Cave, Joseph
Whittington and his Cat, 67, 187
Cecil, Arthur, 60, 168, 187
Chambers, Charles Haddon
Idler, The, 186, 195
Chart, Nye, 189
charades, 1, 23, 24, 72-3, 200

218 *Lewis Carroll and the Victorian Stage*

Chatterton, F. B., 156, 159, 162
Chevalier, Albert, 173, 195-6
child performers, 1, 2, 3, 108-17,
    133, 156-9, 161, 173-4, 193,
    201, 202
Christ Church, 5, 32, 34-41, 47,
    133, 135, 199, 201
Church and Stage Guild, 1, 41,
    48, 50
Clarke, Henry Savile, 53, 58, 61-
    6, 184, 199
  Alice in Wonderland, 62-8,
    184, 191, 193, 199-200
  Rose and the Ring, The, 56, 62,
    184
Clay, Cecil
  Pantomime Rehearsal, A, 177
Clay, Frederick, 159, 171
Cockton, Henry
  The Life and Adventures of
    Valentine Vox The
    Ventriloquist, 17
Coe, Thomas, 59, 109
Compton, Edward, 196
Coote, Bert, 146, 158, 159
Coote, Carrie, 147, 158, 159,
    190
Coote, Charles, 148
Coote, Lizzie, 56, 110, 146, 155,
    158, 159, 165, 190
Courtney, W. L., 42, 43, 44, 45
Cowell, Sam, 36, 45
Coyne, Stirling
  Willikins and his Dinah, 36
Craig, Edith, 97, 103, 104, 105
Craig, Edward Gordon, 97, 104,
    105
Craven, Henry Thornton
  Done Brown, 16-17, 24, 198
Cremorne Gardens, 9-10
Croft, 1, 5, 11, 18, 23, 45, 125,
    198, 200

Currey, Henry, 191, 192

D'Alcourt, Dorothy, 64, 112-3,
    191, 193
Daguerre, Louis, 124, 126
Daresbury, 5
Darlington, 17
Dent, J. M., 17
Devonshire, (seventh) Duke of,
    191, 193
Dickens, Charles, 26, 35, 88,
    146, 153, 188
diorama, 126
Dodgson, Revd Charles, 1, 4, 5-
    8, 19-20, 28-9, 40, 78, 198
Dodgson, Edwin, 26, 59
Dodgson, Frances Jane
    Lutwidge (Mrs), 5
Dodgson, Hassard Hume, 28
Dodgson, Skeffington, 19, 23
Dodgson, Wilfred, 19
Dubourg, Augustus, 43, 60, 110,
    175
Du Maurier, George, 58
  Trilby, 122, 169

Eastbourne, 61, 62, 67, 86, 122,
    191-7
  Devonshire Park Theatre, 122,
    191-7
  Theatre Royal, 193-7
Eliot, George
  Silas Marner, 151, 164
Emery, Winifred, 169-70, 173,
    187
Eton College, 21

Fairbrother, Sydney, 149
Farnie, H. B., 197, 202
  Blue Beard, 183
  Les Cloches de Corneville, 171,
    183, 193

Index

Paul Jones, 195
Madame Favart, 171, 182
Olivette, 182
Rip Van Winkle, 187
Faucit, Helen (Lady Martin), 59, 160
Fechter, Charles, 178, 181
Fitzgerald, Percy, 13, 44, 55, 59
Forbes-Robertson, Johnston, 82, 187, 200
Flexmore, Richard, 14-15
Freiligrath-Kroeker, Kate, 61
Furniss, Harry, 158

Gatti Brothers (Agostino and Stefano), 157, 159, 162
Gielgud, Kate Terry, 97, 164, 187
Gilbert, W. S., 2, 75, 164-5, 180, 197, 202
Broken Hearts, 98
Dan'l Druce, Blacksmith, 98, 164
Engaged, 165
Happy Arcadia, 171
Mountebanks, The, (with Alfred Cellier)188
Pygmalion and Galatea, 98, 165, 189
Rosencrantz and Guildenstern, 177
Wicked World An Original Fairy Comedy, The, 164
with Arthur Sullivan:
Gondoliers, The, 174
H.M.S. Pinafore, 172
Mikardo, The, 75, 174, 193
Patience, 173, 174, 193
Pirates of Penzance, The, 173
Sorcerer, The, 175
Utopia Limited, 174

Gilchrist, Connie, 157-8, 159, 181
Godwin, E. W., 91, 97, 105, 200
Gould, Nutcombe, 119, 186
Grain, Richard Corney, 61, 194-5, 197
Gray, Warwick, 192
Green, Frank W, 162
Dick Whittington and his Cat, 190
Hop-o'-my-Thumb, 110
Jack and the Beanstalk, 159-60, 190
Little Red Riding Hood, 190-1
Greet, Philip Ben, 123, 196
Greet, W. Mrs
Little Squire, The, (with W. Sledger) 140-1
Grundy, Sydney
Sowing the Wind, 187
Guildford, 64, 76-7, 138, 139

Hare, John, 166, 174, 187
Hatch, Beatrice, 80, 123, 134
Hatch, Ethel, 134, 136
Hatch, Evelyn, 134, 138
Hatch, Dr Edwin, 79
Hatch, Mrs Edwin, 79-80
Hatfield House, 80-1
Headlam, Revd Stewart, 8, 50
Holland, Henry Scott, 42, 44
Honey, George, 166, 181
Hood, Tom
Harlequin Little Red Riding-Hood, 75
House of Lords, 113, 116, 123
Hunt, Dr James, 18-19, 83
Hughes, Arthur, 82, 83
Hughes, Thomas
Tom Brown's School Days, 24-5
Hull, Agnes, 97, 100, 102

220 *Lewis Carroll and the Victorian Stage*

Ibsen, Henrik, 2, 202
Irving, Henry, 42, 98, 106, 108,
   163, 166, 179-80, 196, 197
Irving, H. B., 122, 196

Jefferson, Joseph, 156, 172
Jerrold, Douglas
 Back-Eyed Susan, 197
 Paul Pry, 195
Jones, H. A., 2, 202
 Dancing Girl, The, 140
 Masqueraders, The, 186
 Michael and his Lost Angel, 98
 Hoodman Blind, 148
 Silver King, The, 67, 120, 148,
   191
 Triumph of the Philistines, The,
   186
Jowett, Benjamin, 42, 44, 45,
   199

Kean, Charles, 2, 12, 23, 31, 58,
   88-9, 108, 127-30, 138, 142-
   7, 149, 153, 201
Kean, Edmund, 44, 142
Kean, Ellen, 23, 90, 108, 141,
   142, 145, 146, 148, 153
Kemble, Fanny, 45, 199
Kendal, Madge, 89, 164, 174-5,
   185-6
Kendal, W. H., 164, 174
Kingsley, Charles, 19
Kitchin, Xie, 130, 133-4, 136,
   190
Knowles, Sheridan
 Hunchback, The, 155

Laroche, Martin, 127-8, 201
Lewis, Arthur, 96-7
Liddell, Alice Pleasance, 35, 36,
   133
Liddell, Edith Mary, 35, 36

Liddell, Revd H. G., 24, 27-32,
   34-6, 44, 46-7, 199
Liddell, Lorina Charlotte, 35, 36
Liddell, Lorina Reeve (Mrs), 31,
   38, 41, 47
Liddon, Henry Parry, 1, 12, 46,
   47-8, 49-50,
Living Miniatures, 59, 109-10,
   164
London theatres:
 Adelphi, 55, 58, 95-6, 110,
   155-9
 Avenue, 187
 Comedy, 187
 Court, 122, 131, 174-8
 Covent Garden, 56, 69, 78,
   159-62
 Daly's, 187, 188
 Drury Lane, 56, 69, 110, 126,
   157, 159-62
 Gaiety, 180-1
 Gallery of Illustration, 170-1
 Garrick, 187
 Globe, 67, 183-5
 Haymarket, 13, 98, 122, 162-70
 Lyceum, 91, 122, 166, 178-80
 Lyric, 187, 188
 Olympic, 2, 13, 48, 91, 94,
   150-5, 197, 201
 Opera Comique, 171-3
 Prince of Wales, 63
 Prince of Wales's, 63, 165-6
 Princess's, 2, 12, 81, 88-91,
   126, 138, 142-7, 197, 201
 Queen's, 185
 Royal Polytechnic, 60
 Royalty, 91, 188
 Sadler's Wells, 52, 146-7
 Savoy, 173-4
 St James's, 98, 185-87
 Standard, 56
 Strand, 181-2

Index

221

Surrey, 56
Terry's, 172-3
Toole's Theatre, 118, 187, 188
Westminster, 55
Lutwidge, Charles Robert
Fletcher, 11-12

MacDonald, George, 19, 59, 82-6, 200
MacDonald, Mrs George, 83-5
MacDonald, Greville, 82-6, 200
MacDonald, Lilia Scott, 84-6
Macmillan, Alexander, 158, 164
Macready, William Charles, 21, 24-5, 29, 39, 58, 170
magic, 15
magic lantern, 125, 198
Mansfield, Richard, 184-5
Martin-Harvey, John, 122-3, 196
Martin-Harvey, Mrs, 122-3, 196
Mathews, Charles, 126
Adventures of a Love Letter, 185
Maude, Cyril, 169, 187
Maurice, Frederick Denison, 83-4
Mayhew, Henry
Wandering Minstrel, The, 36, 150
Morton, John Maddison, 147, 156, 185
Away with Melancholy, 15-16, 17, 40, 198
Box and Cox, 15, 58
Most Unwarrantable Intrusion, A, 40
My Wife's Second Floor, 181
Thumping Legacy, A, 40
Moss, Hugh
Bootle's Baby, 183, 195

Neville, Henry, 91, 95

Newry, Lord, 180, 186
Danischeffs, The, 177

Oberammergau Passion Play, 50
Offenbach, Jacques, 171, 182
Oxford, 27, 34-48, 139
OUDS, 1, 44, 122, 199
Oxenford, John
My Brother Sam, 163
Porter's Knot, The, 153
Two Orphans, The, 155
Oxford Movement, 6, 24

pantomime, 1, 2, 3, 54-8, 73-4, 156-62, 190-1, 202
Paris, 49, 126
Parry, John, 171
Wedding Breakfast, The, 171
Payne, John W Howard,
Maid and the Magpie, The, 108
Philothespians, The, 42
photography, 35, 124-5, 201
Phipps, C. J., 63, 167, 173, 189, 192
Pinero, A. W., 2, 202
Magistrate, The, 177
Schoolmistress, The, 177
Second Mrs Tanqueray, The, 96, 140, 186
Squire, The, 185-6
Sweet Lavender, 46, 177, 195
Phelps, Samuel, 146-7, 160
Planché, J. R., 147, 153
Young and Handsome, 151
Playfair, Nigel, 44
Punch, 13, 41, 58, 62
Pusey. Edward Bouverie, 6, 24, 34, 48
Prinsep, Mrs Sarah, 92, 131
Prinsep, Val, 131, 180
Cousin Dick, 131, 176

222   *Lewis Carroll and the Victorian Stage*

Quin, Menella (Minna), 1, 2, 13, 103, 119-20, 122-3, 169, 177

Reade, Charles
  Masks and Faces, 13, 196
  Robust Invalid, The, 156
Reed, Mr and Mrs German, 45, 60, 91, 170-1, 177, 192, 195, 199
Rehan, Ada, 189
Richmond, 5
  Richmond School, 21-4, 198
  Richmond Theatre, 2-3
Ripon, 5
Robertson, T. W.
  Constance (with Frederick Clay), 159
  David Garrick, 163, 196
  Ladies' Battle, The, 176
  School, 167
  Society, 165
Robson, Frederick, 2, 36, 48, 127, 150-4, 201
Roselle, Percy, 54, 59, 160-1
Rosmer, Ernest
  Children of the King, The, 122-3, 177-8
Rowe, George
  Uncle Tom's Cabin, 147
Rowe, Saville
  Vicarage, The, 167
Rugby School, 21, 24-6, 29, 71, 198-9
Ruskin, John, 36-7, 81
Russia, 1, 48-9

Salisbury, Marquis of, 80-1, 104, 113, 117, 164, 180
Salvini, Tommaso, 49, 160
Scudamore, F. A.
  Our Eldorado, 196
Selby, Charles

  Boots at the Swan, 153
Shakespeare
  As You Like It, 25, 118, 146
  Cymbeline, 160
  Hamlet, 26, 108, 118, 160, 168-9, 178, 179
  Henry IV.i, 15, 16, 160
  Henry V, 127
  Henry VIII, 1, 12, 15, 16, 45, 58, 127, 138, 144, 180
  King John, 12, 52, 142, 145, 185
  King Lear, 180
  Macbeth, 35, 142, 180
  Merchant of Venice, The, 31, 42-3, 98-9, 102, 104, 166, 179
  Merry Wives of Windsor, The, 142
  Midsummer Night's Dream, A, 118, 126, 127, 143, 145, 185
  Much Ado About Nothing, 98, 99-100, 102, 179
  Pericles, 146
  Richard II, 127, 129, 143
  Richard III, 35, 184-5
  Romeo and Juliet, 40
  Taming of the Shrew, The, 121
  Tempest, The, 90, 127, 132, 143
  Twelfth Night, 180, 189
  Winter's Tale, The, 88, 127, 143
Shaw, G. B., 2, 3, 98, 138, 140, 149, 202
  Arms and the Man, 192
Sims, George
  Golden Ladder, The, 183
  Lights o' London, The, 148
  Two Little Vagabonds, The, 149

Index

Siddons, Mrs, 108, 142, 146, 153
Simpson, J. Palgrave
  Daddy Hardacre, 151, 152
Slaughter, Walter, 62, 64
Sothern, E. A. 163-4
Stephenson, B. C.
  Diplomacy (with Clement Scott), 187
St. John, Florence, 182, 183, 202
Sullivan, Arthur, 2, 58, 60, 96, 180, 202
Synge family, 76-7

tableaux vivants, 38, 73, 200
Tait, Revd Archibald Campbell, 24, 33 n 2, 34, 42
Talbot, W. H. Fox, 127
Talfourd, Francis (Frank), 39
  Jones the Avenger, 151
Talfourd, Thomas Noon, 29, 39
Tate I, James, 21-3
Tate II, James, 21, 23
Tate, Lucy, 23-4, 198
Taylor, Tom, 58, 59, 91, 92, 154-5, 180, 185, 197
  Lady Clancarty, 155
  Masks and Faces, 14, 166, 196
  New Men and Old Acres, 175
  Our Clerks, 181
  Retribution, 154
  Serf, The, 94-5, 155
  Sheep in Wolf's Clothing, A, 58, 96, 154
  Our American Cousin, 163
  Ticket of Leave Man, The, 154
  To Parents and Guardians, 177
Tenniel, John, 51, 58, 96, 199
Tennyson, Alfred, 92, 132
  Cup, The, 179
Terriss, Ellaline, 177
Terry, Benjamin, 88-9, 91, 92

Terry, Ellen, 2, 42, 88-91, 96, 97, 98-106, 108, 109, 118,120, 131-2, 136, 138, 145, 155, 166, 175-6, 179-80, 197, 200, 202
Terry, Kate (Mrs Arthur Lewis), 2, 62, 85, 88-91, 93-6, 97, 100, 106, 130, 132, 146, 155, 178, 202
Terry, Florence, 94, 96, 97, 98, 129, 130, 155
Terry, Marion (Polly), 2, 93, 97, 120, 129, 130, 155, 164-5, 166, 177, 181, 186, 187, 191
Terry, Minnie, 66, 67, 183
Terry, Sarah (Mrs), 88-9, 92
Tertullian, 1, 6-7, 48 198
Thackeray, Anne, 76
  From an Island, 92
Thackeray, Thomas Makepeace, 29, 77, 153
  Rose and the Ring, The, 56, 62
Thomas, Augustus
  Alabama, 187
Thomas, Brandon, 187
  Charley's Aunt, 192
Thompson, Alfred
  Happy Despatch A Japanese Opera-Bouffe, 75-6
Thorne, Sarah, 67, 118-9, 120
Toole, J. L., 98, 181, 183, 185, 188, 192
toy theatres, 8-9, 11, 125
Tree, Herbert Beerbohm, 122, 168-9
Tree, Maud Beerbohm (Mrs), 120, 168-9
Trollope, Anthony, 76, 77, 180
Truss, Lynn
  Tennyson's Gift, 92
Twiss, Quintin, 35, 96, 130

224 *Lewis Carroll and the Victorian Stage*

Vanbrugh, Irene, 67, 93, 118-9,
177, 187, 193
Vanbrugh, Violet, 44, 67, 118-9,
173, 189
'Vance the Great' (Alfred Peck),
45
Victoria, Queen, 31, 38, 70, 96,
127, 142, 145, 146, 148
'Villikins and his Dinah', 36-7,
45, 199
Vokes family, 110, 157, 161-2,
177

Wales, Prince of, 29, 38
Wallis family (actors), 22
Wardell (Kelly), Charles, 104.
105, 185
Watts, George Frederick, 91-2,
105, 131, 200
Webster, Ben, 13, 156, 159
Westminster School, 5, 21, 168,
199

The Latin play, 27-32, 38, 39,
199
Whistler, James McNeill, 157
Wilberforce, Revd Samuel, 27,
29, 32, 46, 199
Wilde, Oscar, 2, 140, 202
*Importance of Being Earnest,
The*, 186
Lady Windermere's Fan, 186
Woman of No Importance, A,
98, 195
Williams, T.J.
Içi on Parle Français, 41
My Dress Boots, 39
Wills, W. G.
Charles I, 179
Claudian (with Henry
Herman), 148
Faust, 2, 100-2
Jane Shore, 147
Olivia, 176, 180